one

ancient civilizations.
He has over two million readers in Europe and America alone, and special societies have formed to study his work in countries as far apart as Canada, Peru and his native country, France.

Also by Robert Charroux in Sphere Books

LEGACY OF THE GODS

Masters of the World

ROBERT CHARROUX

SPHERE BOOKS LIMITED
30/32 Gray's Inn Road, London WCIX 8JL

First published in Great Britain by
Sphere Books Ltd 1979

Published by arrangement with Editions
Robert Laffont and Berkley
Publishing Corporation

This book is dedicated to Sanchuniathon, a pioneer in primal truths

'Our ears, accustomed from early childhood to hearing their false stories, and our minds, imbued with those preconceptions for centuries, preserve those fantastic suppositions as if they were a sacred trust . . . so that truth seems incredible, and adulterated stories have the appearance of truth.'

– Written by Sanchuniathon four thousand years ago

Set in Intertype Times

Printed in Great Britain by
Hunt Barnard Printing Ltd,
Aylesbury, Bucks.

Acknowledgements

I thank my friends of the Round Table, who have helped me with their knowledge, and the correspondents and friends who have provided me with valuable documentation: Jeannine Baussant, the archaeologist Michel Danguy, the writers Roger Delorme, Jean-Albert Foëx, Jimmy Gieu, Guy Lacalu and Michel Ponge-Helmer, the historian Jean Roy, Michel Simkine and M. Stark.

I am also grateful to my faithful collaborator, Yvette Charroux, and to Catherine Krikorian for her photographic documentation.

Contents

Masters of the World

Introduction

THE MASTERS OF THE WORLD

It is hard for most people to accept the fantastic truth of their own time and they ignore its logical consequences. Similarly, they are reluctant to imagine the past as being any different from the stereotyped images presented in their old school textbooks. Yet the moon will be colonised in the near future and that first step will inevitably lead to the conquest of other planets.

That is the truth of tomorrow.

When our astronauts reach Venus, Mars or even more distant planets, they may find a human race that will regard them as the true Masters of the World. And what may happen tomorrow was certainly experienced by our ancestors thousands of years ago. We have abundant evidence that our planet was visited by extraterrestrial beings who were called gods, angels, initiators or demons.

Twentieth-century man can no longer believe in those gods and angels who reorganised social life, taught agriculture and the smelting of metals, brought wheat and initiatic potions and seduced pretty women. He can no longer believe in clouds and heavenly chariots inhabited by ethereal, immortal creatures.

His experience, technological achievements and intelligence make him inclined to give rational explanations for those outdated images, assign human identities to those gods and demons and give substance to those visions. Someone who comes from space is an astronaut. A self-propelled object in the atmosphere is an aeroplane. A 'revelation' of a secret is information given by one human being to another.

Such is truth in the twentieth century and it was the same in ancient times, before facts were shrouded in legend or distorted for political or religious reasons. Seen in this light, events take on their rational meaning: astronauts came from another planet and *they were genuine Masters of the World.*

By 'world' I mean our planet, of course, but the powers of those Masters may have been greater than we think. In any case they placed their mark on all the earth's civilisations, since we find a universal root, still discernible in Sanskrit, at the origin of all languages.

The same is true of the symbols that suddenly appeared all over the world: the winged serpent or dragon, representing a spacecraft; a horse, emblem of the Masters of the World before the Deluge; the bull, emblem of the Masters after the Deluge, and of their original planet: Venus.

The first Masters, those who have become identified with the Biblical angels, came more than twelve thousand years ago and formed two antagonistic blocs: one in Atlantis, the other in the Land of Mu. The Hebrews called them the *nephilim*, which means 'giants', 'brilliant ones', 'workers of wonders'.

The rivalry of the two blocs led to an atomic war which caused the destruction of mankind by the Universal Deluge. Then there was a new cycle, again marked by the arrival of beings alien to our planet.

Five thousand years ago a spectacular phenomenon occurred in our sky and 'gods' reigned in civilised countries. The best-known ones were Viracocha in Peru, Quetzalcoatl in Mexico and Baal in Asia Minor. They were all associated with the planet Venus, they all came on a flying serpent and they all bore the sign of the bull.

It was during this period, as in Egypt and India several thousand years earlier, and by the same phenomenon, that five civilisations flourished: among the Phoenicians, Assyrians, Babylonians, Incas and Mayas.

Is it possible to deny the clear evidence of the facts?

The 'newcomers', as they were later called by prophets,

had great power derived from their scientific knowledge. They had aircraft and probably atomic weapons, since they annihilated Sodom, Gomorrah and other cities.

The Hebrews, Hindus and Greeks spoke of their 'clouds' and 'flying chariots'. Ezekiel described them and reported seeing six men, carrying 'weapons of destruction', take control of Jerusalem, which must have had thousands of inhabitants and armed soldiers!

They punished, rewarded, taught, moved through space at will and ruled the nations. They were unquestionably the Masters of the World. It was not until long after they were gone, whether because they died or left our planet, that they came to be regarded as either gods or demons, depending on whether men wanted to pay just tribute to them or efface their memory in favour of a more absolute master: God.

It is this story of the Masters of the World that I will evoke through our secret history, referring to the documents they left, the events they produced and the accounts of their coming contained in manuscripts, tablets and books.

Chapter 1

THE CONSPIRACY OF FALSEHOOD

The true history of civilisation is forbidden. Powerful conspiracies try to allow only a distorted version to be expressed. People who consider themselves free of preconceived ideas because they are freethinkers, anarchists or Freemasons are actually under the sway of a dictatorial power that conditions their activities and behaviour.

Our social and religious history has been falsified for thousands of years, ever since the Egyptians, forgetting or ignoring the truths handed down by their ancestors, gave themselves the title of first initiators and first civilised people of our planet.

The Greeks also forgot to pay tribute to their Celtic and Egyptian teachers, and presented their country as the cradle of mankind.

Then came the Hebrews. That was the final blow.

The change was brought about by means of strong religious dogmas. New myths and religions were launched for the purpose of hypnotising the masses and turning them away from the original truths.

In our time, two million human beings have intellectual and emotional patterns conditioned by Biblical archetypes. They may exercise their free will on a multitude of subjects, such as science, commerce and industry, but they invariably put on blinders as soon as they approach human genesis, prehistory, history or religion.

To help liberate and awaken those hypnotised minds, two things must be proved: first, that conspiracies of falsehood exist; and second, that history as it is commonly taught is the *reverse* of the facts. That is what I will try to do in this book.

Words That Are Not Allowed to Be Spoken

The word 'angel' is so dangerous to utter that it was banished from Jewish rites, and at the Laodicean Council of 366 the Christians forbade referring to angels by name. (See Chapter 7 of my *The Legacy of the Gods.*)

For two thousand years another word has terrified historians engaged in reconstructing Phoenician and Assyro-Babylonian history. It is the name of the brightest planet in the sky: Venus. The writers of the Bible, and those who comment on it, avoid writing or even hinting at that abhorred name.

Why? Because that name, closely associated with the word 'angels', is the key to the genesis of mankind, the real genesis, precisely the one that the conspiracies of falsehood want to suppress.

Briefly stated, five thousand years ago the gods of mankind were aliens from space. They were mortal. It was to them that our ancestors owed their civilisation, as I will show in this book. This view obviously contradicts history as it is ordinarily presented to us.

The idea that Venus was the homeland of the gods is easily explained by the fact that five thousand years ago that bright planet took its present place in our solar system, between Earth and Mercury. It had previously not been part of our visible universe.

The history of Asia Minor is governed by Venus, with which the main gods are identified: Baal, Astarte, Ishtar, Marduk, Bel, Ashur.

The three ancient American civilisations – in the northern plain, Peru and Mexico – had gods identified with that same planet: the Morning Star or Great Star, Orejona, Viracocha, Quetzalcoatl, Kukulkan.

It can therefore be said that all civilisations earlier than 3000 B.C were typically Venusian, with initiators or deified men who were rightly or wrongly considered to have originated on Venus and come to Earth in flying machines.

The principle of the solar myth was inculcated in hypnotised peoples to prevent them from thinking that the 'angels' had been human beings. This eliminated the ideas of space travel and vanished civilisations, truths which would have demolished the elaborate structures erected by the Egyptian, Greek, Hebrew and Christian conspiracies to show that their origins went back farther than those of other peoples.

The psychosis still continues in our time: textbooks, books on mythology and encyclopedias conceal the truth and present only the traditional, mandatory version.

The Europeans Live in Asia

It is interesting to study how the continent of Europe got its name. It is said to come from the Hebrew *oreb* or *ereb*, 'evening', 'west', or from the Greek *europe*, 'dark place'. It would thus be valid from the viewpoint of Oriental countries but not from that of America, which is west of Europe. Moses called Europe the Island of Nations and sacred writers referred to it as Japetia. The name is used for the first time in a Homeric hymn to Apollo in which Europe of the west is opposed to the Greek islands and the Peloponnesus.

Be that as it may, the etymology of the word 'Asia' interests us much more because it is related to our most ancient traditions. It is said to come from the Phoenician *asir*, 'central', derived from the Scandinavian *ase*, 'god'. This is the most probable root because the Phoenicians descended from the Pelesgians, 'ancestors from the northern seas', whose gods were called Ases. And the Phoenicians, Phrygians and Assyro-Babylonians gave their gods and goddesses names in which the Celtic-Scandinavian root appears: Astarte, Astarot, Asmodeus, Asherah. The Egyptian name of the god Osiris was Asar and the Babylonian name for Marduk was Asari.

Europe, from Gaul to the Caucasus, should rightly have been called Asia.

According to Strabo and Ptolemy, the people of the Ases lived at the foot of the Caucasus in the region of the Seas of Azov and Astrakhan, the first home of the Aryans when they left the plateau of Iran after the Deluge. The people of the Ases therefore had no relation to the peoples now known as Asians.

In Western mythology and old Scandinavian poems, the sacred land where the gods live is Asgard or Asaland.

The Ancient Gods of the French

History thus sets off from a false beginning, with Asians becoming Europeans, good being regarded as evil and vice versa.

For religious reasons that were quite praiseworthy, considering the nature of the times, the Hebrews wanted to impose the One God and therefore had to Satanise the ancestral gods.

Since the oldest civilisation of the white race was developed by the Celts, the Celtic gods were attacked with special vigour. Those gods, or Ases, were Cernunos, Esus, Teutates and Thor, among others, but at the time when the attempt at segregation was launched, the most formidable enemy was the Baal of the Phoenicians, who was both the god of the planet Venus and the Lord of the North, since his name had been given to him as a tribute to the ancestral Celtic gods Bel, Belin, Belenus and Belinus, as well as the goddess Belisama.[1]

The second adversary was, of course, Astarte (the planet Venus itself), so named in tribute to the Ases, who probably came from the sky, since their name is at the origin of the Latin word for 'star': *astrum.* But in ancient times the 'star' in question was the planet Venus.

The Ancient Gods of the Hebrews

In those times, the Hebrews whom Moses wanted to convert worshipped Baal and Belenus, gods of the Aryan ancestors.

Hosea deplores this in the Old Testament:

'Plead my cause with your mother; is she not my wife and I her husband? Plead with her to forswear those wanton looks, to banish the lovers from her bosom.' (Hosea 2:2.)

'On that day she shall call me "My husband" and shall no more call me "My Baal".' (2:16.)

'Your men sacrifice on mountain-tops and burn offerings on the hills, under oak and poplar and the terebinth's pleasant shade.' (4:13.)

The idea of sacrificing under oak trees inevitably has Celtic, Druidic associations, and that is precisely how it should be understood.

It is now easy to see why so many of our demons and devils have names beginning with As, Az, Bal or Bel. This is the case with Azazel, the mysterious demon to whom the Hebrews delegated the scapegoat; Astarte and Astarot, avid for human sacrifices; Asima, likened to a donkey or a goat; Baal, identified with Moloch, the devourer of children; Belial, the demon of pederasty; Belphegor, the phallic god; Beelzebub, the prince of demons; Balltis, the demoness of licentious love and the goddess of prostitution.

How hard it now is to make anyone believe that those vilified gods were innocent victims! How hard it is to reform history!

The Hebrews Are Aryans

Startling as it may seem, the Hebrews are Aryans; that is, descendants of the white race that left the plateau of Iran after the Deluge. Because of an atavistic urge to return to the Atlantean source, the Aryans made their first new home in the ancient lands of the Celts, but finally they spread throughout Europe and into Asia. It was to the Druids, who had inherited the most learned traditions, that Pythagoras went for initiation.

The youngest of the Western nations, since it dates only from about 1500 B.C., is that of the Hebrews. The Hebrew people had previously been composed of Phoenician, Babylonian, Phrygian, Chaldean, Assyrian and Arab tribes. Judging from their customs, writing and religion, most of them were of Phoenician origin.

According to tradition, the Phoenicians descended from 'the sons of the wind', who were no doubt the Pelesgians, but we know that they honoured a Venusian god with a Celtic name: Baal, whose worship was celebrated, for lack of a temple, under oak trees, as Hosea says. They even represented the star of Baal and Astarte as having eight rays, in memory of the figure 8, sacred to the Druids and the Celts, among whom the world's first knighthood flourished.

The horse, symbol of the Atlantean Poseidon, was held in such high honour by the Gauls that they used it only for noble endeavours, particularly war. When Vercingetorix surrendered to Caesar he gave him his shield and weapons but not his horse, because he regarded it as part of himself.

In later times the Templars, who inherited Celtic courage and integrity, maintained the sacred nature of the figure 8.

As for the Phrygians, they were pure Pelesgians and therefore Scandinavians and Franks.

Ollivier de la Marche, a fifteenth-century chronicler, wrote that when Francio, son of Hector, was exiled and driven away from Troy after the capture of the city by the Greeks, he went to the Western land now known as France and settled in Lutetia, which he named Paris after his uncle, Paris of Troy. This story is by no means as fantastic as one might think.

According to Claude Fouchet in his *Antiquités Gauloises*, the Druids maintained that the population of Gaul included people who had fled from the Greeks after the destruction of Troy.

It is interesting to note that the iris, emblem of French royalty in the form of the fleur-de-lis, was also the emblem of the Salian Franks and the ancestor of the Phrygian cap, the symbol of liberty mysteriously adopted by the French revolutionaries of 1789.

The historian Laurence Talbot, who reports these traditions, adds that when the Phrygians settled in northern and western Europe they were only returning to their ancestral lands.

As for the name Israel, it is related to the Ases, *as* and *is* being interchangeable, which also explains the geographical names of Ys, Yseel, Ière, etc., as well as the name of Isis, sister and wife of Asar (Osiris).

These data enable us to understand why Stanislas de Gaita wrote to Péladan, 'I maintain that Saint Yves d'Alvèdre (in *La Mission des Juifs*) unquestionably and irrefutably establishes the common pre-Celtic origin of the Semites, the Aryans and the European Celts.'

The Semites were originally Aryans. Moreover, the erudite philologist Eugène Burnouf classified the Semites as Indo-Europeans.

Prehistorians vainly try to find a monkey ancestor from which all the races descended. It is as ludicrous as trying to make a cleavage within the white race, which exacerbates the horrors of racism.

Who was responsible for the initial distortion of history? Was it the Hebrews? No. It was a conspiracy of initiates that included Moses and Pharaoh Ikhnaton, who launched 'Operation One God' with the intention of avoiding the worst.

We cannot know if the worst was really avoided, but perhaps we can bring charges against that God. After all, he is responsible for many misfortunes and his story, as it has been reported to us, is strongly subject to doubt.

In the Beginning, God Re-created the World

The first verse of the Bible is probably the world's best-known sentence and most absolute dogma: 'In the beginning God created the heaven and the earth.'

That is the primordial assertion: God is the creator of a universe that had a beginning, which seems reasonable. Yet it appears that the opening sentence of the sacred book has unfortunately been misinterpreted and mis-translated. The Hebrew scholar J. M. Vaschalde attributes this error to the 'divine complex' that has always affected translators of the Bible, and he offers a version that I will present below.

בראשית ברא אלהים את
השמים ואת הארץ:

These Hebrew words, the first sentence of the Bible, are usually translated as 'In the beginning God created the heaven and the earth.' The word translated as 'in the beginning', however, is a compound word which can have two meanings (as is true of the first word of many initiatic and hermetic texts). It can be divided into a particle and a noun, the latter meaning 'beginning'. But the particle can mean either 'in' or 'with', so the compound word can mean either 'in the beginning' (the usual translation) or 'with what remained from the past' (a translation closer to a historical truth).

The third word, 'Elohim', is translated as 'God'. But it is strange that in the sacred book of a monotheistic people the name Elohim is plural, whereas all the other names of God are singular. This would seem to indicate that God is not referred to here, but rather what might be called 'divine beings'.

It should also be noted that the Elohim are universe builders, working gods, creators, while the wrathful, avenging God always bears the name of YHWH. Orthodox Jews never produce this name and it has such an aura of awe that it is usually written not in Aramaic, but in Phoenician.

Here, then, is an alternate, grammatically possible translation of the first verse of the Bible: 'Using what remained [after the cataclysm?], beings from the sky [re-]created the sky and the earth.'

That changes everything! The sentence now reports a recent phase – only a few thousand years old – of the re-creation of the world by beings from the sky (the Elohim), who must not be confused with God (YHWH).

The re-creation probably took place after a cataclysm, since it was done with 'what remained', that is, with the debris of an earlier world that had been destroyed.

Elohim in Flying Machines

Continuing his interpretation, Vaschalde notes that in the second verse of the first chapter of Genesis there is a reference to 'the blast from the engines of the intergalactic spacecraft used by the Elohim.' The words are usually translated as 'And the Spirit of God moved upon the face of the waters,' which does not convey anything very intelligible, but they can also mean 'And the breath of the divine beings agitated the surface of the waters,' which is less puzzling to a physicist or an astronaut.

It is not my intention to lend support to those who believe in what are known in our times as 'flying saucers', but all mythologies and sacred texts lead us to study the mystery of those 'clouds', 'chariots', 'winged discs' – in other words, flying machines – used by the 'angels' and 'gods' who were the Masters of the World.

Even the Roundness of the Earth Was Concealed!

During the first thousand years of the Christian era, scribes did their best to make all authentic historical works disappear.

It was during this same period that the benevolent ancient gods were depicted as diabolical, lewd and cruel.

The unenlightened masses had neither the right nor the intellectual means to react against this, but it is hard to excuse the silence of the cultivated classes: scholars, writers, priests.

Historical works reflecting the decrees of conspiracies maintained that the earth was flat. Even today, 'historians' say that Christopher Columbus' conviction that the earth was round ran counter to the belief of his time. And everyone feels sorry for poor Galileo, who had to proclaim that the earth was motionless, as stated in the Bible: in 1633 the

Inquisition forced him to abjure the Copernican view that the earth revolves around the sun, which led him to say his famous words, *'Eppur si muove.'* ('And yet it moves.)

The historical truth is quite different: *in the fifteenth century, cultivated people all over the world, including not only Columbus but also the Queen of Spain and the whole Spanish court, knew that the earth was round!*

And in Galileo's time it was known that the earth revolved around the sun. It had been known for two or three thousand years, in fact, but it was concealed in obedience to orders, out of fear and cowardice.

The Greek historian Musaeus, who lived in about 1400 B.C., wrote a treatise – which has not come down to us – entitled *The Sphere*. He was a high priest of the Elusinian Mysteries and a great initiate; it is hard to imagine how he could have written a treatise on that subject without having known that the earth was round.

Aratus of Soli, a Greek physician and poet of the third century B.C., wrote an astronomical treatise in which he described the spheres so precisely that there could be no doubt about the roundness of the earth and universal gravitation. He was not an unknown; on the contrary, he was a famous man in his time. He lived with Ptolemy Philadelphus, King of Egypt, who had the Hebrew Scriptures translated into Greek (the Septuagint). Aratus was translated or commented on by Eratosthenes, Hipparchus, Cicero, Caesar, Ovid and others.

Several centuries earlier the Hindus,[2] Mayas and Incas proved that they had excellent cosmological knowledge, and two centuries before Aratus the Greek philosophers Pythagoras and Plato taught the sphericity and rotation of the earth. In about 450 B.C. Pythagoras learned from the wise men of Egypt that the earth rotated on its axis and revolved around the sun, as is reported by Ovid in the last chapter of his *Metamorphoses*.

In his book *Meadows of Gold and Mines of Gems*, the tenth-century Arab historian Masudi wrote, 'The sphere revolves around two pivots, or poles, which can be likened to the pegs of the carpenter or turner who makes balls, bowls and other wooden objects.'

In the year 1000 Sylvester II, the most learned pope that Christendom has ever known, demonstrated experimentally, with three spheres of his own invention, that the earth was round and revolved around the sun.

Copernicus, in about 1500, and Tycho Brahe and Kepler, in the sixteenth century, published works and formulated laws that aroused indignation but were known to be based on scientific truth.

How could the prelates who judged Columbus and Galileo have been ignorant of this?

The cultivated classes undeniably had that elementary cosmological knowledge, but for centuries and centuries the whole world remained silent on the subject; it was as if no one knew, as if everyone were in good faith.

What prodigious power did the conspiracies have to impose that hypnosis?

Moses Did Not Write Genesis

According to tradition, Genesis was revealed by God and written by the Hebrew patriarchs; it is also said to have been written by Moses.

This explanation fails to stand up under rational criticism. It is probable that Genesis was based on the *Phoenician History* written by Sanchuniathon long before the Hebrews were known, and long before they had written the Old Testament.

It would obviously be to the advantage of certain people to deny the great antiquity of Sanchuniathon's book, which is immensely valuable to the study of human history even though it destroys allegations regarded as sacred. If Genesis is a forgery, a copy, the Bible has no worth, the ancient Hebrews were only tellers of amusing stories and the Lord is an imaginary being whom it would be futile to invoke, pray to or fear. It is easy to see why believers had a great interest in trying to establish the idea that Sanchuniathon's book was either a pure literary invention or a work more recent than the Bible. But since it would have been dangerous to stir up public debate on the matter, the best policy was to plunge the book into oblivion, and that is what was done.

Have you ever heard of Sanchuniathon?

The orders for a 'blackout' were well obeyed! Atheists, who often had little historical knowledge, overlooked Sanchuniathon. Cultivated historians, who could have spoken of him, were careful not to bring down the wrath of Christian justice upon their heads.

The *Phoenician History* has not come down to us. It was translated in the first century by Philo Byblius. His translation mysteriously disappeared. In the early centuries of the Christian era the same thing happened to all authentic works of history that might have cast doubt on the Biblical version of history: they mysteriously disappeared.

Nothing would have remained of Sanchuniathon's work if, in the third century, there had not been a resounding controversy between the Greek philosopher Porphyry (of Syrian origin) and Eusebius, Bishop of Caesarea.

Referring to Philo's translation, which still existed at the time, Porphyry maintained that Moses had copied the essential parts of Genesis from the *Phoenician History*. Eusebius tried to refute him by quoting from that book. (His quotations will be given in the next chapter.)

Whom are we to believe: the man who categorically accused Moses of plagiarism, or the man who said that Genesis was the fruit of a divine revelation given to the great patriarch?

To attack Porphyry's arguments, Eusebius first quoted from the *Phoenician History*, then stated that Sanchuniathon had never existed and that the book had actually been written by Philo to combat Christianity. This gave a new turn to the controversy: Eusebius implicitly acknowledged that part of the text was the same as Genesis, but he claimed that Philo was a forger.

It was a clumsy tactic because several ancient authors had spoken of Sanchuniathon and, referring to their quotations, the grammarian Suidas was able to give the titles of three of his works, parts of which were collected in C. Müller's *Fragmenta Historicorum Graecorum.*

Eusebius therefore did not maintain his accusation and contented himself with confusing the issue to sow doubt.

'Moreover,' wrote the historian Ernest Renan, 'Porphyry was not a forger, but an erudite book lover. His character, as far as we can judge from his own works, was that of a conscientious writer on a variety of different subjects . . . We are immediately struck by his tone of good faith . . . He forthrightly describes his desire to know the truth, the effort he has made to do so, the mass of books he has read, the doubts that have been aroused in him by disagreements among various accounts . . .'

We must choose between the honest Porphyry and the pious Eusebius.

It should be pointed out that although Eusebius is the author of the valuable *Historia Ecclesiastica,* he has an extremely dubious reputation for accuracy.

The English historian Edward Gibbon reproaches him with having been a courtier of Emperor Constantine and having constantly lacked good faith in his descriptions of events. According to Gibbon, Eusebius dwells at length on everything that may uphold the honour of Christianity and systematically suppresses everything that might tarnish it. His partiality with regard to Constantine is notorious.[3]

It is worth knowing that one chapter of Eusebius' *Evangelical Demonstration* bears this curious title: 'To what extent it is permissible to use falsehood as a remedy for those who may be converted by that means.'

Without discussing the pros and cons of pious fraud, I will simply say that it is easy to choose between Philo and Eusebius.

In spite of everything, however, it is only fair to point out that Eusebius was a well-intentioned man even though he was blinded by his faith, and that we owe him a great debt of gratitude because it was through him that we received the only existing fragment of the authentic history of our civilisation. I believe it will convince a sceptical but open-minded reader that the existence of a conspiracy of falsehood is at least a real possibility.

Chapter 2

THE OLDEST MANUSCRIPT OF THE WESTERN WORLD

The *Phoenician History* is the oldest non-coded document of our historical archives. Furthermore it is particularly valuable because its author was a free man who did not hesitate to denounce myths.

Here is what the *Encyclopédie* says about Sanchuriathon: 'Judging from the fragments of the *Phoenician History*, he appears to have been a contemporary of Semiramis, two thousand years before Christ. If so, his book would go back into fabled antiquity . . . Sanchuniathon, like Vgasa in India, is said to have been a compiler of extremely ancient theogonic and historical documents that had been transmitted to him either by oral tradition or in writing.'

I regret that the entire text has not come down to us because it is certain that Eusebius did not reproduce the plagiarised parts and that the essential element, that is, the beginning of historical times, is totally absent. This is no exception to the general rule, whether Genesis is a copy or not, since we have countless proofs that history has always been falsified.

Since the *Phoenician History* is a fundamental document of human culture, but the surviving fragments of it are hard to obtain, I believe the truth-seeking reader will appreciate an opportunity to study them. I will therefore reproduce them as they appear in Eusebius' *Evangelical Preparation*, where they are interspersed with long commentaries in several different chapters, which explains a certain lack of coherence.

In the extracts given below, the subheadings, footnotes and passages in italics are my own additions.

1. Extracts from *Evangelical Preparation*, by Eusebius of Caesarea

Eusebius Complains of Having Been Slandered

In the fourth chapter of his slanderous work directed against us, Porphyry mentions these things, testifying in favour of Sanchuniathon as follows:

Sanchuniathon of Berytus relates with great truthfulness everything concerning the Jews because he alters neither places nor names, having had access to the writings of Jerombal, priest of the god Jeuo.

'Jerombal dedicated his history to Abibal, King of Berytus. It was accepted by him and by those he had instructed to examine it with respect to its veracity.

'The time when those men lived is earlier than the Trojan War and is very close to the time of Moses, as is shown by the successions of the Kings of Phoenicia.

'As for Sanchuniathon, whose name means "Friend of Truth" in the Phoenician language, he gathered all the ancient history in the documents found in each city and formed it into a body of writings. He lived in the time of Semiramis, Queen of the Assyrians, whose reign is believed to have preceded or at least coincided with the events of Ilion.

'Philo Byblius translated Sanchuniathon's writings into Greek.'

As he continues writing, he does not speak to us of the Supreme God, or even of the celestial gods, but of mortal men and women, and not even of those whose outstanding moral refinement makes them worthy of being admired for their virtues or being taken as models because of their philosophical minds, but of persons guilty of all the perverse and shameful aspects of depravity. Yet he admits that it is these same persons who have been and still are regarded as gods by all men, in different cities and places . . .

Philo divided Sanchuniathon's entire collection into

nine books. In his preface to the first book he writes as follows:

Taautos Was Thoth

'Things being thus, Sanchuniathon, a very studious and active man who desired above all else to know the principles of things and that of which all that exists is formed, diligently inquired into the writings of Taautos, having learned that of all the men who have ever appeared under the sun, Taautos was the first to conceive the invention of letters, and open the way for written documents. He therefore made him the foundation of his entire discourse. It was Taautos whom the Egyptians called Toyt and the Alexandrians Thoth, which the Greeks translated as Hermes (Mercury).'

Having said these things, Philo denounces the newcomers who, after those writings, wrongly and untruthfully introduced allegories, theories and expositions of physics into fables concerning the gods.

He continues: 'But more recent religious scholars destroyed all vestiges of events that occurred after the origin of things, inventing allegories within fables and combining them in such a way as to unite them with the movements of the universe.

'That is how they instituted mysteries and spread such thick shadows over all those things that it was no longer easy to determine what had really occurred. But Sanchuniathon discovered the secret writings of the Ammonians, which were known to very few people, and studied everything they contained. He then achieved his goal by setting aside the fable based on allegories until in later times there appeared priests who wanted to dissimulate the truth and restore to honour that fable which was the origin of the mystery that had not yet penetrated among the Greeks.'

After more observations, Philo continues in his preface:

'It must be stated at the outset, for greater clarity and partial knowledge of everything that follows, that the most ancient of the barbarians, notably the Phoenicians and Egyptians, who have served as guides for all other men, considered the greatest gods to be those who made discoveries to aid our existence, or who conferred benefits of any kind on various populations. They called them benefactors because of the many benefits they owed to them. They worshipped them as gods, and for that purpose they rededicated already existing temples to them. They erected pillars and branches to them, and worshipped those objects with great devotion.[4]

'The Phoenicians dedicated their greatest festivals to them and gave the constellations the names of their kings, some of whom were already regarded as gods. They recognised as natural gods only the sun, the moon, the planets, the stars and other things in that general category, so that there were mortal gods and immortal gods.'

Theology of the Phoenicians

'He supposes that a dark and windy air, or a breath of dark air and a muddy, infernal chaos, were infinite in both time and extension. When that wind, he says, fell in love with its own principles a conjunction resulted, and that coming together was called desire. Such was the principle of the creation of all things.

'That wind had no knowledge of what it had produced.

'From that cohabitation of the wind came Mot.

'Such was the sole germ of the creation and origin of all things.

'Animals appeared, but they were lacking in sensibility. They gave birth to intelligent animals named Zophasemin, that is, observers of the sky.

'Mot had the shape of an egg when he was formed. He became luminous and produced the sun, the moon, the stars and the great constellations.'

Such is the cosmogony of the Phoenicians, which openly introduces atheism.

Next comes the generation of animals: the male and the female were on the earth and in the sea.

'These things,' writes Philo, 'were found in the cosmogony and dissertations of Taautos, supported by the conjectures and convictions which Sanchuniathon conceived and made known by means of his insight.'

After speaking of the winds Notus and Boreas, which were deified, Philo adds:

'Such were the inventions of religious worship that were in conformity with the weakness and cowardice of their inventors.'

Birth of Mortal Men of a Divine Race

'The mortal men Aeon and Protogonos were born of the wind Kalpia and his wife Baau. Aeon discovered the food provided by trees. They were the parents of Genos and Genea, who lived in Phoenicia. Great droughts came and they reached up their hands towards the sky and the sun.'

He says that they regarded the sun as the master god of the sky and named him Beelsamen, which in Phoenician means 'master of the sky'. He was the Zeus of the Greeks. Then Philo attacks the error of the Greeks:

'It is not without reason that we make this distinction known: it is in order to establish the true meaning, which has been misinterpreted, of these names applied to objects. Misled by the uncertainty of translation, the Greeks took them in another meaning.

'From Genos, son of Aeon and Protogonos, were born new mortal children named Phos, Pyr and Phlox ('light', 'fire' and 'flame'). They invented fire by rubbing pieces of wood against each other, and taught its use. They had children of great size and marked superiority who gave their names to the mountains of which they were the sovereigns.'

It was from them that Mount Casios, the Lebanon Mountains and the Anti-Lebanon Mountains took their name. They gave birth to Samemrumos and Hepsurianos ('celestial height').

Sanchuniathon observes that men were named after their mothers, and that women shamelessly gave themselves to any man they saw. Then he says: 'Hysurianos lived in Tyre and invented huts made of reeds, rushes and papyrus. He had a dispute with his brother Usus, who was the first to think of taking the skins of animals he had killed and making them into a covering for his body.

'Torrential rains and violent winds devastated Tyre and broke the trees. The forest was swept by fire. Usus took a tree, stripped it of its branches and was the first to venture on to the sea. He consecrated two steles to fire and the wind, and worshipped them by spilling on them the blood of animals he had taken in his hunts . . .

'Many centuries had gone by since the age of Hypsurianos when Agreus and Alieus, inventors of fishing and hunting, were born. It was they who provided those arts with their implements. From them came two brothers who invented iron and the production of all things that make use of it. One of them, Chrysor, devoted himself to sorcery, prediction and the composition of discourses.'

He was the same as Hephaestus, who invented the fishhook and bait, the fishing line and the raft. He was the first of all men to sail on the sea, and that is why he was worshipped as a divinity after his death. He was called Zeus Michius.

Birth of Men of an Earthly Race

Next, he says that from this race came two young men: Technites ('artisan') and Autochton[5] ('earthly'). They conceived the idea of mixing wet clay with hay, drying it in the sun and making bricks with it; they thus invented the construction of roofs.

Others came after them, including Argos, then Agrueros or Agrotes, whose statue and portable temple are highly venerated in Phoenicia. The inhabitants of Byblos regarded him as the greatest of the gods.

It was they who conceived the idea of placing courtyards in front of houses and forming enclosures and grottoes. From them are descended those who hunt with dogs; they are called wandering tribes and Titans.

They procreated Amunon and Magon, who invented market towns and sheepfolds, and from whom were born Misor ('dauntless') and Sydic ('just'); they discovered the use of salt.

From Misor was born Taautos, who discovered writing

and formed the first letters. The Egyptians named him Thoor, the Alexandrians Tuth, the Greeks Hermes.[6]

From Sydys were born the Dioscuri, or Cabiri, or Corybants, or Samothracians. They invented the ship. From them were born other men who found medicinal plants for curing venomous bites and invented magic words. In their time were born Elium Hypsistos[7] and his wife Beruth, who settled in the land of Byblos. From them were born Epigeios or Autochthon, later named Uranos.

Uranos married his sister Ge and had four children by her: Ilus, known as Cronus,[8] Betyle, Dagon, known as Siton ('fish'), and Atlas . . .

Cronus Was a Mortal

Cronus had two daughters, Proserpine and Minerva. Proserpine died while still a virgin. Following the advice of Minerva and Hermes, Cronus used iron to make a scythe and a spear . . .

In this time the descendants of the Dioscuri combined all the parts of rafts and ships and began sailing the sea. When they were driven back to Mount Sasios they consecrated a temple there. The allies of Hel (Cronus) were called Eloim, which corresponds to Cronians. It was they who were thus named after Cronus.[9]

We learn from Philo's account that Uranos, a descendant of Hypsistos and his wife Beruth (the region of Byblos), was fought by Cronus and exiled. Where? It is not said.

In later times Uranos sent from the place of his exile his daughter Astarte and two of her sisters, Rhea and Dione, to kill Cronus.

The god Uranos invented and composed animated stones (*abadir* in Phoenician).

After having discovered wheat and the plough, Dragon was surnamed Jupiter the Ploughman.

Here, then, are the acts of Cronus and the venerable compacts of that life under Saturn, so celebrated by the Greeks that they declare it to have been the first age, the golden age of men endowed with the organ of the voice and the epoch of that felicity of the Ancients which is praised so highly.

The Coming of Astarte

The great Astarte, Jupiter Demarun and Adad, king of the gods, reigned over the earth with the consent of Cronus.[10]

As a sign of royalty, Astarte placed on her head the head of a bull.

Having travelled through the universe, she found a heavenly body that cut through the air and, having taken it, she consecrated it on the sacred island of Tyre.[11]

She whom the Phoenicians name Astarte is for us Venus.

Travelling through the universe, Cronus gave Athens and the kingdom of Attica to his daughter Minerva.

When a plague and a great loss of life occurred, Cronus sacrificed his only son to his father Uranos. He circumcised himself and made all his allies do the same. A short time later, after the death of the son he had had with Rhea and Pluto, he consecrated him; the son's name was Muth, and it is thus that the Phoenicians name death and Pluto.

After this, Cronus gave possession of Byblos to the goddess Baaltis, the same as Dione, and he gave Berytus to Poseidon and the Cabiri, ploughmen and fishermen. It was they who consecrated the relics of Pontus in the city of Berytus.

Before these things, Taautos, having initiated Uranos, traced in relief the facial expression of the gods Cronus and Dagon and the others who are the sacred characters of letters. He also conceived, in favour of Cronus, the emblem of royalty: four eyes distributed in the anterior and posterior parts of the body, two of them slowly closing, and on the shoulders four wings, two spread and two folded.

The meaning of this symbol is that Cronus saw while asleep and slept while awake; and for the wings, that he flew while resting and rested while flying.

As for the other gods, he placed two wings on their shoulders to show that they accompany Cronus in his flight. He also gave Cronus two wings on his head, one to indicate commanding intelligence, the other to indicate sensation.[12]

Cronus having come from the regions of the south, he gave all of Egypt to the god Taautos so that it would be his empire.

The seven Cabiri, sons of Sydysc, were the first of all men to record these facts in order to preserve their memory, as did their eighth brother Asclepius, following the order of the god Taautos.

History Has Been Altered

Then the son of Thabion was the first hierophant of Phoenicia. Having allegorically translated these facts, and having mingled them with the physical movements of the universe, he transmitted them to the directors of orgies and the prophets of mysteries.

The latter, wishing to increase the obscurity of all those traditions, added new inventions to them and taught them to their successors and those they initiated.

'The Greeks, who excel among all peoples by their brilliant imagination, first appropriated most of these things and added various embellishments to them in order to give them a dramatic form; then, intending to beguile by the charm of fables, they completely transformed them.

'Hence Hesiod and the vaunted cyclical poets fabricated their own stories of gods, giants and castrations and carried them from place to place until all truth was extinguished.

'Our ears, accustomed from early childhood to hearing their false stories, and our minds, imbued with those preconceptions for centuries, preserve those fantastic suppositions as if they were a sacred trust, as I said at the beginning. When time had corroborated their work it made that usurpation almost impregnable, so that truth seems incredible, and adulterated stories have the appearance of truth.'

Let us end here our quotation from the work of Sanchuniathon interpreted by Philo Byblius and recognised as true after examination by the testimony of the philosopher Porphyry.

A little farther on, we read:

In his work on the Jewish people, Philo reports the following:

'The genius of Taautos, whom the Egyptions call Thoth, surpassed that of all the Phoenicians. He was the first to regulate religious worship among them. He drew it out of coarse inexperience and made it into an enlightened experience.'

The Mysterious Serpent

This same Philo, in speaking of Phoenician letters and interpreting Sanchuniathon, says:

'Consider venomous reptiles and animals which are of no benefit to mankind; they cause death and loss of limbs to those in whom they inject their terrible poison.[13]

'Taautos, and after him the Phoenicians and Egyptians, deified the species of dragons and serpents as having the strongest breath of all crawling animals.

'He declares that the serpent belongs to igneous matter in that it has a speed that nothing can surpass, because of its breath.[14] Without feet, hands or any of the external means that other animals have, it performs all movements and exemplifies the most varied shapes. It gives whatever speed it wishes to the helixes[15] it describes in its motion. That is what makes it an essential part of temples and mysteries . . .

'This animal does not die a natural death . . . The Phoenicians call it Agathodaemon,[16] the good spirit, and the Egyptians call it Kneph, giving it the head of a hawk because of the energy of that bird.'

Epies, the foremost Egyptian hierophant and temple scribe, who was translated into Greek by Areius of Heracleopolus, writes on the subject as follows:

'The first and most eminent divinity is the hawk-headed serpent which, when it opens its eyes, fills all the first-engendered earth with light; and when it closes them, light is succeeded by darkness.'

Epeis used that grandiloquent language to convey the idea that, being brilliant, it illuminated everything, for the nature of light is to illuminate.[17]

Pherecydes, who took all his fundamental ideas from the Phoenicians, celebrated in his theology the god Ophioneus[18] and the Ophionides, of whom we shall speak later.

The Egyptians, representing the universe in accordance with the same concept, drew an airy, flaming circle with a hawk-headed serpent stretched across it. The entire figure resembles the Greek letter theta. They interpret the world by a circle, and the serpent at the centre of it by the good deity Agathodaemon.[19]

In the sacred ritual of the Persians, Zoroaster says, 'The hawk-headed god is the first, eternal, indivisible and peerless, the guide to all that is beautiful, never letting himself be won over by gifts.'

Ostanes says the same things about him in a work entitled *The Eight Prayers.*

Taking this as their point of departure, philosophers built their system, as has been reported: in the sanctuaries of the temples they consecrated, they represented the first heavenly bodies in the form of serpents. They offered sacrifices to those reptiles, dedicated festivals and mysteries to them, and believed them to be the greatest gods and the moderators of all things.

Such are the traditions of Sanchuniathon concerning serpents.

Philo writes:

'Among the Ancients, in situations of grave danger, it was customary for the rulers of the city or the nation to ward off general destruction by sacrificing the most cherished of their children as an appeasement offering to the vengeful gods; their throats were cut in secret.

'When Cronus, whom the Phoenicians call Il [Hel, Bel], and who after his death was consecrated in the heavenly body that bears his name, was ruling the country, he had an only son, Jeud. He adorned him with the emblems of royalty and sacrificed him on an altar he had erected for that purpose.'

If Sanchuniathon was born during the reign of Semiramis and if, as it generally agreed, she lived long before the time of Troy, then he also lived before that time; but it is said that he received documents by writers earlier than himself, and those writers are said to have lived at approximately the same time as Moses. Porphyry writes as follows in the fourth book of his diatribe against us:

'Sanchuniathon of Berytus relates with great truthfulness everything concerning the Jews because he alters neither places nor names, having had access to the writings of Jerombal, priest of the god Jeuo.

'Jerombal dedicated his history to Abibal, King of Berytus. It was accepted by him and by those he had instructed to examine it with respect to its veracity.

'The time when those men lived is earlier than the Trojan War and is very close to the time of Moses, as is shown by the successions of the Kings of Phoenicia.

'As for Sanchuniathon, whose name means "Friend of Truth" in the Phoenician language, he gathered all the ancient history in the documents found in each city and formed it into a body of writings. He lived in the time of Semiramis, Queen of the Assyrians.'

2. Comments

The Flying Serpent

In my opinion, the most important passage in the fragments of the *Phoenician History* is the one in which the flying serpent is described: it has 'the strongest breath'; 'it has a speed that nothing can surpass, because of its breath'; 'it gives whatever speed it wishes to the helixes it describes in its motion'; it has exceptional energy; it is represented with the head of a hawk; 'being brilliant, it illuminated everything.'

It is clearly not an actual serpent, but a flying machine, since it moves at great speed and is represented with the head of a hawk.

This flying machine 'gives whatever speed it wishes to the helixes it describes'. The sentence is enigmatic, but it appears from the general description that the 'serpent' is propelled through space by a 'breath' from the rear that strongly suggests a rocket or a jet engine, and by a helicoid system in front.

The word 'helix' comes from the Greek *helissein*, 'to wind', from which was derived *ilinx*, 'whirlwind'.

It is this 'whirlwind' that most strongly strikes my imagination. It is at the front of the serpent, but the serpent itself does not constitute a whirlwind, because otherwise it would not have a propulsive blast at the rear.

The whole craft might be a kind of Archimedean screw, but a parallel with twentieth-century aeronautics suggests that the flying serpent was an aeroplane with a turbojet engine and a propeller in front. It is interesting to note that aeroplanes are now assuming more and more the elongated shape of rockets and snakes.

It is also worth noting that the craft had a brilliant appearance and that its source of energy belonged to igneous matter. This is no doubt a reference to the fire ejected from its jet engines, whose roar ('breath') made a strong impression on Sanchuniathon.

This 'serpent' was known to the Phoenicians and Egyptians, and it closely corresponds to the definition that was finally given of it: an extraterrestrial flying machine piloted by initiates. For it is both the craft and the astronauts. Furthermore it is ofen represented as having the head of a ram; that is, a guide.

'When it opens its eyes, it fills all the first-engendered earth with light; and when it closes them, light is succeeded by darkness.'

This sentence and the cosmological symbol that follows it, in which the universe is represented as an airy circle containing a serpent, are richly instructive despite the confusion that Philo creates by introducing Zoroaster's thought into the circuit. I see in them a revelation of our genesis: the first-engendered earth has been formed, and may already be populated by indigenous human beings but men will not become self-aware and enlightened unless initiators from space bring them knowledge. And when men no longer help each other, civilisations decline or collapse.

What is involved here is not God – the whole description of the serpent obviously refers to a material object – but it may be the gods, and we have seen that this is the name Sanchuniathon gives to civilisers and inventors.

The serpent in the middle of a circle is closely related to the primordial electric wave known to the Celts, which I identify with Agathodaemon: electricity.

Sanchuniathon's *Phoenician History* thus takes us into extraterrestrial adventure and, amazingly, the same is true of the Bible (the angel-initiators), the Book of Enoch, the Mayan and Tibetan manuscripts and the Vedas.

I do not know if we should believe in the mysterious 'flying saucers' that are said to be visiting us. The evidence is weak, and in any case we cannot know whether extraterrestrials will make any contribution to our civilisation, in spite of the knowledge we attribute to them. One thing is clear, however: all civilisations born five thousand years ago bore the mark of extraterrestrial contributions: first, because the gods were recognised representatives of another planet; and second, because inventions that were extraordinary for the time were revealed to mankind and lasted only a few generations, during the period when the initiators were present.

Five Thousand Years Ago the Gods Flew

Five thousand years ago there were prestigious civilisations in Asia Minor and America: those of the Assyro-Babylonians, Phoenicians, Mayas and Incas. And at the same time the older civilisations of the Persians, Hindus and Egyptians experienced a revival. The whole world was under the sway of alien gods who came from the sky.

These gods are represented everywhere by the same mysterious symbol: the flying serpent, or dragon.

In Egypt, Isis, Horus, Hathor, Thoth and Khonsu-Ptah are placed under the sign of a winged disc flanked by two asps.

In Persia, the great god Ahura Mazda is shown in a flying boat that has the shape of a helicopter; in Assyria and Babylonia this same symbol is used for Ashur, the husband of Ishtar.

In Phoenicia, the two great gods are Baal and Baal Tsaphon, Lord of the North, whose symbol is the begetting bull.

In Carthage, the outstanding Phoenician colony, the great goddess associated with Baal is Tanit. She is represented in steles by an enigmatic symbol called the Sign of Tanit, which historians refrain from interpreting.

In its most purified version, the Sign of Tanit is a disc hovering over a truncated cone or pyramid. Below the disc there is sometimes a kind of boat resembling two raised arms.

The Flying White Goddess

In Honduras the myth changes but keeps its main characteristics: extraterrestrial gods and flying machines.

Legend says that an ineffably beautiful, white-skinned young woman came from the sky and landed in the city of Cealcoquin, where she built a palace adorned with strange figures of men and animals. In the temple was placed a green stone which on three of its sides had drawings as mysterious as those on the walls of the palace. It was a magic stone and a true talisman which gave the goddess's kingdom the power to vanquish all its enemies.

One day, feeling that her beauty was declining, she divided her realm among her sons and had herself carried on her flying bed to the highest terrace of her palace. She soon disappeared into the sky in the form of a beautiful bird.

In Peru, Bolivia and Colombia, in the ancient kingdom of the Incas, there are obvious representations of spacecraft, particularly on the Puerta del Sol at Tiahuanaco. Here, too, the gods used flying machines: Viracocha is closely linked to those shown on the Puerta del Sol. Orejona, the first mother of mankind, came from Venus in a 'vessel brighter than the sun', wrote Garcilaso de La Vega.

Astronauts All Over the Earth

In 1963, Soviet archaeologists in eastern Siberia discovered a stone wall that bore carvings of bird-headed creatures with human bodies. Professor Alexander Lipsky pointed out that they were quite similar to the Egyptian gods Thoth and Horus. They have been dated at about 3000 B.C., during the period when religions all over the world were conditioned by an obsession with gods and flying machines.

An even more important discovery was made at Perghana, Uzbekistan, in central Asia, where Professor G. V. Shatsky found, near a grotto, a drawing of a kind of prehistoric astronaut wearing an airtight helmet with antennae and carrying on his back a device that suggests the kind of equipment used by astronauts outside their spacecraft.

In India, the gods travelled in *vimanas*, flying machines propelled by mercury, and the Ramayana states that the hero Kubera usually travelled in a flying dragon.

Celtic traditions report that in the time of Belisama ('flamelike'), who is easily recognisable as the comet Venus entering our atmosphere, King Bran, a traveller to mysterious regions, went to the West in a winged chariot that did not touch the water.

In all parts of the globe at the same time, a phenomenon occurred which resulted in the advent of new gods, reputed to be from beyond the earth. This correlation makes it impossible to doubt the reality of the events.

Chapter 3

THE WRATH OF THE SKY

Groping our way, selecting probable truths and eliminating proven adulterations, we can re-establish the order of the great events that give a face to the past. But history is also a matter of dates and we have no chronological markers that give the exact times of those events. In a century when distances are measured in thousandths of a micron and times in millionths of a second, we still have only grossly empirical means of delimiting the vast periods of protohistory.

Venus in 3000 B.C.

The birth of Jesus Christ is not an accurate standard for measuring time because there is no way of knowing exactly when it happened. The margin of error is several years at best, and there are no documents from the period to prove that Jesus ever really existed.

Farther back in time, we can situate Pythagoras and Buddha approximately, but with Homer and the Trojan War we enter the mists of the so-called Iron Age and Bronze Age, which are nothing but ludicrous inventions of prehistorians.

A civilisation as scientific and rational as ours should establish an astronomical calendar. It will inevitably be done some day, perhaps on the occasion of the year 2000.

Two periods, however, can be dated with a certain precision: those of the two events that caused the great and lesser Deluges.

We have many accounts of the lesser Deluge. It occurred when Venus entered our solar system in the form of a comet, was caught by the sun's gravitation and began orbiting it as a planet. Reliable astronomical data such as the Tirvalour Tables of India (now hidden somewhere in France), the Chaldean astronomical tables, the testimony of traditions all over the world and the simultaneous advent of many Venusian gods make it impossible to doubt that the phenomenon actually took place, as I showed in *The Legacy of the Gods.*

The date, which could be calculated precisely, is in the vicinity of 3000 B.C.

The great Deluge could also be situated in time, but although it is not denied by most scientists it is so upsetting to prehistorians and astronomers that a rigorous investigation of it would be considered unseemly.

But in recent years geology and especially glaciology have made amazing progress and provided not only proof that the great Deluge occurred, but also facts that enable it to be dated.

Prehistorians have no desire to accept that cataclysm, which was a veritable end of the world, because it overturns their theories based on an obscure relation between man and the ape, and on the eras known as the Paleolithic and the Neolithic, whose misinterpretation I have proved in Chapter 4 of *The Legacy of the Gods.*

Astronomers have decreed that the order of the planets has undergone no notable disturbance for many thousands of years. The idea that Venus abruptly burst into our sky deeply troubles their tranquillity.

Historians, committed to a dogmatic religious mythology with no scientific foundation, cannot accept an order of events which differs from that of the Bible. But it seems clear to me that human history has been falsified from the Deluge to the Christian era. I would like to make corrections and present new views based on events as they must actually have taken place.

The starting point of those views is the Deluge that brought about a new configuration of the globe and was the true Year 1 of the present human race.

Light on the Lascaux Caves

The cave paintings at Lascaux, France, date from the Magdalenian period and are one of the great wonders of the world. Their conception is sober and precise and they show a sense of observation and movement that the painters of the Renaissance did not possess. Yet it was the supposedly primitive and brutal 'cave men' of the Magdalenian who created that exhibition of painting for the sole purpose of showing their knowledge and artistic talent.

In the first publicity folders praising the Lascaux caves, pundits were quoted as saying that the paintings were between twenty-five and thirty thousand years old. Then the figure was revised: fifteen to twenty thousand years. And now they are dated at only twelve thousand years ago.

To err is human, of course, and it is easy to excuse those variations in dating; what is inexcusable is that the significance of the discovery has been concealed.

One thing is obvious to any unprejudiced observer: those Magdalenians, capable of drawing and painting with such consummate art, were not primitive brutes.

It is well established in anthropology that the notion of art, and particularly painting without a utilitarian purpose (the Lascaux paintings have no detectable magic character), shows that a civilisation has reached the crucial period when great inventions will soon appear: agricultural machines, organisation of cities, weapons industry, and so on.

The people of Lascaux, who produced those prodigious paintings, unquestionably knew *at least* how to build a stone wall and a house with a fireplace. In one or two centuries they should have achieved the smelting of metals, farming, stockbreeding and the construction of stone cities. In a thousand years they should have invented wagons, gunpowder and printing. In two or three thousand years they should have reached our level and developed automobiles and space rockets.

Yet despite clear evidence of a coming era of civilisation and great inventions, *nothing happened*! And not only did the people of Lascaux fail to invent gunpowder and the bicycle, but *they disappeared*!

Why have our learned prehistorians not studied that amazing phenomenon? Because they would have to recognise the truth and admit the reality of a primordial event that they are determined to deny: the Universal Deluge. (Strictly speaking, of course, it was not universal, since it affected only our planet, but the term has become commonly accepted and I will continue to use it.)

Only one thing explains the abrupt, total disappearance of Magdalenian civilisation, whose people wore hats, jackets, trousers and shoes, and whose less highly developed members painted in caves: a gigantic cataclysm that annihilated them. Could anything be more obvious?

Unimpeachable Witnesses

Traditions all over the world – among the western Europeans, Scandinavians, Celts, Greeks, Hebrews, Chaldeans, Hindus, Iroquois, Sioux, Mayas, Incas, Africans, Polynesians – speak at length of a great deluge. Such unanimity makes it highly improbable that people on isolated islands and continents so far away from each other could all have invented the same legend with similar if not identical details.

To deny that our planet was repeatedly disrupted by internal or cosmic cataclysms in prehistoric times would be to maintain that the cooling of the earth took place magically, that mountains rose with majestic slowness and that the ocean beds were hollowed out so gradually as not to disturb the sleep of fish.

One would also have to maintain that comets cannot collide with planets, that novas cannot explode; in short, that the universe is a perfectly regulated mechanism in which no abrupt, violent phenomena can occur.

No scientist would venture to defend such a view.

The fact is that there have been upheavals which are

revealed by the study of cosmic, meteorological and geological phenomena.

There have been many deluges since the beginning of our planet, and there is good reason to believe that they follow cycles alternating from one pole to the other.

Beginning in 1248, the northern hemisphere has been cooling and the southern hemisphere has been warming. Since the complete cycle takes place in twenty-one thousand years, we may assume that there will be another Universal Deluge in the year 11,748.

Quasars and the Deluge

Quasars, or quasi-stellar objects, are relatively small heavenly bodies which emit colossal energies much more intense than that of our Milky Way.

Variations in the luminosity of quasar 3 C 273 seem to show that quasars periodically expand and contract, as though to compensate for losses and growths of our universe, thus functioning as cosmic regulators.

This phenomenon has led the British astrophysicist Fred Hoyle to formulate a theory that may seem fantastic, but is in agreement with tradition. The scientific writer André Schnubel states it as follows:

> For more than ten billion years the universe has been progressively reaching higher levels of organisation: galaxy, star, planet, life. But some day all that matter will become atomic dust again, and everything will begin all over again without us . . . A time for architecture will be followed by a time for self-destruction, and so on . . .

In this theory, the mass of any material body depends on the total contents of the universe, which undergoes fluctuations (expansion, explosion, reorganisation).

If so, is it surprising that our little planet should be subject to periodic deluges and upheavals, related to cosmic fluctuations?

'The study of geological phenomena shows the existence of cycles,' writes the prehistorian Furon, and the glaciologist Milankovitch attributes an extraterrestrial cause to the phenomenon of glaciations: cycles of solar radiation.

Meteorites and the Deluge

Every year, thousands of meteorites fall on the earth, varying in weight from a few grammes to several tons. Statistics show that a meteorite weighing several thousand tons should strike the earth every seven or eight thousand years. There are multiple causes of deluges!

It has been calculated that if a meteorite thirty miles in diameter fell into the ocean off Cape Verde, Africa, it would cause a tidal wave capable of submerging cities on the coasts of the Atlantic Ocean. If it fell on land, it would cause a worldwide cataclysm and might produce a shift of the poles, which are not in a very stable state of equilibrium. A meteorite more than sixty miles in diameter would bring on another universal deluge.

We must also consider the possibility of a collision between our planet and a comet or asteroid. This is not as unlikely as one might think, since in 1966 several astrophysicists, including Professor S. T. Butler of the University of Sydney, expressed concern over a possible collision between the earth and the asteroid Icarus.

Icarus is not very large and it is about four million miles from Earth, but its explosive power in a collision would be greater than that of a thousand hydrogen bombs. There have undoubtedly been many such asteroids in the lifetime of the solar system and some of them must have had devastating collisions with our planet.

It should be noted that several asteroids, probably fragments of a destroyed planet, gravitate around the earth:

Hermes, with a diameter of about 4,000 feet.

Adonis, a sausage-shaped rock 1,200 feet long.

Amor, a wandering rock several hundred feet wide.

Eros, in the shape of a dumbbell, 25 miles long.

Halley's Comet, which will pass near the earth in 1986.

Is it unreasonable to assume that a large asteroid struck the earth at the time of the cataclysm?

Meteorites and Mysterious Stones

It is hard to identify the largest meteorites that have fallen, either because they are at the bottom of the ocean, or have formed hills or rocky masses that are difficult to recognise, or lie underground at the bottom of the craters they dug when they struck.

The great craters are:

New Quebec Crater, Canada, diameter two miles.
Meteor Crater, U.S.A., 4,000 feet.
Wolfe Crater, Australia, 2,800 feet.
Aouelloul, Mauritania, 820 feet.
Henbury, Australia, 720 feet.

The largest meteorites have been found at:

Cape York, Greenland, weight 80,000 pounds.
Bacubirito, Mexico, 60,000 pounds.
Otumpa, Argentina, 33,000 pounds. (It was once thought to be an outcropping of a metallic lode.)
Willamette, U.S.A., 30,000 pounds.
Bemdego, Brazil, 20,000 pounds.
Krasnoiarsk, U.S.S.R., 825 pounds.
Paragould, U.S.A., 740 pounds.
Molina, Spain, 255 pounds.

Mysterious stones that fell on the earth were called 'thunder stones' or 'animated stones' by the Ancients. They were believed to be capable of floating on water at the sound of a trumpet, or of sinking into the ground when impious names were spoken. Some of them were thought to be inhabited by gods and for this reason they were either kept in temples or worshipped at the places where they had been found.

The most famous of these stones are as follows:

1. The black stones of the Temple of the Sun on the

island of Lake Titicaca, Bolivia-Peru. They are said to have been brought by Orejona, the mother of mankind, who came from the planet Venus.

2. The three black stones of the Kaaba, in Mecca, brought from the sky by angels.

3. The Stone of Apollo. Black, hard and heavy, believed to be a meteorite.

According to legend, Helenius, son of Priam and a famous Greek soothsayer, could foretell the future by means of a stone that had been given to him by Apollo. To obtain the oracle of the gods, he shook the stone above his head and recited incantations. The stone then spoke in a strange, faint voice and announced the future.

4. The Stone of Cybele on Mount Ida in ancient Phrygia, east of Troy. A mass of iron believed to be a meteorite.

5. The 'Mother of the Gods' at Pessinonte, ancient Phrygia.

6. The Stone of Diana at Ephesus.

According to tradition, the statue of the goddess and the stones of the temple fell from the sky. The worship was of Diana-Artemis, that is, the planet Venus, and not the moon, as some have maintained. Diana was the sister of Apollo, who was the Gwyon and the Bel-Heol of the Celts and the Hermes of the Egyptians.

7. The Ancylus of the Romans, a mass of meteoric iron which fell during the reign of Numa Pompilius in about 700 B.C. According to a prophecy of the Sibylline Books, its loss would announce the fall of Rome.

8. The Stone of Argos, which fell in Thrace in 465 B.C. It made the philosopher Anaxagoras believe that the vault of the sky was made like a stone wall and sometimes lost part of its facing.

9. The Algabal of Emesa, in Syria. A conical black stone worshipped by the Phoenicians.

When he became Emperor of Rome, Varius Avitus Bassianus took the name of Heliogabalus in memory of the temple where the sun is said to have been worshiped. Here again, there was a deliberate false identification: the stone of Emesa was not related to worship of the sun, but to an unknown worship, probably the same as that rendered to Asima, divinity of the nearby city of Hamath.

Aside from these famous stones – or perhaps in close connection with them – we should also mention magnetic mountains whose black, shiny, compact iron, oxidised to a relatively small extent, has two poles and acts as a natural magnet. The most noteworthy are those at Dannemora, Sweden, north of Lake Watter; Taberg, south of the same lake; and Utoe, Finland.

The Deluge According to Glaciologists

Fifteen years ago it was believed that the latest ice age, that of Würms, had lasted between 100,000 and 150,000 years, with very slow melting. But today, on the basis of recent work by such great glaciologists as J. Jelgersame, V. Romanowsky and André Cailleux, we can establish certain fundamental points which put events back in their proper place:

1. The last glacial melting took place about twelve thousand years ago (with a margin of error of two thousand years).

2. It was extremely abrupt and was probably caused by a collision with our planet or a cosmic phenomenon with similar effects, such as the close passage of a comet.

3. The cataclysm was worldwide, with all the glaciers melting at the same time. The earth was swept by a gigantic tidal wave.

And geologists are now convinced, on the basis of scientific evidence,[20] that about twelve thousand years ago the rate of sedimentation on the sea bottoms was considerably reduced, while at the same time an abrupt change of climate affected the whole earth.

The Universal Deluge, caused by an abrupt glacial melting and a shift of the polar icecap, is thus a well-established and reliably dated fact.

With that golden key to history, prehistoy and geology,

we can now open the forbidden door of the past and put an end to the imaginings of certain pundits who are determined to invent our genesis.

Ironically, the good Abbé Breuil, a world-renowned authority on prehistory, developed a number of theories that were worthless because he did not give credence to the Bible and the story of Noah; he did not understand the lesson of Lascaux and vainly sought Darwinian links all his life.

In the ocean depths two hundred miles east of Caracas, Venezuela, probes have shown that the sediment on the bottom was exposed to air and sunlight twelve thousand years ago. This would seem to indicate that waves a mile deep raced across the earth in that area. Such waves would break against mountains at a height of six or seven thousand feet. They would be sufficient to wipe out the human race in most parts of the world, except for groups scattered over high plateaus above the level of the flood.

Chapter 4

THE FIVE ISLANDS OF THE GLOBE

The Deluge is thus no longer a hypothesis: it has become a historical certainty.

Imagine the Year 10,000 B.C.

In about 10,000 B.C. (that is, twelve thousand years ago), polar glaciers much smaller than in our time bordered the Green Land, or Hyperborea, where according to tradition an excessively advanced civilisation flourished – excessively advanced because it had exceeded certain limits and its members, arrogant, learned and dangerous, were soon to return to the clay of their original state.

Traditions state that the cataclysm began with a gigantic fire that swept over the whole planet. People were burned alive or drowned, and the Popul Vuh says that some of them were transformed into animals. We should also note the metamorphoses in Greek mythology and the fantastic beings, half-human and half-animal, that abound in all other mythologies (and also in the Bible).

Those mutations suggest the idea of radiation. In Chapters 2 and 3 of *The Legacy of the Gods* I presented the view that there was an atomic war between Mu and Atlantis, a view supported by the Vedas and the Popul Vuh, the sacred book of the ancient Mexicans.

Even if there was not an atomic war before the Deluge, however, we must accept the probable occurrence of an event like the passage of a comet, which would have been more than sufficient to cause violent atmospheric perturbations and disrupt the Van Allen belts. There would have been an intense bombardment of cosmic particles (radiation) and accelerated mutations in human beings, animals and plants. Such things have happened thousands of times in the billions of years of our planet's existence.

There has probably been too much speculation on the slow evolution of species. Evolution has not always taken place over vast stretches of time, as conventional anthropologists believe; it has sometimes been produced by abrupt mutations resulting from accidental factors.

In the Universal Deluge, the rain of fire that preceded the flood may have had at least four causes:

1. Passage of a comet, a light or glancing collision, a rain of meteorites or the bursting of asteroids.

2. Volcanic eruptions.

3. Nuclear explosions or an atomic war fought by inhabitants of the earth.

4. An extraterrestrial signal. A too-sudden manifestation from an extraterrestrial civilisation to awaken the attention of earthlings. Impact of an enormous spacecraft that crashed in the U.S.A. or Mongolia; something like the 1908 explosion in Siberia multiplied by a thousand or a hundred thousand.

The polar glacier broke loose, crumbled the mountains of Scandinavia, scraped across the continents and plunged into the ocean.

The region inhabited by the Celts was abruptly divided by the English Channel, with England, Ireland and the Isle of Man on one side and Gaul on the other.

A large part of Brittany and Aquitaine was submerged. Disaster struck the whole planet: some continents emerged from beneath the ocean while others disappeared, swallowed up or scraped away by drifting mountains. As a whole, the globe was a smoking, formless magma, a roaring chaos in which the geography of future times was being shaped.

I have no desire to play the part of a visionary, but was this not how the Ancients described the cataclysm? Was this not how it must have happened before the horrified eyes of the survivors?

But on that globe where the flood had finished the destructive work of fire, there were a few islands of relative security in the midst of the general desolation. Those islands were the great plateaus of the globe, whose average altitude is of six thousand feet and whose peaks have an average height of twelve thousand feet.

Waves Six Thousand Feet High

I estimate that during the Deluge waves broke at heights of six to twelve thousand feet, depending on latitude. This estimate is supported by several factors:

1. Since there were only a few survivors, we may assume that the flood spared the high plateaus where a handful of people lived: hunters, shepherds, woodsmen; that is, the least advanced members of pre-Deluge civilisation.

2. Traditions say that the only survivors were those who were able to climb to the tops of high mountains. People living in valleys must not have had time to make such a climb, which ordinarily took several hours or even days, since we know that the flood happened suddenly.

3. The Bible tells us that Noah landed on Mount Ararat; Xisuthrus, in Chaldea, brought his boat to rest on Mount Korkura; the Manu of the Hindus went to the Himalayan plateaus; Bochica in South America took refuge on the Altiplano of the Andes; and Coxcox, the Mexican Noah, did the same in the Sierra Madre. The North American Indians spoke of the Rocky Mountains and African tribes stated that their survivors gathered on the Ethiopian plateau.

All these mountain ranges have peaks higher than twelve thousand feet.

4. Mammoths caught by an abrupt upheaval of the ground have been found frozen at altitudes of twelve thousand feet in central Asia. This means that the cataclysm must have caused gigantic wrinkles in the earth's crust.

The mammoths were killed by the upheaval and remained frozen in the post-Deluge ice.

Five Islands Emerge

If we imagine the earth flooded and ravaged by waves breaking at altitudes of up to twelve thousand feet, what do we see behind the reach of the cataclysm? We see five high plateaus, in Mexico, Peru, Ethiopia, Iran and the Himalayas.

These plateaus were practically the only parts of the globe that were spared by the Deluge, though there were probably other places that might have served as a refuge for a few people, such as Greenland, where the tidal wave was less massive because it started from the north pole. There are peaks in Greenland more than nine thousand feet high. Since the flood began in the north and moved towards the equator, constantly increasing as it went, mountains that were relatively low but located near the north pole must have remained above water.

The tidal wave must have risen to twelve thousand feet in America and to only nine thousand feet at the latitude of the Caucasus. It is logical to assume that, at the beginning, mountains six thousand feet high were not covered.

This view is in agreement with the laws of physics and the tradition which states that Hyperborea and Thule were in a temperate oasis surrounded by mountains of ice. This tradition is supported by the example of Iceland, with its geysers that are a veritable hot-water heating system, and by the fact that before the earth was tilted in relation to the plane of the ecliptic there were no seasons.

A group of Hyperboreans could therefore have survived the Deluge and bequeathed initiatic knowledge to the Scandinavians and Celts who descended from the survivors on the Iranian plateau.

Very Few Survivors

The Universe Deluge, which corresponds to the deluge

of Ogyges, wiped out nearly the whole human race, since traditions mention the following numbers of survivors:

Eight according to the Bible.

Two after the deluge of Deucalion in Greek mythology.

Two thousand nine hundred and one in Persian mythology.

Two to six in the Assyro-Babylonian deluge (attributed to Venus).

Ten to a hundred in the Chaldean deluge of Xisuthrus.

One in the deluge of Manu (the oldest), of the Catapatha Brahmana.

Four or five in the Greek version in which the deluge of Ogyges is older than that of Deucalion.

Eight in the deluge of Manu (Mahabharata).

Eight in the deluge of Satyavrata.

Two in the deluge of the Kymris (Belgian Celts).

Two in the Eddas of the Scandinavians.

Two in the deluge of the Lithuanians.

Two according to traditions of the Canaris in Ecuador.

Fifty to a hundred in the deluge of Bochica (Colombia).

Fifty to a hundred in the deluge of the Chichimecas in the first age, known as Atanotiuli ('Sun of the Waters'). This deluge is specifically said to have been worldwide.

Two in the Mexican deluge of Coxcox.

Four in the traditions of Brazil.

A small number in the deluges of New Caledonia, the Incas, etc.

I would not want to accept all these figures literally, but the testimony of traditions all over the world shows that the number of survivors was extremely small.

Most animal species survived and it is probable that they had a premonition of the danger. This premonition cannot be rationally explained; it escapes scientific analysis but it is a proven fact.

Even if it is not totally groundless, the legend of Noah's Ark cannot explain the survival of animals. If it had existed, the Ark would have had to be as scientifically advanced as our modern laboratory ships. To preserve a multitude of sensitive species from excessive cold, heat, dampness and dryness, and to give each species the proper temperature and food, the resources of electricity and perhaps even electronics would have had to be used.

The Egyptian Case

Another enigma, one that involves the human race, solicits our curiosity: the 'Egyptian case'.

Until about 4000 B.C., no notable civilisation was developed in the world, except in Egypt. Farther back in time, it seems impossible to find architectural traces (except in caves), since the Deluge razed part of the earth's surface, particularly the valleys where cities and other evidence of human activity existed.

The cataclysm, abundantly cited by the Hindus, Babylonians, Chaldeans, Hebrews, Scandinavians and Amerindians, was all but passed over in silence by the Egyptians, which may have led prehistorians to deny its reality.

Everything seems to indicate that the populations of the Nile had never known the Deluge. And the truth is that they had not, for the valley of the Nile is only twelve thousand years old; before, the river did not flow into the Mediterranean.

It was thus in a new country that the most ancient of our historical civilisations was born about eight thousand years ago. We may therefore assume that Hyperboreans or Atlanteans settled in the upper valleys of the Nile shortly after the Deluge. (By Hyperboreans I mean the white populations living between Greenland and Florida before the Deluge, and by Atlanteans the red populations living in South America and the continent of Atlantis, which was later submerged.)

Did they come from the sky, like the 'angels' of the Bible? We find no other mention of such an intrusion in Egyptian mythology. It should be noted, however, that the symbolic winged disc, as among the Assyro-Babylonians, is the mysterious sign found on most temples.[21] This sign apparently dates from only five thousand years ago; that is, from the period when gods travelling in a flying serpent landed in Phoenicia and Assyria.

The initiators could only have come from the nearby Ethiopian plateau, but it is unthinkable that the survivors there, who were herdsmen and hunters, could have had the intellectual resources necessary for reinventing the vanished civilisation. The presence of scientists among them can be explained only by the existence of a strategic or scientific base similar to the laboratories that great nations of the twentieth century have built in such high places of the globe as Mount Wilson, Mount Palomar, the Pic du Midi, and so on.

That base must have had enough supplies to last at least several months. When the globe had regained its tranquillity, the survivors went down to less hostile lands and they naturally settled in the upper valleys of the Nile.

They had to face formidable problems, of course, probably including radiation and certainly epidemics and lack of fresh food,[22] but it is obvious that the survivors of the Deluge and those in Ethiopia were in a relatively privileged position.

The 'Egyptian miracle' in art and science can be explained only by considerations of this order.

After five or six thousand years of social life during which civilisation blossomed in the valley of the Nile, from Thebes to Sais, the Egyptians had almost totally forgotten the horrors of the Deluge, which is all the more understandable because floods were a blessing for them.

The 'end of the world' that I have been describing shows correlations among fire from the sky, a great flood and the moral deterioration of mankind that is affirmed by ancient texts. But such correlations fall within the universal norms that govern our human adventure.

When times of cosmic cataclysm are near, civilisations

are too highly advanced, too dangerous, and then the inevitable disruption occurs. Like the fruit and the husk at the beginning of the cataclysm of winter, man rots and bursts at the approach of a new cosmic cycle.

This view is in accord with the laws of evolution, since nature herself subscribes to it. From our human standpoint it would be stupid for such a vast revolution to take place before civilisations had ripened to their culmination. It would be illogical and disorderly, whereas it is rational to believe that everything, including intangible factors, is regulated by laws that are often obscure, but always scientific and universal.

Cosmic Antiracism

Traditions and the Bible state that after the Universal Deluge 'unnatural' couplings produced hybrid beings, half human and half animal, that nearly brought about the disappearance of the human race. Was that hybridisation actually in accord with secret universal laws? We must have the courage to consider this hypothesis if we are to avoid racism. Black, yellow and white men are all brothers, of course, but why should they not also regard themselves as brothers of the monkey, the cow, the tapir, the lion, the oak and the cabbage?

Are we about to relive the experience of those people who, after the Deluge, vanquished the hybrids they had created?

Our proud space rockets will soon land men and women on Venus and Mars. There is almost no chance that they will find another human race on those planets, and it is not much more likely that they will be able to acclimate themselves and procreate outside our earthly atmosphere.

Acting on this assumption, American and Soviet specialists have worked out a plan of hybridisation in which a human foetus or fertilised ovum, brought directly from Earth, would be made to develop in an extraterrestrial plant or animal. It is quite possible that such a procedure could lead to the formation of a viable creature, assuming that the necessary chemical elements were supplied to the incubation medium. Development might also be favoured by eliminating harmful secretions in the medium.

After the conclusive experiments conducted in 1964, on the cellular level, by Professor Henry Harris and Dr J. F. Watkins of Oxford, there can be no doubt that in the near future new races will be created by crossbreeding between species and even between plants and animals.

For a biologist, there is no fundamental difference between matter and energy, or between minerals and highly organised living matter. Pygmalion loved a marble statue and poets love with all their senses an ancient oak, a river, a field of daisies, a mountain or the sea. Animal lovers adore their pet dogs, cats or monkeys. For them, there is no barrier or physical repugnance against crossbreeding, but only a moral barrier known as racism; that is, opposition to the natural laws of life.

Eve, Isis and Lot's Daughters

There was no racial problem in the past when earthly women let themselves be impregnated by 'angels', and neither the Lord nor the writers of the Bible saw the slightest immorality in it.

The Virgin Mary had a child by the 'Holy Ghost'; in Egypt, the goddess Nut copulated with her brother and Isis even had a child (Horus) by her sexual relations with her husband's corpse: in Greece, Zeus gave birth to the virtuous Athena. In history, legend and mythology we find many examples of bizarre unions, going from incest to marriage with extraterrestrials.

When the fate of the human race is at stake, all scruples give way to the superior law of necessary reproduction. Eve had only male children; she assured descendants for herself by having sexual relations with her sons.

After the atomic destruction of Sodom and Gomorrah, the daughters of the patriarch Lot thought that the whole world had disappeared and the elder said to the younger, 'Our father is old and there is not a man in the country to come to us in the usual way. Come now, let us make our father drink wine and then lie with him and in this way keep the family alive through our father.' (Genesis 19:31-2).

Later in Hebrew history the Lord showed himself to be more moralistic, more of a stickler for principle, and he even gave a racist mission to his 'Chosen People'.

After this exposition, it is easier to understand the problem that mankind faced after the Deluge, and how it was solved.

Some people believed they were the only survivors in the world and copulated with animals until more or less human births occurred. There was then a biological experiment on a large scale, much more conclusive than the few artificial inseminations timidly attempted by twentieth-century biologists.[23] The experiment was successful; monsters were born and unmixed human beings had to wage a war of extermination against them.

Strange Lovers

Among the Celts the mother of mankind was named Dana, Danu or Ana[24] and was associated with the flying ram that came from the sky. She was the Mama Quilla of Peru and the Ma of Asia Minor, as well as the Maia of the Greeks, who gave birth to Hermes in her 'shadowy den'. In the Eleusinian Mysteries the symbols of the Mother, the serpent and the cave were fundamentally associated with worship of Demeter, and in Greek mythology Dionysos (the Initiator) was resuscitated in the form of a ram-headed serpent.

Esoterically – that is, in their deeper meaning – these myths are directly related to our genesis and hybridisation.

Professor André Bouguenec notes that in most plant species, in which evolution is more rapid, fecundation requires the coming of a 'foreigner',[25] an external agent, such as the wind, insects or man, which transports pollen, usually by air. Is that 'foreign' agent analogous to the 'extraterrestrial lovers' who came and will no doubt come again to fecundate the earth, earthly women and our intelligences? Are hybridisations, transplants and mixtures necessary to the evolution of species?

Chapter 5

INITIATION

> If man wants to be recognised, he must simply say who he is. If he lies or remains silent, he dies alone and everything around him is doomed to misfortune. If he tells the truth, he will no doubt die, but after having helped himself and others to live.
>
> —Albert Camus

1. Initiation in Early Times

The population of the earth from the recent past to the present can be represented by a graphic curve, and approximate figures for the future and the more distant past can be obtained by extending the curve in both directions. Starting with a population of about three thousand million at the present time, this method gives an estimate of 500,000,000 for the fifteenth century, three hundred million for the beginning of the Christian era and ten thousand to a million for the post-Deluge period between ten and twelve thousand years ago.

This shows not only that there was a worldwide cataclysm but also that, contrary to the claims of prehistorians, it was impossible for man to have vegetated for millions of years without increasing his intellectual powers in an arithmetical progression.

There were necessarily civilisations before the Deluge and their most enlightened survivors tried to preserve knowledge that was still fresh in their minds. The first initiates formed cells in which priests who were not required to be celibate – quite the contrary – were both guardians of secrets and agents of genetic transmission. Religions had a grandiose nature in that period: the future of the world depended on it.

The First Guarded Secrets

What knowledge was retained by the members of that reviving human race? Very little, probably. Imagine what would be known by two hundred or two thousand Russians or Americans who escaped a Deluge in our time. There would be only one chance in a million of an atomic scientist being among them, and even if such a man survived he would have almost no means of transmitting his knowledge.

When men tried to take stock of their knowledge a few years after the cataclysm, they recalled only isolated bits and pieces; they had no coherent, scientific notions of things. Yet certain memories were so vivid and powerful that they were all but imperishable: the Deluge itself, of course, and also machines that flew through the air, a weapon capable of annihilating everything, images that magically appeared in a mirror, words mysteriously transmitted from one end of the earth to the other. And here we find the essential features of their civilisations, and of ours: aeroplanes or space rockets, the atomic bomb, television, radio, writing.[26]

Those memories, and a few others of lesser importance, made up the core of ancient initiation and the constantly altered and adulterated secrets transmitted by initiates. We find them in scores of different forms, behind scores of veils, in the traditions and documents that have come down to us.

In Peru, people who still retain some of the old knowledge carved images of motors and space suits on the Puerta del Sol. In Mexico, someone drew a spacecraft almost identical to our modern rockets. The Mayas described the fantastic destruction of their world in the Popul Vuh. The Hindus related the atomic war that must have annihilated Mu. Various peoples left descriptions of flying men and wondrous vehicles.

Another memory persisted, though in a more confused form: that the Masters of the World who came from another planet.

The names of some of those initiators have come to us in altered or completely different versions: Azazel, Lucifer, Prometheus . . . Their arrival took place in extremely remote times and it was easier to call them 'gods', 'angels', 'watchers', 'saints', and so on. They had all stolen fire from the sky, they had all wanted the happiness of mankind and they were all of unknown origin, from beyond the earth.

Several decades after the cataclysm, people tried to organise their knowledge and sometimes drew pictures, from memory, of machines whose functioning they had never understood. Those people were probably not survivors of the cataclysm, but children or grandchildren of survivors.

Secrets were reported by 'initiates' who were climbing back up the slope towards civilisation and it is easy to imagine what became of descriptions of electronic robots, television or jet engines a century or two after they had disappeared, after human beings had fornicated with animals and during the period when many of them had degenerated almost to the point of ceasing to be human.

It was then that the more backward elements of mankind developed a primitive kind of occultism that was a deformed and degraded vision of primal truths. From that occultism came the crude magic that still exists among all peoples of the earth.

Mysterious Writing

In his book *La Clé des Choses Cachées,* Maurice Magre writes, 'A tradition related to that of the Agartha states that after the great cosmic catastrophe in which Atlantis was submerged, there were men who survived and restored the task of perpetuating the human moral heritage. They had taken refuge in the heights of the Himalayas. It was there that they buried astronomical tables, documents engraved on sheets of metal and everything else that represented the elements of knowledge.'

It is widely accepted that post-Deluge mankind had a universal language, at least among learned men.

If, as it is claimed, there are documents engraved in metal in Peru, Tibet and the Gobi Desert – the Bible of Anahita, according to Swami Matkormano – they should all be in the mysterious writing that Sanchuniathon found in the temples of Phoenicia.

Several words of that universal language have come down to us, such as *mama*, 'mother', and *dam*, 'mistress of a household' in the Vedas. *Dam* is older than Vedic Sanskrit, which took it 'from a language that is now lost'.

Spiritualistic sects maintain that before the Deluge initiates had knowledge of a premonition of the cataclysm and took refuge in a safe place: in Tibet according to some, in the Pyramids according to others. This seems unlikely to me because it assumes that initiates, knowing in advance that an early cycle was about to end, were able to build shelters that would protect them from floods and earthquakes, something that would have been nearly impossible.

We now know that the end of our cycle is near, that an end of the world will inevitably occur; but who would be able to build a shelter the size of the Great Pyramid or equip caverns like those of the Agartha?

Would it be possible to use the Agartha or the underground sanctuary of Hawaii? No, for if the continent of Mu was engulfed by the Pacific Ocean, how could the caverns in the Himalayas and the Hawaiian Islands have remained intact?

Finally, it seems unthinkable to me that initiates should have been willing to survive, to sequester themselves in a refuge they judged to be safe, while above or below them billions of men, women and children were dying in the 'apocalypse' of evolution.

Furthermore, the nature and transmission of secrets indicate that the survivors were people of only an ordinary intellectual level, since major pieces of knowledge were not transmitted, such as the harnessing of horses, crop rotation and grafting.[27] No reasonable person will grant that initiates worthy of the name would have had the arrogance to conceal such knowledge if they had possessed it.

Masked Men Who Go Out Only at Night

In most sects, however, it is good form to believe that initiates have maintained an unbroken chain from the Deluge to the present, passing on their fabulous knowledge in writing and stone carvings and by word of mouth, always in skilfully veiled terms.

As occultists see him, the initiate is typically an unknown, untouchable man who has nothing in common with ordinary mortals and probably goes out only at night, wearing a mask! He knows the how and why of all things. He can make alchemical gold, double himself, see and hear at a distance. He has the gift of ubiquity, he knows how to use the quintessence of human psychic powers and, if he wanted to, he could release forces more powerful than those of the atomic bomb. Silent and invisible, he knows the secrets of the universe. God confides in him. His wisdom and faith are boundless. It would be unseemly to try to put his knowledge to the test.

All that is nothing but occult drivel, say rationalists, tired of waiting for the first inkling of any significant revelation.

The problem has been misinterpreted.

There have been and still are genuine initiates: Pythagoras, Plato, Poincaré and Einstein, to name only a few whose knowledge cannot be placed in doubt. Not all of them have revealed their entire message, but they have all proved their initiation and made an immense contribution to human development.

The problem has been misinterpreted because occultists have come to view initiation as entirely a matter of alchemy, numerology and mysterious psychic powers, all of which have been in the same rut for the past two thousand years.

The 'initiate' ritually drapes himself in great mystery and proclaims that 'if he could speak' he would say wondrous things. But he has taken a vow of secrecy, or else the right time has not yet come. He could reveal the formula for squaring the circle, or a cure for cancer – if only he could speak!

It is the same with some alchemists who seek the Philosopher's Stone. If they ever found it, it would give them a thoroughly materialistic means of making gold that could be converted into money, but to soothe their conscience they piously (and falsely) claim that in 'esoteric truth' the goal of their quest is wisdom. As if wisdom could be materialised in a stone! As if it could be found by heating mercury, lead sulphur, phosphorus and other chemicals! Alchemy, which was once simply chemistry, is now a good illustration of how truth can deteriorate.

How can anyone take seriously the intricate gibberish and deliberately confused drawings of pseudo-initiates? Is it initiation to untie the Gordian knot of the Cabala by means of inversions, numerations and permutations of a text that has probably been falsified? Is it initiation to see nothing in the Argonaut's expedition but hermetic symbols of a science whose goal is the transmutation of base metal into gold.

If real initiates were so reticent, devious, crafty and cryptic, and if their initiation consisted only in taking intellectual tests and undergoing physical trials such as going down into a dark well, taming a lion and overcoming fear, they would deserve no more confidence than the charlatans of a travelling medicine show.

Genuine Initiation

The real initiate has always been a man who, by patient, skilful work and clear-sighted intelligence, is able to draw out the threads of the skein of knowledge that has been diabolically tangled by conspiracies of evil and ignorance.

Initiation is knowledge, not of the fabrication of gold or the satanic wisdom supposedly derived from the quest for the Philosopher's Stone, but of man's true history and of what his destiny can be within the framework of the perceptible universe in which he has his being.

Man wants to know where he comes from and where he is going. He wants to see what is around him and discover, if he can, the essential elements of genesis, science, the Mysterious Unknown and other hidden things that appeal to his curiosity.

Those who go farthest in that discovery, and they alone, are initiates.

Except for a small number of things that would be too dangerous to reveal, the initiate tells what he knows, so that the experience of the past can help the present and the future.

From this viewpoint, the alchemist is not an anonymous man who allegedly knows how to make gold, but the scientist who unquestionably transmutes metals in his laboratory and effectively though alarmingly juggles with matter.

I believe, however, that truths have been hidden, adulterated or lost. It is known that symbols conceal true keys and that mysteries veil a knowledge that millions of people, for thousands of years, have tried to eradicate from history.

Those Who Slew the Dragon

It would be less difficult to reconstruct the unknown history of mankind if the Egyptians, Greeks and Hebrews had not transmitted it in fables and if the Catholics had not Christianised ancient rites and destroyed documents alien to their doctrines. All of man's past was submerged by that enterprise, which was strangely glorified by the symbol of Saint George and Saint Michael slaying the pagan dragon.

In esoteric truth, Saint George and Saint Michael are emissaries of Satan extinguishing the light of knowledge and murdering the guardians of the treasures bequeathed by our ancestors.

In history, those who 'slew the dragon' have left prestigious names: Julius Caesar, Augustus, Alaric, Omar, Charlemagne, Genghis Khan, Torquemada, etc.

330 B.C. Burning of the Persepolis Library by the troops of Alexander the Great. (Extremely doubtful.)

240 B.C. The Chinese emperor Shih Huang Ti destroyed all books of science and history.

75 B.C. The Sibylline Books of the priests of Apollo perished in the burning of the Capitol.

48 B.C. First burning of the Alexandrian Library, by Julius Caesar.

A.D. 1 (approximately). Augustus destroyed more than two thousand volumes of oracles.

54. Saint Paul, at Ephesus, burned all books dealing with 'strange things'.

296. Diocletian burned the Christian libraries, with their Egyptian and Greek documents.

Third century. The Christian emperors of the West burned and destroyed wonders of the ancient world, including the Temple of Diana at Ephesus and archives called pagan. The real history of the world was effaced by that criminal enterprise.

389. Theodosius burned the Books of the Sibyl.

390. Second burning of the Alexandrian Library, by the Christians.

405. Stilicho destroyed copies of the Sibylline Books.

410. Alaric pillaged the libraries of Rome.

Seventh century. Ignorant Irish monks burned ten thousand runic manuscripts on birch bark, containing the traditions and annals of Celtic civilisation.

641. Third burning of the Alexandrian Library, by order of Caliph Omar.

728. Leo the Isaurian burned three hundred thousand manuscripts in Byzantium.

789. Acting on the decrees of the Councils of Arles, Tours, Nantes and Toledo, Charlemagne forbade worship of trees, stones and springs and ordered the

destruction of all objects and documents related to pagan rites.

1221. Genghis Khan burned the books of the ancient city of Bamian, the Thebes of the Orient.

Thirteenth century. The Catholics destroyed the books of the Cathari.

Fourteenth and fifteenth centuries. The Inquisition burned heretical manuscripts.

Sixteenth century. The Christian conquistadores of Bishop Diego de Landa destroyed nearly all the sacred books of the Mexicans.

The books of Garcilaso de La Vega were burned by the Inquisition.

1566. Francisco Toledo, Viceroy of Peru, destroyed an immense stock of Incan cloths and painted tablets relating the ancient history of America.

Eighteenth century. In the little port of Ouardan, in Egypt, Father Sicard burned 'a papyrus dovecote covered with magic characters'.

1709. The Inquisition burned Gusmao's scientific documents in Lisbon.

Twentieth century. The Hindu astronomical tables known as the Tirvalour Tables were sequestered in Paris. They may have been destroyed.

1926. The credibility of Glozel, the world's richest archaeological deposit, was fraudulently undermined.

1937. The prehistoric library of Lussac-les-Châteaux was sequestered.

It is enlightening to examine this partial list of 'witch-hunting' activities.

2. Science and Initiation

The first task of the initiate is discovery of genesis (knowledge). Next, he must identify himself with his knowledge; that is, he must become a model. Finally, he must speak in order to aid the evolution of others.

The great cosmological secrets are revealed by Thoth-Hermes, Hesiod, Empedocles, Pythagoras, the Druids and most sacred writings. They are often hard to penetrate and they have sometimes been mutilated by sectarians, but in general they remain in the form of more or less hermetic symbols.

Only the Bible plays almost no part in reconstructing the great jigsaw puzzle of the past, because it came from a people, the Hebrews, who did not experience the cataclysm. (The Hebrews spoke of the Deluge only from hearsay, since they did not form their nation until about 1500 B.C.)

The Secret of the Swimming Serpent

It is likely that the first group of initiates knew – approximately – the secret of creation. At least they had a very elaborate idea of it because of the importance of the civilisations that had flourished in Atlantis and Mu.

That is what appears from the study of mythologies in which the creation of the world is represented by the symbol of the 'serpent swimming on the waters'.[28] This must be seen as a striking condensation of cosmology as it is viewed scientifically in the twentieth century: an electric wave (the serpent) propagated in a universe of stationary waves (the waters), thereby producing concentric circles in the image of universal expansion.

The Celts, perhaps closer than other peoples to the primal tradition,[29] represented the primordial waves of creation by a single undulating or spiral line of the kind seen on the carved rocks of the famous tumulus on the Island of Gavrinis in the Gulf of Morbihan.

To the uninitiated, a spiral is only a geometrical figure; to the initiate, it suggests the winding and unwinding of cycles. It can become a serpent again, then an electric wave. From that point on, the initiate knows nothing more – and neither does anyone else.

There was no veil deliberately spread, but a natural occultation, with only one nearly hermetic concept remaining: the word was created by the Word or by Light (a wave).

Atomic Energy

Like his thirteenth-century homonym Roger Bacon, Francis Bacon, the sixteenth-century English philosopher, was a true initiate. In his book *De Sapientia Veterum*, with regard to Love and Cupid, he writes these lines which show profound scientific knowledge.

'This love seems to be the appetite or goad of primary matter; or, to state it better, the natural movement of the atom, for it is the ancient and unique force which forms all matter. It has neither father nor mother, since it depends on no cause (and the cause is the father of the effect), but only on that sole force. We can assign no cause to nature, if we except God.'

In the fifth century B.C., Leucippus and Democritus had knowledge of atomic science. More empirically, the Gauls, the Mayas and prehistoric men had preserved the symbols of atomic energy.

Rationalists will dismiss this as a figment of the occult imagination. Sanchuriathon foresaw their reaction when he wrote, 'Our ears, accustomed from early childhood to their false stories, and our minds, imbued with those preconceptions for centuries, preserve those fantastic suppositions as if they were a sacred trust . . . so that truth seems incredible and adulterated stories have the appearance of truth.'

Ancient Truth Is Incredible

The patriarch Enoch, grandfather of Noat, related in detail the first arrival of initiating 'angels' on our planet fifteen to twenty thousand years ago, and the history of our world to the time of the Deluge. (See Chapters 6, 7 and 10 of *The Legacy of the Gods.*) He also describes his journeys to the 'sky of the First Fathers,' a 'sky' that was located on earth, 'between the north and the west.'

That story has not come to us directly from Enoch. It

was probably transmitted by post-Deluge initiates and finally transcribed by a copyist who must have had qualms of conscience. Enoch surely spoke of real journeys by airplane or rocket, but the copyist, seven thousand years after the event, could not bring himself to reproduce what he believed to be a lie or at least a wild exaggeration: a flying machine! He solved the problem by changing the journey through space to a dream, or 'vision', implanted in Enoch's mind by God. And all the important information conveyed by the story – atomic war, space rockets, astronauts, television, helicopters, radio – was distorted *out of a concern for truth*!

Four or five thousand years ago, people could not believe in such a prodigious, fantastic reality. Most people still do not believe in it, even in the twentieth century! But primohistory becomes logical and rational only if we identify the Lord with an astronaut, the flying rams and serpents with rockets, Ezekiel's 'wheels' with a flying saucer, and the destruction of Sodom with a nuclear explosion.

The Initiates of Hawaii

It often takes a great deal of goodwill to accept the accounts of cosmogenesis (creation of the world) given in sacred writings. Some of them – the one in the Bible, for example – are ludicrous and childish. In this area the original inhabitants of the Hawaiian Islands, isolated in the middle of the Pacific, could have given lessons to modern civilised peoples. Here is the ancient Polynesian account of the creation of the world as it is reported by Professor G. H. Luquet of the University of Paris, in *Mythologie Générale*:

> In Hawaii, animal and plant forms emerged from dark chaos by gradual evolution. First came zoophytes and corals, followed by worms, mollusks and algae, followed by rushes. Then, when the silt resulting from the decomposition of earlier creatures had raised the land

above water, insects, birds and leafy plants appeared. Then the sea produced its highest types, such as jellyfish, fish and whales, while monstrous creatures crawled in the slime. Later, edible plants appeared; then, in a fifth period, the pig; and in a sixth, mice on land and porpoises in the sea.

Finally, after a seventh period had seen the development of abstract physical qualities that were later embodied in the human race, an eighth brought the birth of women, men and some of the great gods.

In Samoa we also find, in a less sharply defined form, the concept of a transformistic succession of plants.

What do you think of that cosmogenesis elaborated by 'savages'? Moses and even Darwin could have learned from it!

In Hawaii there is an underground sanctuary for initiates. It must bear some relation to that superior tradition, which may represent a survival of knowledge from the Land of Mu.

It is also interesting to note that Hawaii is on a major fracture line of the earth (the wombs of Gaea), which always seems to favour exceptional development of man's intellectual and psychic qualities.

Who could have conceived such a learned cosmogenesis, if not initiates? Real initiates who spoke and were even able to escape the Deluge, since several peaks in Hawaii are higher than twelve thousand feet.

Several particularly important points in the Hawaiian cosmogenesis are worth stressing: gradual evolution, earlier creatures, abstract physical qualities later embodied in the human race, the birth of woman before man, the birth of mankind before the gods, a transformistic succession of plants.

Here, beyond doubt, is an initiatic revelation worthy of serious meditation by the most cultivated Western philosophers.

The Sphinx Speaks

True initiation always has a scientific character and

always brings valid knowledge to mankind, even if it is veiled by symbols.

In a manuscript written in Aramaic, *El Fellahat en Nabatiat* ('Nabataean Culture'; the Nebataeans lived in ancient Arabia Petraea), there is a description of vast libraries whose books contain extraordinary scientific and philosophical knowledge. This manuscript is apparently very old, since it speaks of Noah.

Twenty-five hundred years ago, Aristagoras of Miletus wrote a history of Egypt on the basis of inscriptions carved in the pyramids. This work has not come down to us; it was probably destroyed like Sanchuniathon's *Phoenician History.*

The staffs of the great Pythagorean masters bore carved characters relating to initiation into the Mysteries. They are thought to have been our multiplication table, which is still known as the Pythagorean table, but other secrets written on those staffs have been lost, unless our scientists have rediscovered them without realising that they were known before.

On the ancient temple of Sais, in the delta of the Nile, the initiate Plutarch read this inscription:

I am all that has been, is, and will be. No mortal, to this day, has been able to lift the veil that covers me.

'This day' refers to a time far in the past; the veil is now being lifted from secrets that were forbidden to our ancestors.

The Sphinx is speaking again. It says that secrets are terrible to know and that they announce the end of the world.

3. God and Initiates

Is God known by initiates? For spiritualists, the answer is clear, since they believe that the supreme privilege of initiation is precisely to know God. Actually, however, initiates do not believe in God; they are ignorant of him.

Pythagoras had no precise idea of God. His disciple Plato believed that God was not omnipotent and had not created the world. As for Pherecydes, teacher of Pythagoras and therefore of Plato, he openly stated his disbelief or, more exactly, his ignorance.

The Forbidden Name

If a scientist is asked whether he believes in an eternal, omnipotent God who created heaven and earth, his answer is likely to be evasive, and even if it is affirmative it will be highly qualified. If the same question is asked of a Spanish picador, a Mexican woodsman or an Italian beggar, he will answer yes without hesitation. As a general rule, the ignorant person is a believer.

Buddha did not believe in God.[30]

Buddha, Pherecydes, Pythagoras, Plato . . . The case should be judged, but it would play into the hands of atheists. Although they are ignorant of God, initiates are not atheists.

For subtle reasons, initiation on this point consists in not naming God, not writing his name. But while the name is forbidden, the idea remains, which is esoterically sacrilegious, and unless we are simply to refrain from speaking of him, as Buddha did, God must be symbolised by a word or a sign.

It has become customary to replace the name with an abstraction, and the more confusing that abstraction is, the more initiatic it is. Since, through the millennia, God had become a concept used too freely and exploited by charlatans, initiates decreed out of respect that it was forbidden to name the Unnameable.

In ancient China, God was an active and inexhaustible principle, infinite in every way, that could not be represented by any image or named by any word, and to which nothing could be added.

Lao-tse, like Buddha, was completely ignorant of God.

Confucius was an initiate, no doubt a recessive case, since at the age of six he amazed those around him with his great wisdom. According to Chu Hsi, the authoritative commentator on Confucius, he gave no identity to God, rejected all religion and trusted only in rational science – twenty-five hundred years ago!

'Confucius did not speak of mystical things [as Buddha and Lao-tse did], or of spirits [souls], or of the Celestial Way.'

When someone asked him how spirits and genies should be served, he answered, 'When one is not yet able to serve men, how can one serve spirits and genies?'

Another answer shows his great honesty and humility, and his awareness of the limits of his knowledge: having been asked what death was, he said, 'When one does not know what life is, how can one know death?'

At the end of his life, Confucius withdrew to a mysterious place with a few of his disciples, and it is curious to note that no one has identified that place as the Agartha.

The God of Moses Was Celtic

When they adopted the God of the Egyptian Moses (see *The Legacy of the Gods*, Chapter 7), the Hebrews gave him the pseudonymn of Elohim or Adonai; that is, the unique god Aten of the Egyptians, who was in turn Adonis, the universal god of the Phoenicians.

The Phoenicians originally called God by the name of Beelsamen, which later became Bel or Baal (the Bel-Heol of the Celts), then Hel, Il or Cronus. In his *Phoenician History*, Sanchuniathon says that 'the allies of Hel (Cronus) were called Eloim, which corresponds to Cronians.'

It is thus easy to recognise Elohim or Eloim, the God or gods of the Hebrews, as the god Hel and the Eloim of the Phoenicians, and to go back to the source: the Bel-Heol of the Celts, fathers of all philosophy, according to the initiate Pythagoras.

This identification provides another explanation of the Hebrews' desire to hide the fact that their initiation (which was great) did not come from a special revelation, but from their knowledge of the traditions of Egypt and Phoenicia.

By partially identifying God with the Holy Ghost and Jesus, the Christians deliberately broke with the great initiatic traditions.

The Phoenicians tried for a long time to hide the name of Baal, for fear that, by invoking him, foreigners might gain his favour; but that was only a superstition.[31]

Ritually, the name of God was lost among the Hebrews, as the Word was lost among the Freemasons.

God Is Infinitely Unknowable

According to one hypothesis, God, being the universal Whole, necessarily loses his power as man increases his own. When man becomes all-powerful, God will cease to exist and will then be represented by his creature.

The Scandinavians did not believe in the eternity of the gods and the world. For them, and for the Germans, the gods were long-lived mortals who had to be constantly on the alert. One of them, Heimdall, had the task of standing guard night and day in front of the Bifrost Bridge, which gave access to Asgard, the palace of the gods, the Ases. But it was the destiny of the Ases to succumb one day beneath the blows of their enemies, the Giants, and to bring the entire old Aryan world down with them in their fall. That fall is described in one of the finest poems of the Edda, the Voeluspa, under the title of the 'Twilight of the Gods.'

The idea of the end of the deity has been taken up again in our time by the American theologians who have developed the theme that 'God is dead.' Professor J. Sittler, of the University of Chicago, has interpreted the viewpoint of the group by saying that at a time when man is extending his concern to the whole universe, it is no longer possible to be interested in a Jesus whose action was limited to Galilee.

This 'death of God' school would seem unimportant to me if, in spite of its limited outlook, it did not fall within an evolutionary cycle that may lead to a certain identification of the God of initiates.

While still remaining infinitely unknowable, this God may lose, for the benefit of our perception, some of the seventy-seven thousand veils which according to Hindu theology preserve his anonymity and prevent us from being consumed.

In this view, the universe-God could be regarded as a regulating mechanism, something like a system of electronic robots making an infinite number of calculations governing all events that can occur in all possible universes. There would not be one determinism, but an infinity of determinisms designed to give universal significance to even the smallest detail, such as the choice of buying a ballpoint pen rather than a pencil.

If initiation is knowledge (science), it almost necessarily follows that God must be viewed as an electronic superbrain. Since God and science are infinitely impenetrable, we can deduce that an initiate is only a perpetual adept.

God's inaccessibility, even to those known as great initiates, is pointed up by a statement concerning knowledge (initiation) by Bernard d'Espagnat, Professor of Mathematics at the Collège de France:

'There is only one serious way of perceiving the world: by scientific vision. Any other mode of perception is futile.'

Mathematicians and scientists are convinced of their profound ignorance of even the most commonplace facts, on the level of the absolute.[32] They know that no judgement or calculation can be perfectly accurate in a concept of space-time that fundamentally eludes us.

This humility, this certainty of uncertainty, is the mark of what can properly be called genuine initiation.

4. Ancient Initiation: Sigurd

All the rites of initiation are condensed in the marvellous legend of Sigurd, a hero of Scandinavian mythology (the

Scandinavian Sigurd is the German Siegfried), in whom it is easy to recognise the Rama of the Edda.

Sigurd, son of Sigmund and a descendant of the god Odin, was a handsome, valiant young man with a noble soul. One day the blacksmith Regin, a formidable magician who aspired to initiation, gave him a wondrous sword named Gram, so sharp that if its blade was held in a river it could cut a strand of wool drifting with the current. Then Regin gave Sigurd the horse Grani, which was unmatched in speed and could gallop through flames.

Such a well-armed knight lacked only a great feat to perform. Regin suggested to Sigurd that he kill the dragon Fafnir, which guarded a treasure. Fafnir was not malicious and he never took the offensive, but if he was attacked he had either to die or kill his attacker.

To overcome this formidable adversary, Sigurd dug a symbolic ditch that would become a grave. The dragon came forward and stumbled into the ditch. Quick as lightning, Sigurd plunged Gram into Fafnir's heart and killed him.

Regin, who had witnessed the combat, drank some of Fafnir's blood, cut out his heart and asked Sigurd to roast it.

While Sigurd was doing this, he burned his fingers when he touched the hot, bleeding heart; he put them in his mouth to soothe the pain and thereby swallowed a little of Fafnir's blood.

A miracle occurred: Sigurd suddenly understood the language of birds, and a conversation between two eagles perched in a tree revealed Regin's secret designs to him.

'When Regin has eaten the dragon's heart,' said one of the eagles, 'he will kill Sigurd.'

'No,' said the other. 'Sigurd will kill Regin.'

That was what happened. Guided by a mysterious premonition, Sigurd ate Fafnir's heart, drank his blood and buried him with honours. He then took the treasure and, following the birds' advice, set off for the land of the Franks.

On the way, he saw a castle surrounded by fire. He impetuously rode his horse Grani through the flames and came to a room where he found a handsome warrior whom the god Odin had magically put to sleep. Acting on another intuition, Sigurd took off the warrior's helmet with the point of his magic sword Gram, cut through the coat of mail and discovered the body of an ineffably beautiful woman: the Valkyrie Brunhild. This broke the enchantment. Brunhild fell in love with Sigurd and drew him into her bed.

When he awoke the next morning after a passionate night, she gave him the gift of reading and writing runes. In exchange for that knowledge and that initiatic night, he gave her a golden ring from the dragon's treasure and swore eternal fidelity to her.

He then continued on his way till he came to the Frankish chiefs Ginki, Gunnar and Hoegni. He became their brother in arms, then their blood brother.

Krimhild, mother of the three chiefs and of the fair-haired Gudrun, gave Sigurd a drink that wiped away his memory of Brunhild.

Then came a series of adventures in the course of which Sigurd married Gudrun and Gunnar married Brunhild, even though she was still in love with Sigurd. But one night Sigurd took back the magic ring, named Adavaranaut, that he had given Brunhild. Consumed with anger and jealousy, she succeeded in persuading Gunnar to kill the man she still loved.

It was Gunnar's younger brother who attacked Sigurd while he slept. As he was dying, Sigurd killed his murderer with his sword Gram.

Inconsolable, Brunhild threw the treasure into the river and stabbed herself. Her body was burned with Sigurd's on an immense funeral pyre.

Such is the myth of the Edda in which the initiatic myth

of the Ancients clearly shows through. Its essential features can be expressed as follows:

– A handsome god kills the dragon guarding the treasure (the initiation that must be acquired at the cost of a great feat). In the first stage, Sigurd understands the language of birds.

– The hero comes under the domination of Night and Death. Iniaitic tests and journeys.

– He traverses the circle of fire and discovers the woman of Light whose carnal love raises him to the second stage of initiation: knowledge of runes.

– He gives the ring of the treasure to the initiating woman. This is a solemn commitment: the initiate cannot return to the beginning of the journey to escape from the labyrinth; his commitment is total.

– Having failed, Sigurd must pay. He is pricked by the thorn of death and the treasure is thrown into the river, at the mercy of another questing hero.

5. Initiation and Love

If initiation were pure science, it would be hard to reconcile it with the notion of love. How could one put love into the calculation of the date of an eclipse or the speed of a wave, or even into a simple multiplication? But initiation is also wisdom, a moderating agent in the escalation of forbidden knowledge and a catalyst of the noblest emotions.

Pythagoras cultivated the notion of love and, five centuries before Christ, Buddha gave a lesson in it that has never been surpassed.

A Lesson in Love

The maharajahs of Benares have a motto, adopted by theosophists, that is admirable in its purest sense: *There is no religion higher than truth.* This is the only dogma that can be accepted by an honest man.

Love is not a dogma; if it were, one could say, 'There is

no truth higher than love,' which in a certain sense would be an admirable lie.

The legend I will recount below expresses the concept of love through the Bodhisattva; that is, Buddha before he experienced illumination through love.

The Bodhisattva was wandering across the countryside in search of he knew not what. He was walking slowly, sometimes absorbed in his thoughts and sometimes turning his curiosity to nature, sumptuously arrayed in all her colours and infinitely intelligent.

Suddenly he saw a dove so tired from flying that she was about to fall. With a final effort she flew to him and fluttered down to the ground in front of him.

'Please save me, Bodhisattva!' she gasped. 'A vulture has been pursuing me since morning. I'm exhausted and you're my only hope. Look, here comes the vulture now!'

A big, black bird was approaching, flying so laboriously that his exhaustion was painful to see.

The Bodhisattva picked up the dove, hid her under his tunic and said to her with brotherly affection, 'Put your heart at peace, little dove. I am the Bodhisattva. I offer you the hospitality of my bosom and you have nothing more to fear.'

The vulture wearily landed in front of him, with his feathers in disorder.

'I can't go any farther after this terrible day of hunting!' he said. 'Bodhisattva, I saw you hide that dove under your tunic. Give her to me quickly, before I faint from hunger!'

'I will not give her to you,' replied the Sage, 'because I have guaranteed her safety and the laws of hospitality must not be broken.'

'That dove is mine, not yours,' said the vulture. 'When you picked her up, she was at the end of her strength and on the verge of falling into my power. Give me what rightfully belongs to me!'

'No!'

'Think carefully, Bodhisattva. I'm a vulture; my nature

was imposed on me by the gods, who also imposed on me the kind of food I must eat. I pursued the dove till she was exhausted. She's the reward of my work as a vulture and you must give her to me.'

'No,' the Sage said again, but this time there was less assurance in his voice. 'I'd like to oblige you, vulture, but I can't do it at the price you ask. Go off and find another prey.'

'Find another prey? That's a cruel joke, Bodhisattva! Can't you see that I'm incapable of flying? If a fox finds me in this condition, I'm lost! You're forcing me to die of hunger or be eaten by an enemy. My death will always be on your conscience.'

The Bodhisattva had no need of long meditation to realise that the vulture was right, but the dove was also right to want to save her life, and he too was right to give her sanctuary. Could he tell her that she was the vulture's rightful reward? Could he let the vulture devour his prey?

His heart was torn by pity, love and agonising uncertainty. Should he sacrifice the innocent dove? Impossible! Should he sacrifice the innocent vulture? No!

There was only one solution, and he saw it in a flash of illumination.

'You're right, vulture,' he said, 'I mustn't deprive you of your reward. I will give it to you from my own flesh.'

A pair of scales and a knife miraculously appeared in front of him. He placed the dove on one scale, and on the other a large piece of flesh cut from his own body. When he saw that the balance was tilted on the side of the dove, he added another piece of his flesh, then another, and still another. But the balance remained tilted in the same direction; the mound of human flesh was less heavy than the frail dove. Then the Bodhisattva stood on the scale and his weight exactly balanced that of the dove. A life for a life!

The vulture, who had been watching the scene in silence, flapped his wings and transformed himself.

'I am the god Indra,' he said, 'and I wanted to test you.'

A rain of ambrosia fell from the sky and healed the

Bodhisattva. The god announced to him that he would be reincarnated in the body of the next Buddha.

This story gives us a great lesson in love, complete and edifying: a life for a life; the life of an initiate is worth no more than smoke rising from a chimney. Love is worth nothing unless it is total and is addressed to all our brothers and sisters: vultures, stones, grains of sand . . . Such was the initiatic teaching of the Bodhisattva.

6. True Initiates

Sigurd and Buddha show us that the quest for initiation is not contemplative. Contemplative people – theorists of psychic powers, prayer, rapture, 'revelation' – achieve nothing but the deterioration of their physical and mental faculties.

No initiate has ever been a contemplative man. Nothing truly useful to mankind – the wheelbarrow, the steam engine, electricity, vaccination – has ever become known through revelation. Going into a trance is a procedure that becomes detestable when it is nothing but a selfish experience.

If Saint Teresa of Avila and Saint Teresa of Lisieux had cared for the sick, they would have had no time for visions; the god who inhabited them during their raptures was less useful than a calming potion that would have made them recover their common sense.

Initiates Speak:

The initiates, whose historical existence seems probable if not certain, even though their identity is not always clear, have all divulged secrets and thus proved their knowledge.

Prometheus, Oannes, Quetzalcoatl, Kukulkan and Viracocha taught men the secrets of fire, agriculture and writing.

In India, the first initiator was Mannus or Jina the Mahavira (great man); in ancient Persia, Zoroaster taught men astronomy and how to sow grain and smelt metals.

Among the Celts, Lug the initiate was skilled in all the arts, and he created knighthood.

Khusor, the ancient god of Byblos, is said to have invented porticos, crypts and houses with courtyards in front of them, as well as divination and incantatory formula.

The Egyptians Hermes revealed the arts and sciences through writing. In Greece, Apollo invented the lyre and the seven notes of the musical scale; he had the gift of prophecy and was able to transmit it. Orpheus, who revealed 'sacred mysteries', was skilled in making chariots.

Moses knew the secrets of genesis, explosive powder and electricity. By revelation? No. From direct teaching. It was as if he had been commissioned by a powerful group who had come in a flying machine – the 'cloud' – to give him instructions. Sometimes the enigmatic visitors spoke to him where they found him, and sometimes they took him to a place that I am tempted to identify as either a general headquarters (perhaps on another planet) or, more likely, an initiatic centre in America or Asia, for he remained absent for months or even years.

The case of Enoch, before the Deluge, was similar, but we must assume that after the Deluge the destination was deliberately concealed, which would tend to indicate that it was the Agartha, the secret centre that tradition situates in Tibet.

Buddha was a moral philosopher and a great astronomer; he based his doctrine on the idea that only knowledge leads to full human development.

Leucippus spoke of the atom and the corpuscular universe; Pythagoras, a philosopher and mathematician, revealed essential laws of mathematics.

Apollonius of Tyana, born in the first century, travelled in Greece, Babylonia and India, visiting the great sanctuaries of initiation. He preached more reform, abstinence from the flesh of animals, and the sharing of wealth. He gave his belongings to the poor, lived in temples, went barefoot and worked miracles. In Rome he resuscitated a young girl, which caused him to be banished from Italy by Nero. The people deified him because of his worthy life, his morality and his teachings.

All these men (and there have been many others) were unquestionably initiates, and they all spoke.

They Do Not Know Everything

However great they may have been, there is no reason to believe that they had superhuman powers. They were only astronomers, physicists, mathematicians, philosophers and biologists on the scale of their time, and what they knew was far below the knowledge of a modern scientist. They knew how to formulate theories and rediscover processes, but none of them could have made an aeroplane or a computer.

It is obvious that if they had known useful secrets they would have revealed them and mankind would have benefited much sooner from quinine, vaccination, vitamin pills, printing, the sewing machine, the universal joint, the steam engine, and so on. We do not owe these things to those known as initiates, but to scientists and inventors who, by their genius, rediscovered ancient knowledge that had been lost because of the Deluge and the passing of time.

We thus see how insubstantial initiation is when it is not extended and exalted by scientific work and the genius of the initiate.

It seems that transmission, particularly from Orpheus to Pythagoras, was marred by omissions, errors and adulterations.

The Hebrews took up the torch five hundred years before Christ and we owe them a debt of gratitude for having assembled certain fragments of the ancient secrets.

In the first century, Apollonius of Tyana had to go back to the sources to reconstitute a particle of the heritage; he may have been the last heir of the primal tradition.

False Initiates

As for psuedo-initiates – alchemists, ultra-discreet thaumaturgists, knowers of secrets that have never been revealed or tested – they are nothing but exponents of a crude brand of occultism, devoted to false knowledge inherited from the degenerate period of antiquity. Speculators in a Mysterious Unknown of which they have only hazy notions, they are vanquished by such scientists as Denis Papin, Marconi, Becquerel and Einstein, who have been initiates without being aware of it, and have truly rediscovered the main elements of the ancient secrets.

Once again, flying machines race through the air, self-propelled vehicles move over the surface of the earth, man's voice carries from one pole to the other and his image is magically transmitted through time and space.

Such are the magic secrets of our Superior Ancestors.

Not all of them have been rediscovered,[83] particularly those that constitute what is called the Mysterious Unknown. Perhaps initiators 'from the sky' will divulge them in the near future. If so, a new cycle of universal evolution will then begin, but we must become aware of true values and reject lies and charlatanism.

An initiate is someone who knows a little, keeps a great deal to himself and reveals often.

'For nothing is hidden unless it is to be disclosed, and nothing put under cover unless it is to come into the open. If you have ears to hear, then hear.' (Mark 4:22.)

Z

Chapter 6

THE WORLD BEYOND

Less learned than initiates and physicists, but more capable of penetrating a universe that eludes rational verification, a few privileged people baffle our logic. Furthermore, certain phenomena cannot be fitted into any discipline of our orthodox knowledge.

These people and phenomena belong to a non-perceptible world that has been given the name of the Mysterious Unknown.

For thoroughgoing rationalists, the Mysterious Unknown falls under the heading of occultism in the same way as elves, ghosts and flying saucers. Honest, sober scientific minds, however, admit the existence of unexplained facts whose reality cannot be doubted.

The Inexplicable

In August, 1966, during the week preceding the earthquake in Anatolia, Turkey, extraordinarily large catches of fish were taken in Iranian waters. A coincidence? No, since Oriental tradition says that this has always occurred just before great earthquakes.

We see here one of the elements of the Unknown: precognition. What mysterious information is received not only by fish, but by all animals several days before a volcanic eruption? What mysterious instinct guides birds and eels?

A few months ago my colleague, Jacques Chabannes, who loves animals, shuddered with alarm when he heard the amiable Jean Richard say during a television programme:

'I'm all in favour of bullfights.'

'But the bull is always killed in them,' remarked Françoise Dorin.

'That's exactly why I'm in favour of them. At least the bull dies a noble, dignified death, with a chance to kill his adversary. But think of the poor cattle that are often penned up for three days at the La Villette slaughterhouses, *knowing perfectly well what's going to happen to them.* It's better to die in battle than in a concentration camp!'

In spite of greatly improved rat poisons, including those that produce a delayed-action effect by causing internal bleeding, rats continue to proliferate and foil all efforts to wipe them out. Professors Steiniger and Drummond are convinced that rats exchange information on the food they eat, transmit their knowledge from generation to generation and are able to impose diets on themselves.

Equally mysterious is the case of the two American twins, Charles and George A., who are mentally retarded but can infallibly tell what day of the week will fall on March 26 in the year 2026, for example, or any other date, no matter how far off it may be.

These verified but inexplicable phenomena, along with thousands of others of the same kind, suggest a certain presumption in favour of the Mysterious Unknown that escapes experimental verification.

Strange Coincidences

History and current events are full of coincidences that seem too numerous to be the effect of pure chance.

Vittoria and Erminia Spizzo are twin sisters from Treppo Grande, a small town near Udine in northern Italy. They were married on the same day, had the same illnesses, gave birth and became widows at the same time.

Planetary conjunctions in the week beginning February 7, 1960, were such that Hindu astrologers announced that the end of the world might occur during that time. They were mistaken, but on February 7, 1962, the gunpowder factory at Angoulême, France, nearly blew up because the usual preparation of nitroglycerin began boiling that day. Five hundred workers had to be evacuated from the factory. Chemists explained that the mishap had been caused by decomposition of the nitroglycerin, but they had to admit that they did not know the cause of the decomposition. And that extremely rare event took place during the conjunction regarded as malignant by the Hindu astronomers.

At Zimbabwe, in Rhodesia, are the ruins of an ancient city whose construction date is lost in the mists of time. They include several puzzling towers that have no doors or windows and can be entered only from an opening at the top, facing the sky. According to tradition, they are the 'towers of the flying men'. Archaeologists scoff at this, but skilfully made statues have been found near the ruins, representing men with folded wings on their backs.

The same 'towers of the flying men' are also found in Peru, which suggests a utilitarian reason that escapes us.

1. Mysteries in Search of a Solution

We must not believe everything attributed to the Mysterious Unknown, of course, especially when verification is impossible and evidence is inadequate or totally lacking, but is there any justification for automatically rejecting things which, by their very nature, are beyond our means of investigation?

Thought transmission is a phenomenon that ordinarily has only two witnesses, and their honesty can be either accepted or denied. But some rather conclusive experiments were recently carried out in the Soviet Union under scientific control. A Russian named Nikolaiev succeeded in reading the thoughts of several subjects at a distance of two thousand miles. The subjects were in Moscow and Nikolaiev was in Novosibirsk, Siberia. The written report on the experiment described his reception as 'excellent' for a quarter of the thoughts and 'satisfactory' for another quarter, which, all things considered, is nearly miraculous.

The Fatima Prophecy

In 1958 the American clairvoyant Jeane Dixon had a vision of the Virgin Mary below a luminous tablet with the name Fatima on it. She saw the papal throne vacant and, nearby, the pope's face with blood streaming from it. When that actually happens, she maintains, the head of the Church will have another title than that of the pope, and this is the prediction of Fatima.

It is an attractive story and may explain to credulous people why the Holy See was reluctant to unveil the last part of the message that the Virgin is said to have given to young Lucia Dos Santos in September 13, 1917, at Fatima, Portugal.

The truth is quite different, and easy to guess.

First of all, it is false that there was a sun miracle at Fatima. According to some 'witnesses', the sun turned; according to others, it moved towards the crowd. It must be acknowledged that such testimony is not very solid. It would not hold up in a court of law, and it was not accepted by the Vatican, which was unable to decide whether the sun had turned or not, or in which direction it had moved.

In 1919 Canon Formigao, Professor of Theology at the Santarem Seminary, wrote as follows in a Catholic newspaper:

'I cannot end this letter without adding that my impressions of what happened that day [September 13, 1917] at Fatima are not encouraging . . . I noted only a diminution of the sun's light, which seemed to me an unimportant phenomenon.'

Not one of the thirty thousand witnesses of the scene (and many of them were journalists) took a photograph of the wandering sun, which seems a bit odd! What actually took place was a collective hallucination and, on the most favourable supposition, an aberration, a phenomenon well known to astronomers; but the witnesses may have described their vision in good faith and it would have been hard to convince them that it was false.

A Lie at Fatima

It is easy, however, to prove that a lie was told by the lady whom Lucia Dos Santos identified as the Holy Virgin.

Before thirty thousand witnesses, several thousand of whom heard her words, Lucia Dos Santos, in a trance, said, 'The war is over and the soldiers will come home.'

That evening she said to Canon Formigao, before witnesses, 'The Virgin told us that the war would end today and that we could expect our soldiers very soon.' And she said the same thing when she was questioned six days later. But the war did not end on September 13, 1917, but on November 11, 1918 – a year and two months later, which is not exactly a negligible error!

The sun miracle cannot be proved and it is highly debatable, as I have said, but one thing is certain: the prediction of the end of the war was false. It was therefore impossible for the Vatican to support the rest of the prediction, since an important part of it is a proven error. Consequently Jeane Dixon's interpretation of her vision is groundless.

Because such stories discredit genuine manifestations of the supranormal, they should be carefully separated from a problem in which deception is so easy to practise.

Rosenkreutz's Cave

The Rosicrucian Society is at the peak of the hierarchy of invisible and unverified Mysterious Unknowns.

In 1613 a strange book entitled *Fama Fraternitatis Rosae Crucis* announced the foundation of the Rosicrucian Society by a fifteenth-century German, Christian Rosenkreutz.

One of its statutes was: 'This Order must be kept secret for a hundred and twenty years.' It is still being kept secret, in fact, for despite the initiatic and missionary nature it has assumed in our time – 'Truth must not remain static' – the Rosicrucian Society of the twentieth century has not yet divulged the secrets transmitted by its great ancestors.

Seventeenth-century Rosicrucians called themselves 'invisible', and they may have been (mysterious uncertainty again), because they were not positively identified. They were alchemists and theosophists, but they are thought to have adopted those titles mainly as a disguise to hide their boldness as freethinkers.

The founder of the Order, Christian Rosenkreutz, was initiated at the age of twenty-six by Unknown Masters of Damascus, then by Moslem Cabalists.[34] When he returned to Germany he instructed three disciples, then lived alone in a cave till the age of a hundred and six. He died in 1484 and his tomb, in accordance with his specific orders, was to remain unknown 'until the time had come'.

That time came in 1604: by chance, someone entered the cave and saw the tomb illuminated by a mysterious light. On an altar was a copper plaque on which Rosenkreutz had engraved this sentence: 'Alive, I reserved this epitome of light as my sepulchre.' Four other inscriptions expressed his philosophy: 'Never empty,' 'The yoke of the Law,' 'The freedom of the Gospel,' 'The whole glory of God.'

In the cave were also found burning lamps called 'eternal lamps', small bells, mirrors of several shapes and books, including *The Dictionary of Words* and *The Microcosm*, by Paracelsus. On one wall was written this fulfilled prophecy: *In six score years I shall be discovered.*

Such is the legend published in 1613 in *Fama Fraternitatis Rosae Crucis*, the manifesto of the Rosicrucian Society, attributed to the theologian Johann Valentin Andreä. The society was a forerunner of Freemasonry, in which educated and liberal people could exchange advanced ideas.

There is no proof of any part of this story; it belongs to the Mysterious Unknown, but it is considered authentic and its secret character is explained by the fact that in the seventeenth century Catholic power would not have tolerated the open existence of a society of mystery in which freethinkers expounded their views.

The Four Secrets of the Rosicrucians

There were eight founding brothers (the figure 8 is the symbol of the Templars and the planet Venus, represented by a star with eight rays). Each member of the society swore on his life to keep the secrets that were revealed to him.

According to tradition, these secrets concerned eight subjects, four of which appear to be known: the transmutation of metals (alchemy); the art of prolonging life for several centuries (the elixir of long life); knowledge of events in distant places (clairvoyance); application of the Cabala and the science of numbers to discovery of the most deeply hidden things (the mathematical system of acquiring initiation).

The Rosicrucian rules of life were strictly defined. Members had to practise medicine charitably and without accepting fees, follow the customs of the country in which they lived, go to a general assembly once a year, choose an able successor before dying, and take measures to ensure that the place of their sepulchre would be unknown, if they died in a foreign country.

According to S. Vandé, in *Instructions à la France sur la Vérité de l'Histoire des Frères de la Rose-Croix,* the Rosicrucians stated their intention of preparing a better world, which related them directly to Freemasonry, but they belonged to the Mysterious Unknown through powers that legend had greatly exaggerated.

Still according to Vandé, the Rosicrucians declared:

'That wherever they are, they know what is happening in all other places of the world, better than if they were present there.

'That they are not subject to hunger, thirst, sickness or any natural infirmities.

'That they know by revelation those who are worthy of being admitted into their society.

'That they have a book in which they can learn everything that is in all books that have been written or will be written.

'That they have found a new language to express the nature of all things.

'That by their means the triple diadem of the pope will be reduced to powder.

'That they freely and publicly profess, without fear, that the pope is the Antichrist.

'That their treasures are inexhaustible, that their governing body can suffer no harm from their enemies, and that they are certain that their truth will endure till the end of the world.'

But the powers that were so lavishly attributed to them did not end there. It was said that they worked countless miracles, cured sick people simply by looking at them, knew the secret of the Philosopher's Stone and made gold and silver at will.

Needless to say, genuine Rosicrucians have never given the slightest credence to most of these assertions, though some of them may not be entirely groundless.

They Were Invisible

In 1625 the following strange manifesto was posted on walls in Paris:

> We, deputies of the Principal College of the Rosicrucians, will make a visible and invisible sojourn in this city. by the grace of the Almighty. We show and teach, without books or marks, how to speak all sorts of languages of the countries where we wish to be in order to draw our fellow men away from error and death. If anyone should want to see us solely out of curiosity, he will never communicate with us; but if he truly wills to join our brotherhood, we, who judge thoughts, will make him see the truth of our promises. We thus do not indicate our place of residence, since our thoughts, combined with the true will of the reader, will be capable of making us known to him, and him to us.

There were (and still are) two schools of thought with regard to this manifesto. One considers it a hoax, since posters would not have been necessary to make such a project known if it had been genuine. The other is favourably inclined towards the idea of Mysterious Unknowns with the mission of secretly guiding the world.

It may be that the Rosicrucians belong as much to the invisible world as to the world we perceive.

Alchemy, transmutation and the Cabala figure only in their exoteric arsenal. Esoterically, the Rosicrucians give rise to intuitions and currents of thought attributed to chance or the unknown; they condition human civilisations and even shape their destinies to some extent.

In the personal invisible, forces combine and fashion providential aids, and the privileged beneficiary knows that he belongs to a secret brotherhood whose material existence is not necessarily concretised.

For the Rosicrucian initiate, thoughts, in the words of the manifesto, 'will be capable of making us known to him, and him to us.'

Napoleon, a Rosicrucian Imperator

In *Astral*, a magazine specialising in the Mysterious Unknown, my learned colleague Serge Hutin (who is a Rosicrucian) has written an article presenting Napoleon as an official agent of the Rosicrucian Society:

> In all probability General Bonaparte was admitted, during his expedition in Egypt, into a military lodge of the Knights of Malta, heirs of the Templar traditions. The Grand Master of the Order, then known under the name of Hompesch, bore such a striking resemblance to the Comte de Saint-Germain that the theosophist C. W. Leadbeater was not deceived and identified him as the Master of Transylvania. Hence the extraordinary probability of direct contrast between Bonaparte and Saint-Germain in person, who may have given him a highly privileged Templar initiation.

In Egypt, Bonaparte was initiated by an extremely secret organisation, the Luxor Brotherhood, also known under the name of Misraim. He is said to have received there the title of Imperator, in its traditional Rosicrucian sense.

'According to a Paris legend,' continues Hutin, 'Emperor Napoleon I met the famous "Little Red Man of the Tuileries", who revealed his historic mission to him, and also the dangers that lay in store for him if he ever succumbed to his will to power.'

Napoleon's mission consisted in bringing about the political and spiritual unification of Europe as the Great Monarch, but the Unknown Masters withdrew their support from him when he realised the nature of his personal ambitions.

The Marvellous Unknown of Lola Rofocale

In the caves of the Chamellier hill near Brissac, in the Maine-et-Loire district of France, a young woman – one might say a priestess – lives in retirement from a world into which she can no longer integrate herself.[35] Her name, Lola Rofocale, evokes the murky magic of Andalusia as well as Satan the seeker of treasures. This does not distress her, since she is well versed in initiation as it was understood beneath oak trees in the forests of Gaul.

Lola, who is contacted by members of bizarre sects, has given me a report of an account closely related to the Mysterious Unknown:

> Instructors who came after the Lemurian period created a brotherhood whose temple was in the middle of South America, between Bolivia and Brazil. [Perhaps at Inca-Llajta, a hundred and fifty miles from Cochabamba, where extensive ruins were recently discovered.] The name of the brotherhood was Y.B.E.Z., formed from the names borne by the instructors who came from four planets: Yetsira, Briah, Enoch for the planet Earth, and Zariatnatmik, who has been identified as Melchizedek. Into the black Lemurian race, the instructors who were

white, introduced phallic worship as it later existed in Phoenicia. with raised stones.

In our time, several sects continuing the tradition of the South American temples are said to possess documents seven to eight thousand years old, reputedly authentic. The initiation ceremonies of these sects are in the purest classical form. Adepts are placed in contact with cosmic 'nuclear centres' accessible only to Masters who are able to pass through the 'airlock'. The fluid transfer utilises a 'sceptre' of power and progressively increases the vibratory rate of the adept's body.

A particularly important centre exists in a 'parallel dimension' in the Gobi Desert and is called the Marvellous Diamond because of the precious stone it contains. This stone was taken from the planet Venus by Sana Kumara.

This strange story reported by Lola Rofocale contains all the good old clichés: Lemuria, an unknown temple, extraterrestrial initiators, phallic worship, ancient documents that have never been seen and will never be exhibited; it also has some scientific-sounding elements of the kind cherished by ignorant occultists: 'cosmic nuclear centres', and 'airlock' (or crack through which the initiate passes into a parallel universe), a 'vibratory rate' (which has no meaning here); and finally there is the inevitable Gobi Desert, where the temples are surely overflowing with the most marvellous diamonds on earth.

We find in this story the whole arsenal of the Mysterious Unkown so dear to the hearts of the good ladies who belong to spiritualistic sects.

'And that's where the real miracle takes place,' Lola Rofocale said to me, 'because in those touchingly naïve groups, obsessed with incredible wonders, *genuine supranormal phenomena occur!*'

This will not surprise those familiar with the operational magic that creates *egregores*.

Egregores

Magic is a 'poor relation' of initiation, doomed to

empiricism and the perils of return shocks. Both are able to raise up forces whose nature is not clearly known but whose existence is beyond doubt: egregores.

Egregores are spectral creations or semicreated powers produced by the thought-will of one or more persons. The larger the number of persons, the more powerful the egregores. For this reason, believers or sectarians combine their prayers or invocations, sometimes forming a chain or a magic circle to increase the transmuting forces they emit.

An egregore can be created by brooding over the idea of revenge, or having a fixed idea or a strongly anchored belief (it then takes the form of an obsession).

The being produced by collective thought has no physical consistency but is said to be capable of becoming an apparition with a more or less definite shape. In any case it manifests itself by either providing intuitions or suggesting to the conscious mind a presence that may give help or have a depressing effect. It is easy to scc the consequences that can flow from this magic phenomenon.

Apparitions and hallucinations are often semimaterialised by egregores arising from faith. (Jesus said, in Matthew 18:20, 'For where two or three have met together in my name, I am there among them.') It is therefore not impossible that the sect members mentioned by Lola Rofocale may create, from nonexistent entities, an egregore that acts as a catalyst or supranormal phenomena.

The Memory of Things

In the first issue of *Revue Métaphysique*, Gérard Cordonnier presented a view that parallels this magic and explains it to some extent:

> Man has created memories, magnetic and otherwise. But matter, with the infinite number of parameters in its depths, is essentially memory. All the rhythms of the universe are registered in it, probably at different levels. This gives us a partial idea of how an intuitive person can relive the whole history of an object by taking it in his

hand. It also helps us to understand how certain psychic influences can activate matter and be registered in it.

Mr Lewis' Phantom

Was it an egregore or a 'memory' that drove a whole family from their home in Wales? In 1962 Mr Lewis, a mason in Cardiff, saw the ghost of a young woman, wearing a provocative nightgown, reflected in his bedroom mirror. The 'lady' left behind a scent of perfume that was smelled by Lewis' daughter, Catherine. His dogs, Kip and Lucky, howled in terror. Sometimes the clocks stopped and draughts of cold air went through the house. Finally, unable to stand the nervous strain any longer, the Lewis family moved out.

Such phenomena are beyond the reach of reason, even in cases involving the well-known psychic influence of girls who have just reached the age of puberty.

At La Sauzaie, in the Vendée region of France, Henriette D, age thirteen, became the catalyst of supranormal events in spite of herself. Her parents had rented a house for their vacation. Every night they heard strange noises; the walls vibrated, silverware rattled and there were dull thuds against the outside of the house.

The physical cause of the phenomenon, though not its underlying reason, was discovered by Abbé Boulais of the high school at La Roche-sur-Yon. The reinforced concrete walls of the house had created a magnetic field under the influence of the electric current that ran the household appliances. Henriette, extremely receptive, stored the current like a battery and released it at night, giving rise to egregores responsible for the troublesome manifestations. An antimagnetic device, placed within the Faraday cage constituted by the house, ended the disturbances without clearing up their mystery.

The Ubiquity of Melkom Khan

Whether it is a legend or a report of genuine magic, the extraordinary story of Melkom Khan was told to me by the painter Raffy le Persan, who heard it from his uncle Charrah Seyed-Ali, who claimed to have witnessed it himself.

In Teheran, at the end of the nineteenth century, lived a strange man named Melkom Khan who was said to be a magician and a miracle worker. The king was a little afraid of him and sometimes had him arrested, but as soon as he was in gaol Melkom Khan would disappear from his cell and turn up at home, ironically claiming that he did not know how he had escaped.

All sorts of tricks were attributed to him. One evening he magically appeared beside the king at table; another time he left a shoemaker's shop followed by all the shoes, walking of their own accord.

The king, exasperated, finally ordered him to leave the city and, to make sure he really left, posted guards at all four gates. When the magician passed through one of them, his exit was to be signalled by a cannon shot. The next morning, four shots were fired at the same time and the guards at all four gates swore they had seen Melkom Khan pass through.

Charlemagne and the Magic Ring

Chroniclers state that Charlemagne lived a strange love story that might have inspired Edgar Allan Poe. The woman involved was voluptuous, red-haired, ardent and something of a magician. She died when her idyll with the emperor was at its peak. Overwhelmed with despair, he had her body embalmed and kept it in his bedroom. An incomprehensible passion prompted him to caress her as he had done when she was alive, which horrified Archbishop Turpin despite the fact that he was not easily upset.

One day, taking advantage of Charlemagne's absence, Turpin went into the bedroom, sensed the presence of some sort of enchantment and began a careful examination of the body. Under its tongue he found a magic ring, which he took away with him.

When Charlemagne returned he was surprised to see a corpse whose ugliness was no longer hidden by the talisman. He quickly had it buried.

But the magic ring still kept its power. The passion that the emperor had felt for his dead mistress was now transferred to the archbishop. Charlemagne followed him everywhere and could not bear to be separated from him.

Terrified, Turpin threw the ring into a lake so that it would no longer belong to anyone. But the spell was still not broken: Charlemagne began intensely loving the lake. Near it he built a monastery that took the place in his heart of the Abbey of Charroux in Poitou, where he had placed a relic of the True Cross. The magic place is at Aix-la-Chapelle.

2. The Secrets of Swami Matkormano

Shri Swami Matkormano, Maha Mandaleswar, lives in seclusion on the Rue de l'Arsenal at Marsal, France. In his ashram, where only his disciples are admitted, statuettes move and speak, and will soon prophesy. Their actions have been witnessed by the swami, the priestess Alfeola and a pupil, Michel Vaugrante,

Oracle Statuettes

The statuettes are of wood or clay and were made by Michel Dib, a former student at the École des Beaux-Arts. From my observation, it seems that those made of clay have not been baked, so that they can remain alive.

It goes without saying that no black magic is performed in that ashram devoted to spiritualism, but if the statuettes were in other hands they could be used for much less innocent purposes.

When one of them has just been carved or modelled, it is only a piece of insensitive matter that must first be 'charged'. Its head is mounted on a pivot, so that it can be turned. It must remain for months with an initiate who is able to impregnate the clay or wood with mysterious forces drawn from fire and his own vitality. In the ashram at Marsal, it is the priestess Alfeola who performs the rite, sometimes aided by egregores created by a gathering of adepts.

The ceremony takes place at certain Avestan hours determined by *gahs* (genies). Only the priestess has the power to wield the *shakti* force (energy of Shiva), which is a feminine force comparable to the Holy Ghost of the Christians. She performs *mudras*, or magic gestures, and addresses invocations to an angel whose name is kept secret, in front of a sacred picture that is a copy of the one around which processions in the *firdos* (sanctuary) of Hawaii takes place.

There are then phenomena identical to those produced by a magic mirror: the hieroglyphs of the sacred picture begin dancing. The priestess sees that the statuette is 'charged' when its mobile head turns or bows. It emits sounds that are first inarticulate, then coherent, and finally it speaks in the dull voice of its body, faintly but intelligibly. The words it speaks are often remarks, a repetition of a conversation, criticisms or reproaches – when it has witnessed an unpleasant scene, for example. One day when an adept of the swami had used some crude language, the statuette angrily reprimanded him for it.

When it has reached this stage, the magic object must be educated and trained, like an unruly child. This is also done by the priestess, who uses a magic wand.

Finally, after thousands of 'charges' and years of attentive care, the object has a soul and a superconscious mind, and gives oracles.

'I have statuettes that are still at the primary stage,' the swami told me. 'They can answer yes or no in a rudimentary way, by moving their heads in accordance with conventions. I have another that can speak on certain occasions, but without giving oracles. When it is more highly "charged" and educated, I will make it speak in public to prove the reality of the phenomenon.'

The Magic Mirror

In addition to chemical means, such as hallucinogenic drugs, which produce trance states that allow exploration in time, there are physical methods with similar effects. The most famous through the centuries has been that of the magic mirror.

The Greek historian Pausanias, by no means a gullible man, wrote that he had seen one of those mirrors set into a temple wall and that 'anyone who looked into it saw his own image only vaguely, but he clearly and distinctly saw the statues of the gods and goddesses'. (*Periegesis of Greece*, Book VIII.) The mirrors were probably made of obsidian. 'The images reflected by these mirrors,' said Pliny, 'resembles a shadow.'

In the second century, initiated priests knew how to make glass mirrors (which had been known for a thousand years) by using a sheet of metal instead of silvering. The reflection of images was satisfactory, which was not true of the mirror mentioned by Pausanias. It was therefore a magic mirror reflecting images of the gods, probably for worshippers already prepared for the experience.

In the same book (Chapter XXI), Pausanias speaks of a marvellous mirror used for predicting the outcome of an illness, and he even gives details of its operation. The mirror was taken to a pool in front of the temple of Ceres and placed in such a way that it was barely touching the surface of the water. Prayers were offered to the goddess and perfumes were burned in her honour, then the mirror was withdrawn and in it the officiants – that is, those who had been prepared by incantations and smoke – saw an image of the sick person in his future state.

The Ancients believed that magically prepared mirrors of glass, obsidian or polished metal could reflect images of realities far away in space and time.

The Mirror of Mazda

After years of study at one of the main initiatic sanctuaries in Hawaii, Swami Matkormano has developed a physical method that enables one to communicate with the Mysterious Unknown in which past and future events are inscribed. It is based on a system of colour and sound perceptions that disrupt physical equilibrium and predispose the subject to increasingly elaborate states of trance.

Six thousand years ago the Magi of Persia practised this rite, then known as the Mirror of Mazda, by looking with the naked eye at a concave lens in which the rays of the sun were reflected.

The lamas and sorcerers of Mongolia also use it, claiming to receive colours from the astral world by this means.

To prevent the experience from being dangerous, the adept first undergoes a secret preparation. He must stand in the dark with his back against an opaque wall, perform *mantras* (magic gestures) and receive projections of light, first in one eye, then in the other, at the rate of two projections every four seconds. The swami also recommends hearing modulated sounds, first in one ear and then in the other. Depending on the goal to be achieved, the lights and sounds may be perceived not alternately but simultaneously.[36]

In this complex experience the two personalities of the adept, 'the right man and the left man' (the two lobes of the brain), are stimulated in such a way as to cause *samadhi*, a superconscious state that sensitises the subject to perceptions from another universe.

Horseraces and Lotteries

Although this initiation must not be used in order to force one's luck, the swami's pupils have succeeded in correctly predicting, entirely for research purposes, the winners in horseraces and lotteries.

The same result can be obtained by practising a certain breathing rhythm in a secret posture. When this rhythm is achieved just before going to sleep, it continues during sleep and dreams then become prophetic.

At an advanced stage, holding the breath for a time that seems incredibly long to non-initiates is said to explain the long states of catalepsy achieved by some yogis.

In ancient Egypt, adepts undergoing the initiation test had to 'die for three days' before being resuscitated and admitted into the sanctuary.

The Secret of Eternal Lamps

One of the great mysteries of occultism is that of the 'eternal lamps' whose invention is attributed to either the Rosicrucians or the ancient Avestans. The secret consists in the hermetic preparation of an 'oil of gold' which supplies the wick with all the elements of combustion and constantly renews them.

It is said that in the fifteenth century, in the tomb of Cicero's daughter, Tullia, a lamp was found which had been lighting the body for nearly fifteen hundred years.

When the monastic orders were banished from England during the reign of Henry VIII, two 'eternal lamps' that had been burning since the fourth century were found in a monastery. They are now in the Leiden museum.

On May 15, 1717, an underground Rosicrucian temple was brought to light in England. The discoverers saw a kind of mummy seated on a stone chair, apparently reading 'a large, magic alphabet book' by the light of a lamp. When they began to approach it, the mummy, with a movement that was certainly not involuntary, broke the lamp and the underground temple was plunged into darkness. This incident was reported by witnesses to the discovery.

Were those lamps truly eternal? It seems doubtful for a number of reasons, especially since tradition specifies that eternal lamps are known only to Rosicrucians and great initiates. Such lamps probably exist in the Centre AMORC of the French Rosicrucians at Villeneuve-Saint-Georges, but it is unlikely that they are shown to all adepts.[37] They are said to be miniature nuclear batteries that can function for five thousand years (the disintegration time of radium).

Agreement is so imperfect on this point that another

explanation, attractively rational, has also been advanced: eternal lamps, like those used by Rabbi Jiechele in the time of Saint Louis (see Chapter V of my book *One Hundred Thousand Years of Man's Unknown History*), were simply electric lights using either a battery or a condenser of atmospheric energy, as in the case of the Ark of the Covenant. If this is true, we know the secret of the fuel, but the wick and the flame still remain a mystery.

3. Telluric and Aerial Currents

The earth is covered by a network of electric currents that is something like its nervous system, with centres (*shakras*) and zones which, according to their nature, influence human behaviour and health.

There are places where you live in apprehension and feel ill at ease, with an unreasoning urge to go somewhere else, anywhere else. There are other places where you feel a flourishing of your whole being, places where you would like to live.

Artists are more sensitive to these magic influences than anyone else. They seek out areas where they can write, think, paint or sculpt in the best psychic conditions.

Animals also feed the mysterious emanations and know very well where they should have their dens or nests.

The agronomist Claude Trouvé, one of the best French specialists, has observed that two seemingly identical plots of land, with the same subsoil and chemical components, may have extremely different qualities: in the same field, plants may grow remarkably in one place, yet be sparse and stunted nearby.

These rationally inexplicable facts point up the existence of an underground Mysterious Unkown: telluric currents, almost completely ignored by conventional science.

Magic Places Where It Is Good to Live

Professor André Bouguenec gives a more esoteric explanation:

There are magic places. The earth must be regarded as a living organism with a physiology as complex as ours. Its womb has fecundated several nourishing 'umbilical cords' of which mankind has lost all trace. These zones are *erogenous* in the sense that they engender emanations of love. Man must therefore seek his affinities with his mother the earth, and by finding them he brings the intellectual and physical levels into harmony with each other.

The scientific writer Pierre Devaux has made a study of the problem in which he adds the effect of the electric potential of the atmosphere to that of telluric currents.

'At all points of the globe,' he writes, 'there is a vertical electric field that is usually 75 volts per metre. This singular field conditions our whole lives. If it is amplified (4,000 volts) tempers become frayed and family life is punctuated by slaps . . . Soon there is lightning, then conditions become normal (130 volts at most) and smiles reappear.'

Experiments have been made with infants whose cradles were connected to the earth by a ground wire with a circuit breaker. In a zero field (with a ground) growth was more rapid than in an insulated cradle and the additional increase in the infant's weight was sometimes more than half a pound a week.

Devaux has made a natural classification of geographical locations:

Positive electric field. On plateaus. Suitable for rural populations. Favourable to fecundation. Parsley resists plant lice.

Zero electric field. In cities and forests. Diseases of woodsmen and coal merchants, tuberculosis, cancer. Proliferation of rabbits, flies, ants.

Negative electric field. Near caves and waterfalls. Radishes degenerate. Suitable for salamanders and slugs.

This study is still incomplete, of course, but it brings an order of knowledge which, in conjunction with investigation of telluric currents, may have beneficial effects on human behaviour.

Initiates once had that knowledge and made great use of it in building a sanctuary, choosing a retreat and performing a cure.

The Asgard, or palace of the Scandinavian Ases (gods), had five hundred and forty rooms for the gods and was located in a region called Thrudwang, that is, 'field of force'.

It is interesting to note that German scientists recently rediscovered secrets that illustrate this view, directly connecting initiation with scientific knowledge. In a factory at Bottrop, in Westphalia, they experimented with an artificial climate produced by the difference of potential between the ceiling and the floor. A current of electric particles constantly circulates in the room, artificially reproducing certain characteristics of the atmosphere in high mountains. Results have been highly satisfactory: the workers resist fatigue better and absencces because of illness have been reduced by 60 per cent.

A Secret of the Compagnons du Devoir

The Compagnons du Devoir, heirs of a long tradition of craftsmanship (a notion that has become lost in our time), have secrets that they reveal only in the intimacy of their workshops.

Although it is remarkably well built in comparison to deplorable structures in the style of Le Corbusier, the Sacré-Coeur church in Paris is cracking in some places. The Compagnons du Devoir say that this is not surprising, without explaining any further. But the cause of the phenomenon may lie in the telluric currents that are extremely active at the site of the church: the Butte Montmartre, which has been a consecrated place since ancient times.

The church is built on a north-south axis; the longest walls therefore follow that direction, and so, of course, do the joints between the stones. It is believed that by an effect of electrolysis the north-south telluric currents of the area are able to dissociate the bonds of cement and mortar by polarising them, which leads to their disintegration. Possible fracture lines are thus produced. This is much less pronounced in the east-west walls, where the joints are not aligned with the currents.

The fact that telluric currents usually have a north-south direction is said to be the esoteric reason for the construction of churches and cathedrals on an east-west axis, with the chancel nearly always at the east end.

The curious northeast-southwest orientation of the Chartres cathedral, a particularly venerated sanctuary of Christianity, is said to have been chosen because of the direction of the telluric currents in the area.

Balancing the Positive and the Negative

Nerve impulses can be regarded as an electric current, a steady flow of electrical particles whose charges are either positive (protons) or negative (electrons). Health may be the result of a balance, always the same for a given individual, between the number of protons and electrons. The slightest disruption of that balance is manifested by a deterioration of health stemming from a loss of electrons and consequently a greater proportion of protons. An organic electric positivation then takes place, causing an abnormal increase in nerve tonicity which gives rise to states described under the names of vagotonia and sympathicotonia.

This is the hypothesis formulated by Dr Pierre Chevalier in his *Relaxation Electronique et Vitalité Générale.* He believes that electronisation acts effectively against pathological disorders.

Chapter 7

HERMETIC TOWERS AND THE PYRAMID OF FRANCE

France is a country so rich in mystery that a book could be written on its unknown sites and monuments. In all districts, and even in Paris, the ardent seeker discovers wonders, invisible to many people, that make him think of initiatic sanctuaries. Such sanctuaries, says Swami Matkormano, 'are open to those who deserve to enter them but others cannot find them, for a kind of magic always guides their steps away from the right direction.' If so, there must be many Frenchmen whose eyes have not been opened, and who are doomed to wander aimlessly.

The Vénérand Fountain

At Vénérand, a few miles from Saintes, one can admire a fountain more beautiful than those of Rome, Viterbo or Lyon, or the Médicis fountain in Paris. It is said to be Roman, but that is not certain.

Imagine, in a hill full of caves, a deep cleft of shadow and greenery that you enter by walking under enormous trees growing horizontally. Suddenly the ground gives way to a steep staircase, as wide as a road, and the fountain appears. It has the form of two pools, one below the other. A circular passage, cut into the rock, leads to a cave where the spring seems to have its source. Vines, moss and ferns on the hillside provide a luxuriant setting.

An inevitable Virgin presides in her niche and Christianises the site, of course, but two thousand years ago there must have been a Minerva, a Diana or an Epona in her place.

The whole site suggests a baptistry and could hardly

have been used for anything else; but what kind of baptism was given there?

Very few visitors discover the beauty of Vénérand, which no doubt pleases the gracious André Vinet, whose small estate must be crossed in order to reach the fountain.

The Field of Idols

If the idea of seeing a lunar landscape appeals to you, I suggest that you take a walk some day near Saint-Barnabé, in the Col de Vence, Alpes-Maritimes. On an arid plateau where sheep have difficulty finding enough to eat, you will see a multitude of small basins with a diameter of thirty to sixty feet. There is a little difference of level between the edges and the center, but grass and lichens do not grow there in the same way as elsewhere, which is rather puzzling.

The whole plateau is riddled with craters, like the surface of the moon. Was this caused by a bombardment of meteorites?

To add to the strangeness of the place, there is sculpture scattered all over it: sections of walls, rudimentary towers, entrances to enclosures guarded by stone giants. Are they curiosities of nature or relics of a titanic civilisation?[38]

'This place,' I was told by Guy Tarade and André Millou, directors of the Centre de Recherche d'Eléments Inconnus de Civilisations,[39] 'is truly magic; furthermore it is called "the Field of Idols" and is known only to hunters and shepherds.'

The Falicon Pyramid

Yes, there is a pyramid in France! It is similar to the Pyramid of Cheops, but much smaller. Incredible as it may seem, it is still almost totally unknown.

Yet endless books have been written on the 'unknown' archaeological and prehistoric wonders of France. The Eiffel Tower, Mont Saint-Michel and the city of Carcassonne have not been overlooked, but not one line has been written on the Vénérand fountain, the titanic city of the

Field of Idols, hermetic towers, the Valley of Wonders, the Glozel museum, the 'mediumistic museum' of Brantôme, the troglodytes of Paris or the mysterious underground sanctuary that is said to give continuous initiatic instruction. And no mention of Swami Matkormano's curious ashram at Marsal!

There may be some excuse for ignoring the underground sanctuary, whose existence is kept secret, but it is hard to imagine how anyone can overlook a pyramid as big as a three-storey house, or hermetic towers more than seventy feet high! Yet in the village of Falicon, just above Nice, that 'invisible' pyramid can be seen from a mile away. A few prehistorians and a handful of speleologists know of its existence but, whether from indifference or lack of culture, they have taken no interest in it.

Nicholas Andréa, the mayor of Falicon, did me the honour of guiding me to Mont Cau, crossing a private estate that can be entered only by permission.

A hundred yards from the top of Mont Cau stands the pyramid, made of stones joined by cement that is of better quality than Roman cement.

Its sides are unequal because of its location on a steep slope and it is built over a fissure with an opening about eight feet wide. Its eastern side has a kind of doorway eight feet high. Until 1921 there was a carved swastika above this doorway, but it was then removed or destroyed by vandals. (The swastika was the sacred symbol of the Jains. It was also the sign of Manu, 'he who makes the wheel of events turn,' writes Guénon, 'while remaining motionless in the Invariable Middle.' Such is the meaning of the swastika.)

Under the doorway is the entrance of the fissure. The pyramid stands over the cavity and cannot be entered. The orientation of the opening permits the sun, at ten o'clock on summer mornings, to illuminate the white calcite pillar that supports the vault of the underground temple.

The base and the largest side of the pyramid are twenty-two feet long, but the point is missing. Assuming a pointed design, the original length of the main side must have been about thirty feet.

The First Underground Temple

It takes speleological equipment to go down into the fissure, which is about fifty feet deep. An Italian named Rossetti was its first known discoverer, in 1803.

Accompanied by André Millou, I saw a great central pillar (a stalactite) supporting the vault, fifteen to thirty feet high, of a room with a diameter of sixty feet. The whole scene gave me the impression of an underground cathedral, containing a beautiful triforium of stalactites and stalagmites.

On the east side of the room we identified an initiation altar. Its tabernacle has disappeared, but its seven steps, carved into the rock, are in good condition. Rossetti did not mention these steps in his report, even though they are of great interest.

At the back of the room, to the left, are two holes or wells. One of them is filled in (it may not be very deep) and the other descends vertically to a great depth.

'The eye plunges into a shadowy hole,' wrote Rossetti, 'and despite the strong light that I had sent for, I was unable to dissipate the darkness. Some day, no doubt, a brave man will succeed in exploring the hole. I tried in vain to do so; all those whom I asked to help me were seized with dread and terror.'

We felt no terror, but since we had no rope ladders we could not venture down into the hole, whose narrow sections constitute a serious obstacle.

The Patriarch Gothland

Until 1922 the pyramid remained in oblivion, but in that year a strange patriarch named Gothland (now dead) settled in the nearby village. He was something of a prophet and he founded the sect known as Universalité Pratique.

Initiated into occultism, he rediscovered the monument

and tried to determine its age. On the basis of traditional data he 'measured a sixty-degree difference by the precession of the equinoxes, in the direction opposite to that of the earth's rotation. Knowing that the shift is one degree every seventy-two years, we can place the age of the pyramid at 4335 years.'

Until 1921 a Jain cross adorned the side containing the entrance. And, curiously, the nearest and also the oldest village in the region is called Jaïn or Jaïna on old maps. Its present name is Gaïna.

The Jains of India are said to have built pyramids as far away as Europe and South America.

According to Gothland, the altar at the top of the seven steps in the underground room was used for initiation. And neophytes underwent ordeals by fire, water and air.

The Underground Pyramid

In 1927 speleologists went down into the 'shadowy hole', which is a pit about twenty feet wide, cut by a fissure. Thirty feet down, they set foot on slippery, clayey soil. They saw fissures opening on both sides and disappearing into the mountains. Still farther down, they came to the bottom of a spacious cavern a hundred feet long and sixty feet high.

In this cavern is a second pyramid formed of blocks of stone that either fell from the ceiling or were dropped from the upper room by unknown persons. It is about thirty feet high and sixty feet wide at the base. There are two stalactites in the cavern, which is extended by narrow passages that could be penetrated only by a child. The walls are blackened by layers of soot nearly an inch thick in some places.

Was the cavern a prehistoric hearth? Was it an initiation room that could be reached by an easier passage? For the moment, these questions cannot be answered.

A legend says that a cat was once thrown into the fissure and came out through a cave at Nice.

It is said that in the twelfth century Templars lived in the upper room and knew a secret entrance leading to the room containing the second pyramid, which may have been a hiding place for treasures, like the pyramid of Antiochus I at Nemrut Dag, in the Anti-Taurus Mountains of Turkey.

There is a curious parallel between those two pyramids made of loose stones, which is rare, and both associated with fire: the one at Nemrut Dag by its terraces, the one at Falicon by its sooty walls. It is likely that they were both dedicated to Mithra, the ancient Persian god whose worship was performed only in caverns.

The Autun Pyramid

Such is the information we have on the Falicon pyramid; it is not enough to let us know with certainty why the pyramid was built and for what it was used.

Pyramids are nearly always an enigma, even in Egypt, Mexico and China, where they are found by the hundreds. We are far from having a complete list of them, since the one at Falicon was unknown until recent years and the one whose remains exist at Autun, France, is still unknown.

It stands half a mile from the town, halfway up the slope of Mount Briscou known as the Field of Urns, since several clay and glass vases have been found there, probably intended for use as burial urns. The pyramid, which bears the name of Pierre de Couhard, originally had a height of more than eighty feet and a quadrangular base with a length of about fifty feet. The facing has been completely removed, but the masonry that remains is extremely solid.

Monsieur Desplaces, a learned gentleman of Autun, carefully examined it and noted that it had been built up by a series of hollow pyramids placed on top of each other like upside-down funnels (the pyramids of Mexico are also built in this way), but its intended purpose is unknown. Many have seen it as a tomb of the kind that Mainz erected to Drusus, and some have believed it might be the tomb of Divitiacus. Others have thought of a sepulchral beacon, a kind of observatory or signal tower.

One important detail wipes away all those hypotheses

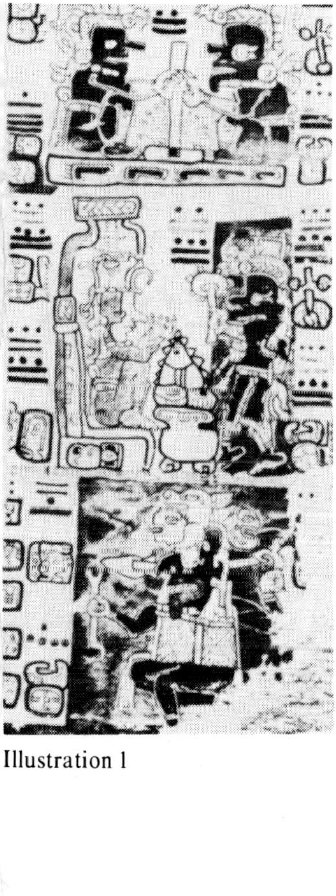

Illustration 1

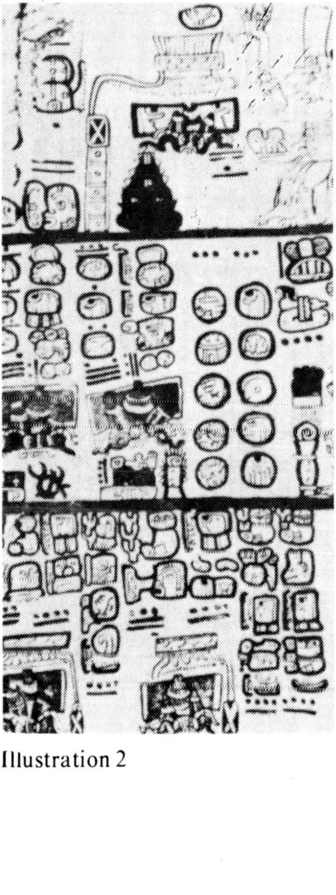

Illustration 2

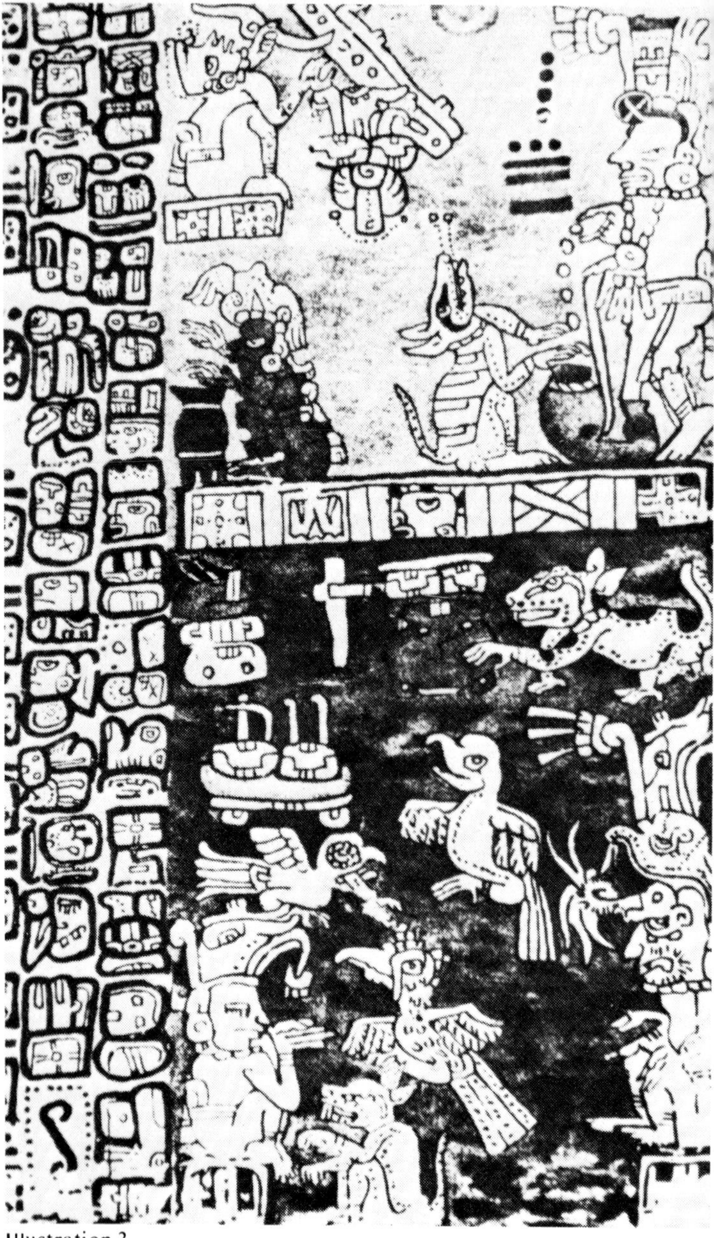

Illustration 3

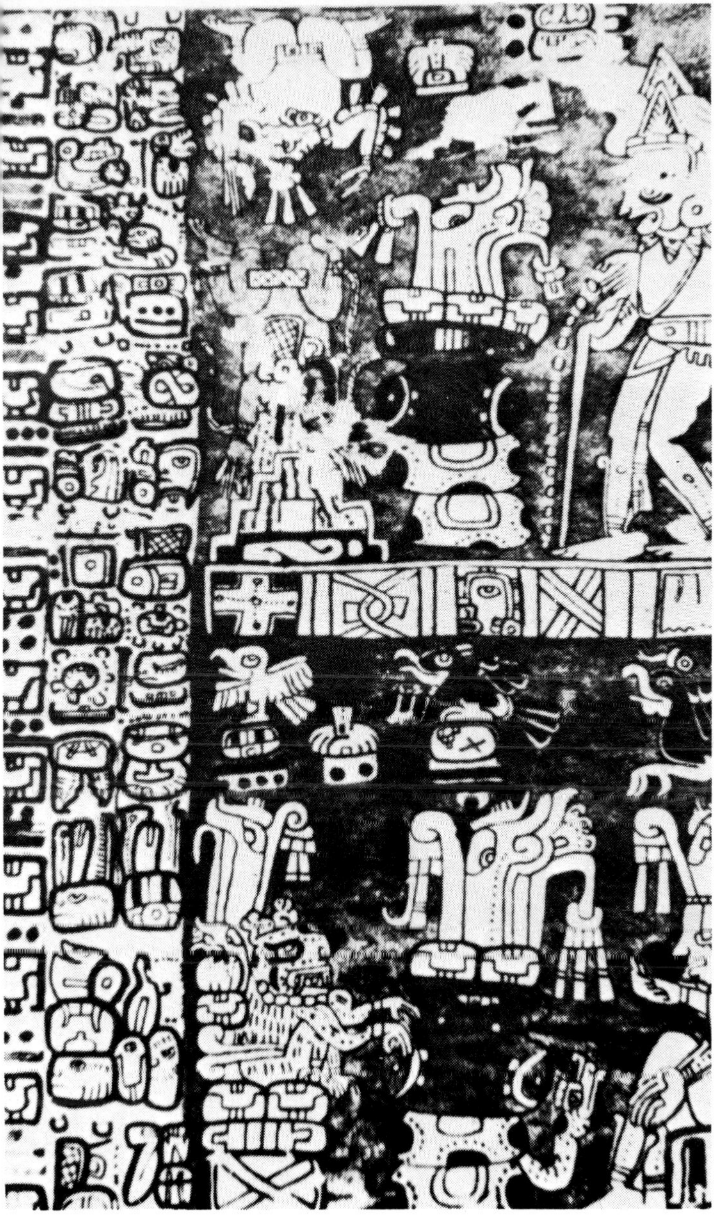

Illustration 4

Illustration 5

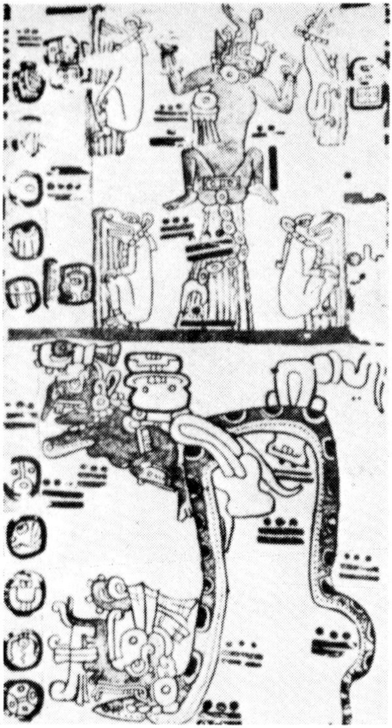

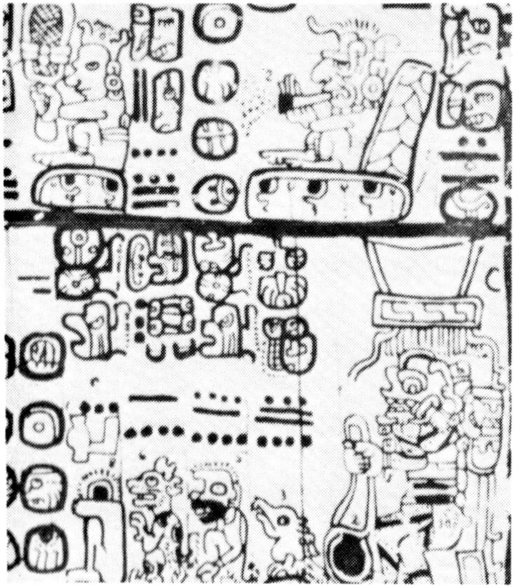

Illustration 6

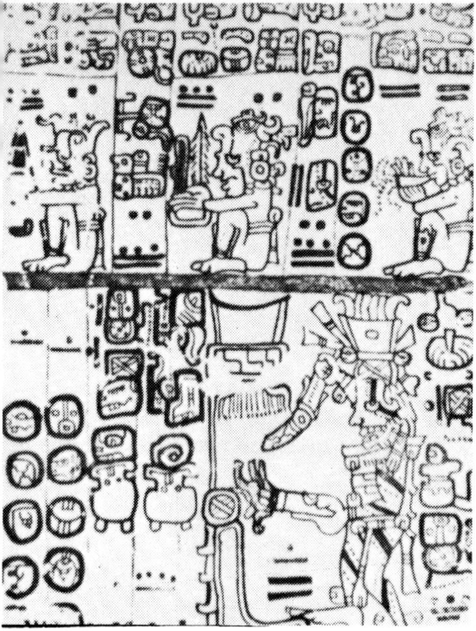

Illustration 7

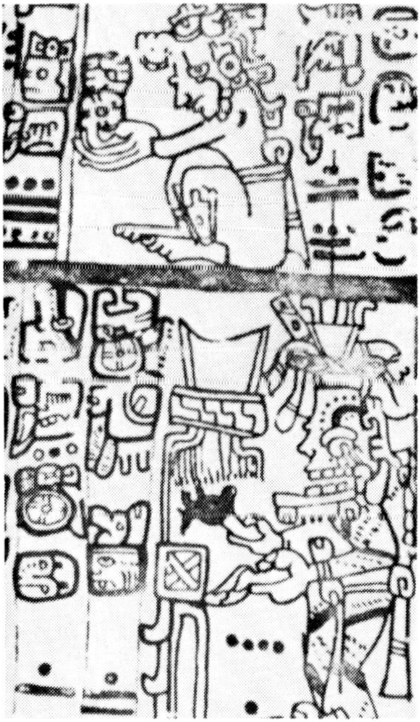

Illustration 8

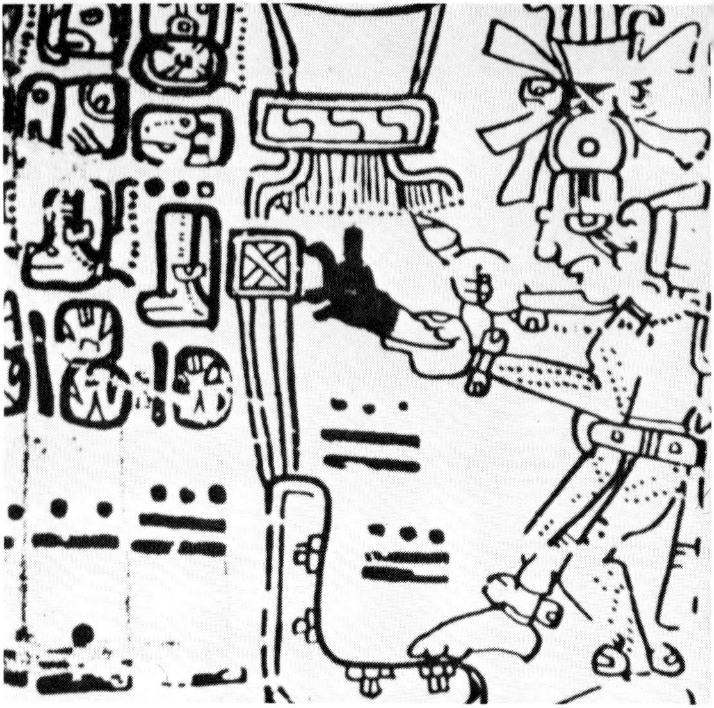

Illustration 9

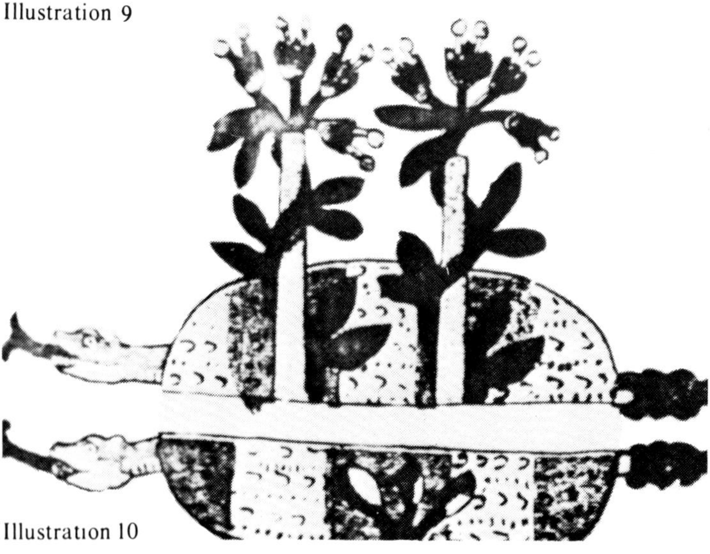

Illustration 10

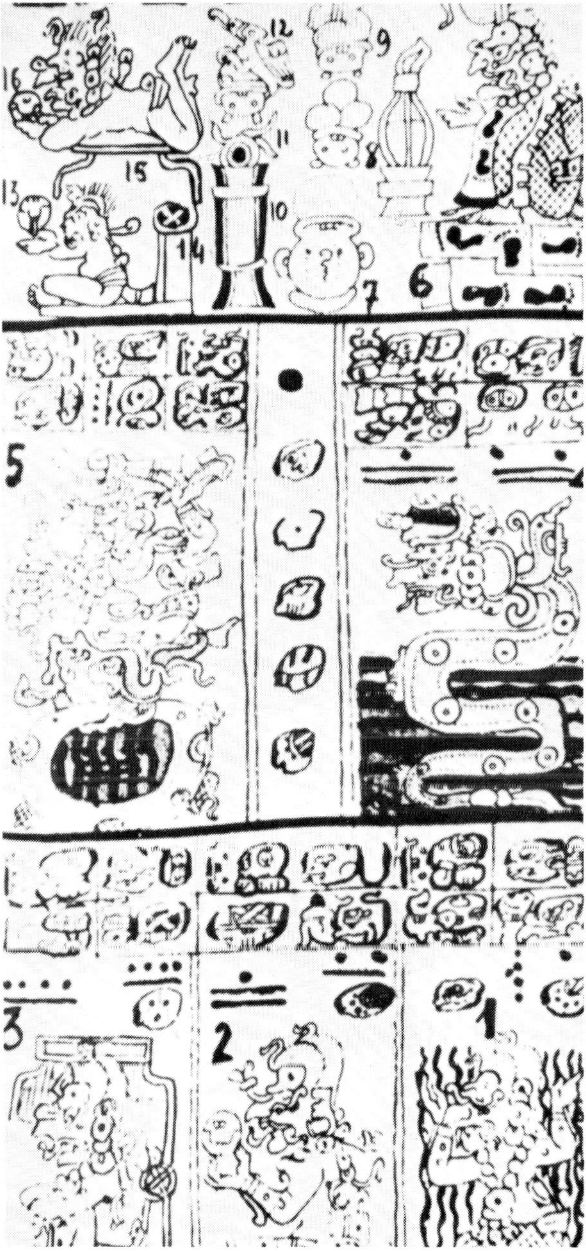

Illustration 11

Illustration 12

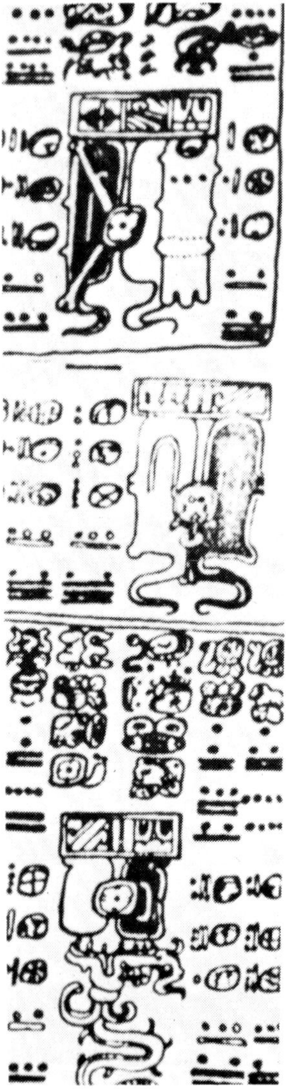

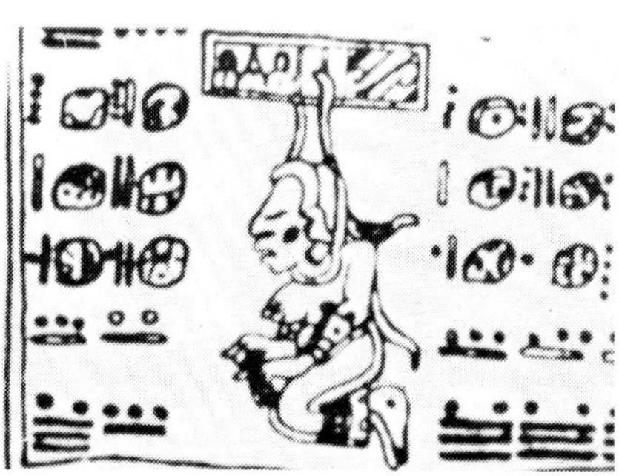

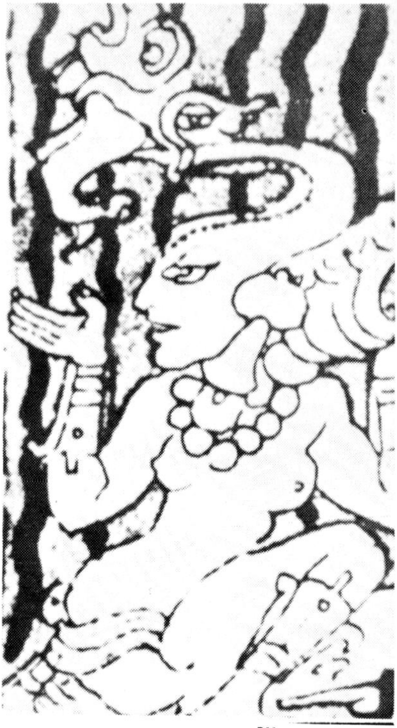

Illustration 13

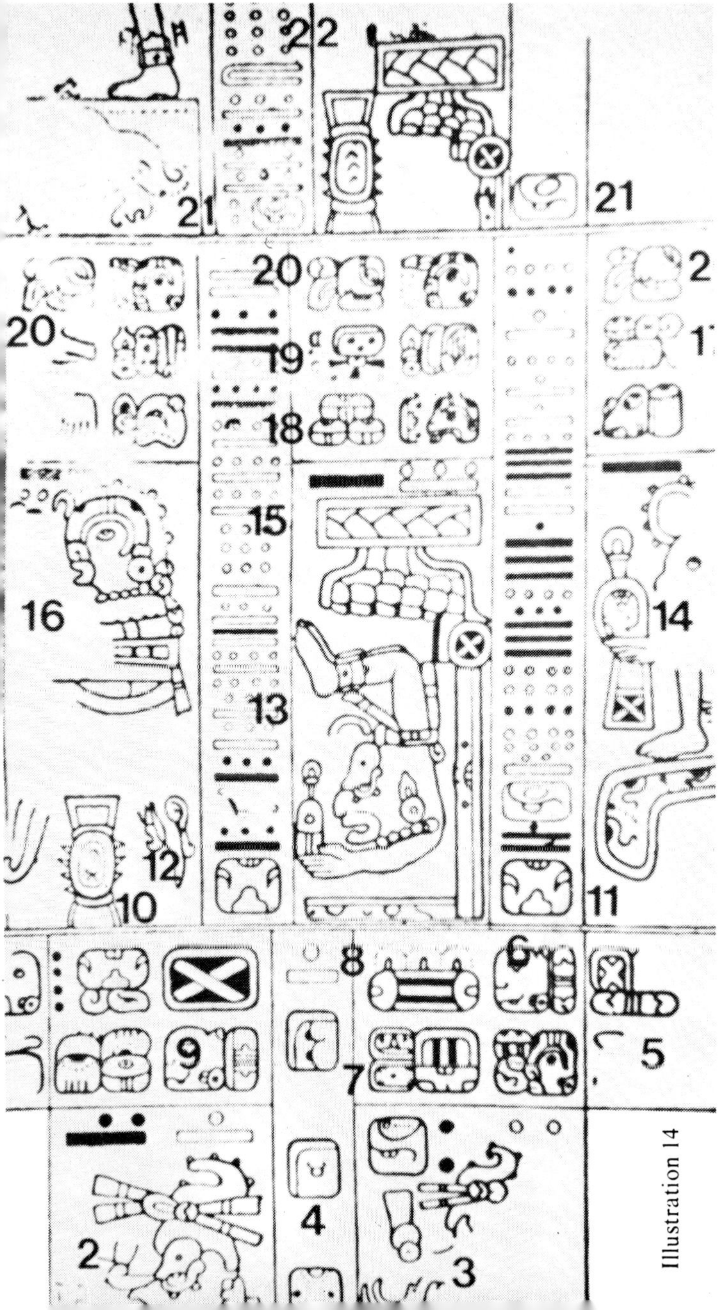

Illustration 14

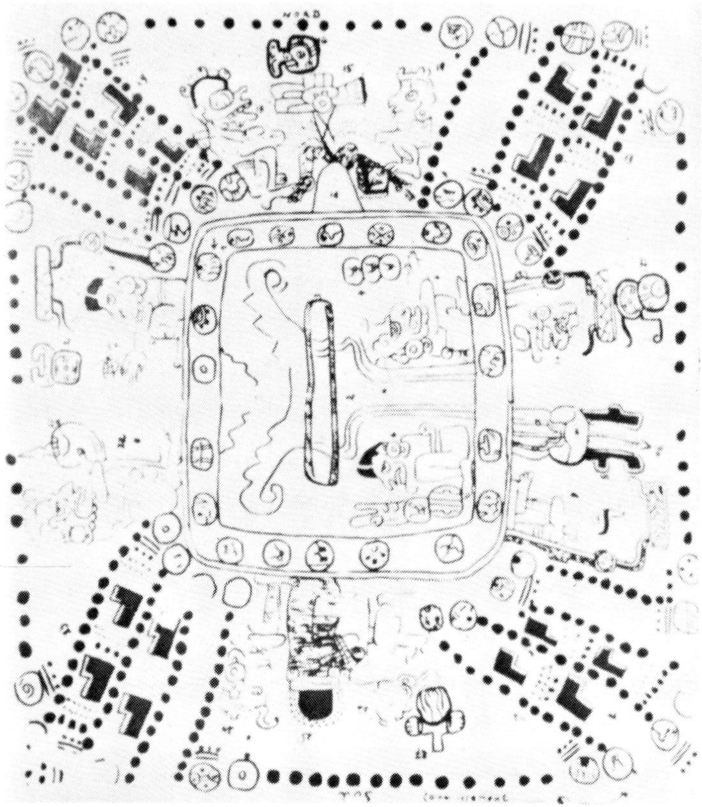

Illustration 15

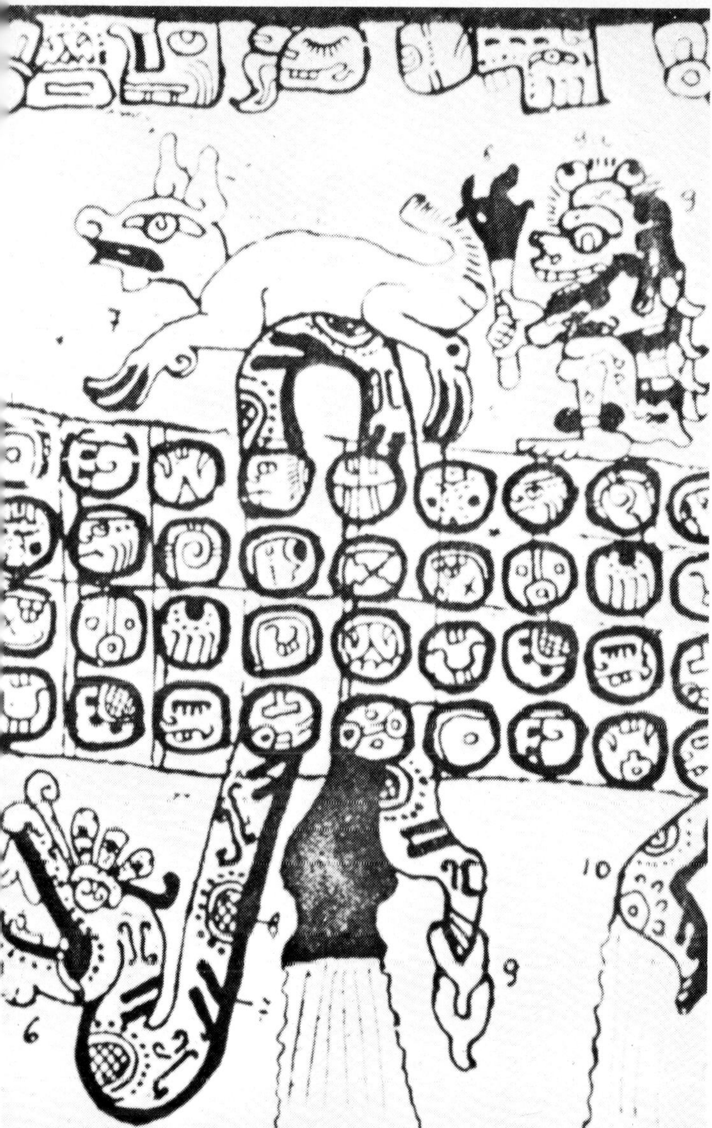

Illustration 16

DESCRIPTIONS OF ILLUSTRATIONS

Illustration 1. (PLATE VI of Troano Manuscript)

Top Section: Ritual preparation of fire. Idea of energy.

Middle Section: Concentration of force and energy (the pyramid) on the sign of upheaval of the earth. The traveler is seated under an exhaust pipe from which no fire is coming (rest), connected to a motor (the rectangle with crossed bars).

Bottom Section: The personage surmounted by a flying monster and an arrow conveys the idea of space travel.

Illustration 2 (PLATE VII of Troano Manuscript)

Top Section: An enormous pyramid of energy and a flying monster under the exhaust pipe, still connected to the motor.

Above: sign of upheaval of the earth toward the starry sky.

Middle Section: Sign of fire and flying monsters.

Bottom Section: Fire, energy, flying monster and pyramids in the form of arches concentrated under an exhaust pipe.

Symbol repeated twice. Each of the exhaust pipes contains the sign of a motor.

Illustration 3 (PLATE XX of Troano Manuscript)

To the left of the drawings, twelve tablets representing the earth lifted up into the sky.

Scattered through the drawings are strange devices and birds representing flying machines. Nearly all of them contain the sign of upheaval of the earth. One of them, resembling a locomotive (with two signs of upheaval) seems to have wheels. Another seems to have a rudder. The general idea of flight in space is clearly expressed.

Illustration 4 (PLATE XXII of Troano Manuscript)

Force poured (the rings) onto the flying serpent. Flying signs.

The upside-down monster may be meant to convey the idea of weightlessness.

On the serpent, the universal symbol of a flying machine, preparation of a lifting force clearly indicated by the tablets.

Numerous symbols of flight, flying staircases and lifting beyond the earth.

Between the two drawings, as in Plate XX, are tablets showing astronomical symbols (stars) and the sign of a motor.

Illustration 5 (PLATE XXVI of Troano Manuscript)

Top Section: General idea: propulsion in space by reaction. The chain starting from the monster signifies an accumulation of energy and ends with a kind of horseshoe which, in the alphabet of the Perez Codex has the meaning of "great, expanding breath."

The black lozenge surrounded by radiations is a symbol of concentrated energy.

Lower Section: The flying serpent seems to be charged with the energy necessary for its takeoff.

The position of Plate XXVI in the Troano Manuscript seems to indicate not action, but the idea of an unrealized action still in preparation. The craft with an exhaust pipe and a motor does not appear in these drawings.

Illustration 6 (PLATE XXVI-a of Troano Manuscript)

Top Section: Two personages are seated under the sign of fermentation; i.e., upward thrust. The one on the left evokes a sound about to be heard. The one on the right holds a racket with a flying symbol.

Lower Section: Test flight of a flying machine? The personage resembles an astronaut, with his harness and space suit. On his back he carries an apparatus marked with a symbol that we do not know. In his hand he holds a bag with a carrying strap, perhaps containing provisions for his journey.

Illustration 7 (PLATE XXVII of Troano Manuscript)

Top Section: The personages hold three clear symbols: sound (coming out of the trumpet) – roar of the motor; an arrow = flight; a pyramid = energy.

Lower Section: An exhaust pipe ejecting gases. The personage is moving fire toward the motor (to start it); the surrounding signs reinforce the idea of space flight.

Illustration 8 (PLATE XXVIII of Troano Manuscript)

Firing of the exhaust pipe and starting of the motor. The object held in the personage's left hand is a torch.

Illustration 9 (PLATE XXIX of Troano Manuscript)

Repetition of firing the exhaust pipe and starting the motor.

As in the account of the cataclysm where the sign of the upheaved earth is reproduced three times, the repetition of identical acts (Plates XXVII, XXVIII and XXIX) indicates the power and complexity of the act.

The drawings in the other plates of the manuscript are incomprehensible to us. They relate events that may have taken place on another planet, but the narrator reproduced them in accordance with his earthly understanding. To interpret them, one would have to give a clear translation of the tablets, which is not possible in the present state of our knowledge of Mayan writing.

Illustration 10: The Magliabecchiano Codex

A strange drawing evoking the image of a "flying saucer." The serpents' heads symbolize a flying machine; their tails are two flaming torches.

Illustration 11: The Dresden Codex

Like most of the other Mayan manuscripts, the Dresden Codex is considered to be a calendar.

In the drawings reproduced here, the theme of space travel appears with motifs similar to those in the Troano Manuscript.

Interpretation of the images, going from bottom to top and right to left:

1. The power (necklace of rings) of fire (vertical waves) which will produce propulsion.
2. He who is about to rise above the earth (symbol between the fingers) where men (crouching personage) live.
3. Powerful flight (rings) produced by the exhaust pipe ejecting fire, connected to the motor.
4. Powerful flight of the serpent in position to spring.
5. The flying serpent containing propulsion, high in the sky.
6. Footprints indicating the walking of God on earth, followed by three symbols of energy and rising from the ground, then a bowl containing subjugated fire. Above, a bird of flight over the upheaved earth. The two personages on the left bear the sign of lifting beyond the earth. The one on top is lying on an exhaust pipe from which fire is no longer being ejected.

Idea of an ended journey.

Illustration 12: Dresden Codex Calendar

The calendar of the Codex contains other symbols evoking the idea of flight.

Three Sections on the Left: Stylized image of a spacecraft with an exhaust pipe and a motor, surmounted by two or three astronomical symbols.

Bottom Right: Idea of the uplifting of a personage suspended from two symbols. The one on the right represents the known sign of space; the one on the left is an ideogram expressing the idea of forces directed upward.

Whatever objections may be raised against this interpretation, it seems to me impossible to deny that these drawings from the

Troano Manuscript and the Dresden and Perez Codices are related to an extraterrestrial adventure that is supported by the whole mythology of the ancient Mexicans.

Illustration 13: Dresden Codex. Goddess listening to space waves

Illustration 14: The Perez Codex

The Perez Codex was discovered in 1863 in the Bibliothèque Impériale in Paris, now the Bibliothèque Nationale, by Professor Léon de Rosny, an eminent Orientalist.

The portion of it reproduced here, like certain drawings in the Troano Manuscript, has so far defied the efforts of translators.

In my interpretation of it below I have used known signs, which I have marked with an X, as well as other signs and drawings that do not appear in the conventional alphabet; the meanings I have given them are more arbitrary, but they seem logical to me.

1. Sky. X.
2. Flying machine with a rotor.
3. A thing about to fly away.
4. Breath. Planet Venus. X.
5. The master who has the power of rising steam. X.
6. The very strong master of steam.
7. Power of the sun linked to the idea of a staircase (elevation). X.
8. Great force using light.
9. The very strong master of steam. X.
10. Uplifting above the original earth (afterward: sign of a motor.)
11. and 12. Earthly object raised into the sky above mountains. X
13. Space flight, weightlessness.
14. Energy enclosed in a vessel above a pyramid (energy) with a motor.
15. Exhaust pipe connected to a motor, causing the personage to be weightless.
16. Astronaut?
17. Symbol of energy, staircase (elevation) and the planet Venus. X.
18. Upraising of the earth (repeated twice). X
19. Flying machine in the starry sky.
20. Three signs of danger. X.
21. Liberation, expansion. X.
22. Exhaust pipe connected to a motor on the right and a symbol of energy on the left.

I will leave it to the reader to imagine the relations among these signs and symbols, but the general idea is logically that of an action or a plan for action taking place in space by means of flight.

Illustration 15: The Cortesianus Codex. (PLATE VI)

The Cortesianus Codex is one of the most important Mayan manuscripts. It belongs to the Madrid Library.

The first figure reproduced gives a precise idea of a journey from Earth to Venus. At the center an earthling is seated with, at his feet, a symbol that must represent the earth. Above this symbol is a tablet bearing the sign of Venus. To the right is a Venusian god with three superimposed signs identifying his planet. Between the two personages is a kind of mushroom expanding like the cloud of an atomic explosion.

According to interpreters, the course marked by black dots begins at the sign of Venus, lower left, and continues toward the right in a winding but circular path. The first stop shows the space traveler under an exhaust pipe. In front of him is the sign of flight away from the earth, followed by an arrow that reinforces the idea.

The other identifiable figures show the personage under a smaller exhaust pipe (sign of slowing down?). Then the astronaut is in front of a god. The dotted lines of their conversation can be seen below the winged symbol.

The astronaut resumes his journey, since farther on he is under another exhaust pipe. He meets a god still more powerful than the first one, with a large necklace of force around his neck, holding a symbol of rising above the earth, surmounted by a little drawing of a space rocket. A third encounter seems to be evoked. The whole series speaks clearly and can suggest no interpretation that does not involve a journey in space.

Illustration 16 (PLATE XIV)

The serpent of the Cortesianus Codex with jet or rocket propulsion.

Here we again find the sign of Venus. The serpent is represented in levitation or, more exactly, as being propelled through the air by gases coming out its tail and an exhaust pipe. The meaning is clear enough to require no comment.

and directly connects this pyramid to those of Falicon, Egypt, China and Mexico: inside it is a pit whose bottom, according to tradition, cannot be fathomed. This is a major clue, for either pyramids are built over a fissure, as in Chichen Itza (Mexico), China and Falicon, or there is no natural fissure and a pit is dug for presumably magic purposes. The Great Pyramid of Giza has one, dug obliquely, which has never been searched because it has not been given the interest it deserves. It is therefore not by chance that pyramids are built over fissures or pits.

There is also a kind of pyramid at Vienne, France, known as the 'Plane of the Needle,' but it is actually an obelisk fifty feet high, with four archways, dating from the Roman period.

In the village of Commelle par Orry-la-Ville is a pyramidal 'lantern of the dead' whose known intended purpose may be a significant indication.

It is in Asia, however, that the mystery of pyramids is most precisely cleared up, thanks to tradition.

The Great Pyramid of China

The great pyramid of China is in Shensi, forty miles southwest of Sian, and it happens to be in a forbidden zone. The secrecy of the Chinese with regard to this monument is no doubt related to the military importance of the area, since not even its exact height is known.

American aviators who have photographed it believe that it is at least twice as high as the pyramid of Cheops (four hundred and fifty feet) and have suggested a figure of a thousand feet, which would make it the world's highest pyramid, if we except the one at Cholula, Mexico, which is built over a mountain. It is dated very approximately from the Hsia dynasty, four thousand years ago.

Archaeological excavations have discovered magnificent jade objects and 'green stones' which, in my opinion, place its construction in the time when the Masters of the World from the planet Venus ruled Mexico, Peru and Asia Minor. (Many pyramids were consecrated to the Venusian rulers who were deified five thousand years ago, but most of them had existed since the second millennium after the Deluge.)

Since the sign of the bull figures persistently in Chinese cryptography, we may deduce that the initiators of Shensi were compatriots of Quetzalcoatl and Baal.

Traces of the original colouring have been found on the great pyramid of China: it was black on the north, blue-grey on the east, red on the south and white on the west. The point was painted yellow.

Another pyramid, east of Sian, served as a tomb for Emperor Shih Huang Ti two thousand years ago, but, as with the great pyramid, we have little information on its measurements.

The Pyramid of Chan-pa-Chan

The pyramid of Chan-pa-Chan, however, is well known. It stands on a mountain in Turkestan and is an object of frequent pilgrimages because the eastern Tartars regard it as the cradle of their people.

Here is what tradition reports on it:

> Discouraged by the confusion of languages and unable to take refuge in towers rising to the clouds, the post-Deluge peoples settled in high mountains to protect themselves, if possible, against the chance of another disastrous Deluge. It was not until their flocks began to lack pastures, and the soil could not produce the food needed by the growing colonies, that they settled in the plains, which they often had to dry out before living in them. Hence the respect that the Orientals have for their sacred mountains. They show that respect by annual visits accompanied by offerings, vows and prayers. (From *La Vierge. Histoire de la Mère de Dieu*, by Abbé Orsini, reported by Louis de Sivry, members of the Société Asiatique.)

An explanation at last! It is so clear and simple that, in my opinion, it has a high likelihood of being true. Briefly, I believe it can be said that pyramids are monuments erected after the Deluge to thank mountains for having saved the human race.[40] That is probably the reason for the construction of most of the world's pyramids, except those of Falicon and Autun.

This explanation is particularly convincing with regard to the pyramids of Egypt, the stepped tower of Choga Zanbil in Iran, and the pyramids of Rapa Iti in Polynesia, perched on the peaks of the highest mountains.

Initiation Caves

Since the Falicon pyramid cannot be a symbol of gratitude to the mountains that saved mankind from the Deluge, hypotheses concerning its magic function have been formulated, notably by Guny Tarade, on the basis of the curious experiments carried out by Professors Bissonnette and Benoit.

According to these biologists, if light shines on the head and eyes it has a stimulating effect on the genital system by means of the pituitary body and its gonadotropins. Yellow radiations are particularly effective.

We may assume that darkness has the opposite effect, and in any case can produce glandular disorders. That is precisely what happens during the polar night, which disturbs the menstruation of Eskimo women.

On Easter Island, writes Francis Mazières, children of both sexes were once raised in dark caves so that their skin would turn white and their intellectual and psychic powers would be sharpened.

Were caves used for genetic experiments, as in the sanctuary of the Agartha in Tibet, where teaching is said to be given under conditions most favourable to chastity and the development of psychic powers?

This view is supported by the initiation altar at Falicon and the dark, secret chambers of all pyramids. They are related to magic, the worship of Mithra and the myth of the 'mysterious cave' of the Egyptians, where the union of the soul and the body took place.

Hermetic Towers

In several French departments, such as Gers, Indre-et-Loire and Charente-Maritime, monuments even more enigmatic than pyramids defy the sagacity of archaeologists: hermetic towers.

They are structures of solid masonry with a rectangular base, between thirty and eighty feet high, without doors or windows. What were they used for? No one knows. For a long time they were thought to have been beacons, observation posts or monuments to the dead, but there is no evidence for those hypotheses.

Villepouge and Pierrelonge

The best-known one is at Cinq-Mars-la-Pile in Indre-et-Loire. It stands on the side of a hill, a hundred and fifty feet from the top, and is made of Roman brick.

At Ebéon, in Charente-Maritime, on the road to Saintes, is a hermetic tower forty-feet high, and there is another, seventy-five feet high, at Pierrelonge, near Saint-Romain-de-Benet.

Holes have been made in the compact masonry, probably by treasure hunters, because wherever there is a mystery someone always thinks of a hidden treasure. Nothing was found, of course, but all the towers were damaged.

In 1896, at the foot of the hermetic tower at Villepouge, Charente-Maritime, archaeologists uncovered a thick wall forming a small enclosure that could be entered through a portico. In it they found coins dating from the time of Antonius Pius in the second century, fragments of Roman pottery, a life-sized 'double woman's head' and two lead tablets on which were written, in Latin, magic imprecations dating from the beginning of the Christian era.

We have no other clues to the nature of those mysterious monuments. They can be compared, however, with the hollow towers of Sardinia, the towers of the Parsees, the towers of the Caucasus and the phallus-shaped towers that are so numerous in Ireland. As on the Sardinian towers, which are three to four thousand years old, there are no graphic representations to aid research.

'But these monuments,' writes Antonio Borio, 'attest to the presence of an unknown people who created a remarkable civilisation . . . no doubt the Shardanas who came from the northern seas and islands and fought in Egypt as enemies or mercenaries of the pharaohs.'

In India there are also what may be called hermetic towers: the *stupas* that contain ashes of Buddha.

The Jains who returned to the land of their Aryan ancestors may have been the magician-builders of the Falicon pyramid and towers like those of Charente-Maritime.

Pyramids and hermetic towers, which have the general lines of the menhirs of the Celts and Pelasgians, may have had the same function, if we think of a kind of acupuncture of the ground and a condenser of forces, unknown in our time.

Charles S

Charles S has few friends, and that is the only reproach that can be made against him. He lives in seclusion in a village on an island off the Atlantic coast of France. His neighbours believe that he concerns himself with astrology and metaphysics, and some of them regard him as something of a sorcerer.

For my part, I think he is a great investigator of the Mysterious Unknown and perhaps an initiate, but he speaks so little that it is hard to learn very much about him.

As a special privilege, he allowed me to visit him; the preliminary approaches took a long time but I was able to apprehend part of that unknown which nearly always eludes our research.

In the garden next to his house is a workshop that looks quite ordinary from the outside, but it contains a kind of *borie* made of carefully cemented stones, about six and a half feet high. (A *borie* is a small, conical stone structure used as a shelter by shepherds in Provence. In Poitou, *bories* often contain a fountain.)

This *borie*, hermetic like the towers of Charente-Maritime, rests on a cement platform and it is beyond doubt that there is no secret opening that would enable a man to enter it. It is used for fantastic experiments that are completely outside conventional science.

Charles S explained the system that enables him, he says, to communicate *by telegraphy* with the world of Elsewhere:

'I built this *borie* myself. Inside it, on a table, is a Morse code apparatus that can send signals by means of a contactor like those that were once used in railroad stations. The only difference is that this contactor is very sensitive, much too sensitive to be used by a human hand.

'I'll point out one detail that doesn't affect the experiment directly: at the top of the *borie* are three openings about a quarter of an inch in diameter. Their purpose is to let moisture escape from inside. To keep moisture to a minimum, I conduct my experiments only in summer or in dry weather.'

The *borie* can thus be considered hermetic as far as the possibility of fraud is concerned. The Morse apparatus inside it is connected to the outside by wires that come through the masonry and lead to batteries and a receiving apparatus consisting of a box containing a coil (I assume), a roll of paper that moves around a drum, an electromagnet and a stylus that must be moistened with stamp-pad ink when the experiment is conducted.

The whole system constitutes a simple transmitting and receiving apparatus that can be worked only from inside the *borie*. Since no one is inside the *borie*, there would seem to be no way of receiving messages. But messages are received, and there lies the miracle.

Someone in the Invisible

'Every year I receive dozens of messages,' Charles S said to me. 'Some of them are laconic, others consist of several words. They're sent in ordinary Morse code: a dot for E, a dash for T, a dot and a dash for A, and so on. Many of the words are incomprehensible to me; the others are in French, German, Italian and especially English.

'The word *mora* comes often and I don't know its meaning. I also receive the words *alval*, *diar* and *metes* rather often . . . The best message I've received in French said, "force of earth impossible," which greatly disturbed me. Since then, I've been trying to find another system, but it would take too long to explain.'

He showed me sheets of paper bearing a record of the attempts at communication made by invisible beings who are almost imponderable but whose strength is nevertheless great enough to be manifested in our world. Some of the dots and dashes were nearly imperceptible, others were quite distinct; sometimes there was a long, continuous line that meant nothing.

I was lucky enough to witness a reception. It was quite modest, since it consisted of only two letters, A and T, but it was convincing.

'That was nothing but a stray impulse,' said Charles S. 'But I'm glad you were able to see a reception for yourself. The trouble is that I have to wait for favourable times. I've become used to it, and now I can *feel* when a communication is about to come. I go into the workshop and wait calmly, sitting in an armchair.'

'Where do the messages come from?' I asked.

He hesitated briefly, then answered, 'I don't know.'

'You must have some idea,' I insisted. 'Do they come from beyond the grave? From a spirit? From another planet?'

'I don't know what you mean by "spirit",' he said. 'There are wandering forces in space, but there are probably also other universes beyond the reach of our investigations.' He hesitated again. 'There are beings on earth who carry out parallel lines of research. I try to receive signals; others emit them, or emit forces capable of being transformed into egregores. There's also interstellar space, full of waves, static and emissions that are unknown to us. It's a vast problem, as you can see. Maybe I should make an apparatus that can receive certain waves that are close to light waves . . .'

Charles S did not open wide the door of his Mysterious Unknown. He spoke to me only evasively about messages in a language similar to Sanskrit. He refused to discuss the unidentified objects that haunt the sky, which may be a clue.

When I left him, he said only these words, as hermetic as the Pierrelonge tower:

'Terrible forces are trying to manifest themselves. They say terrible things.'

Later, he will probably say more. The prohibitions may not come from him.

In mysterious France, and also in the rest of the world, there are enigmatic, hermetic towers and pyramids that were once used in powerful occult work. There are underground initiation centres which we do not know and which are neither the Agartha nor the temple in the Gobi Desert.

The secret is still intact and those who know will not speak until the time has come to make revelations. But there are indications that that time is near, since hermeticism murmurs its name and the doors are already ajar.

Chapter 8

SORCERY-MAGIC

When men had forgotten the ancient secrets, they sank into belief and faith, and since their reason no longer had the function of verification they asked for miracles, invoking an occult power. Thus religions were born. At first they were related to natural forces: the earth, the sun, forests, rivers, reproductive organs. Then came the gods, for nothing is eternal and everything evolves with time.

The first concern of a new religion is to condemn the one that preceded it as evil, pernicious and diabolical. But the basic elements remain the same: a god, a rite, a philosophy.

Religion Equals Sorcery

Believers in sorcery and religions behave identically: they enclose themselves in a magic circle (a clearing in the forest or the enclosure of a temple), invoke an occult power (Satan or God), promise fidelity to him and ask for something in exchange (salvation in the next world, virility, wisdom, luck, money).

They perform ritual gestures with the hand, arm or head to drive away evil forces or summon a benevolent power.

They all practise the rite of water, usually at the beginning of ceremonies (baptism, symbolic ablutions or purifications with lustral water), incantation, the magic of colours and sounds. Many of them engage in erotic magic, with flagellation, mortification and worship of a naked deity.

The philosophies of sorcery and religion are also the same: improvement of the human condition, consolation,

Another common point involves only the meaning given to words: priests accuse sorcerers of addressing themselves to an evil entity, the devil, while sorcerers accuse priests of invoking an evil power that they call God.

In sorcery, Satan takes back the place that God had stolen from him, but he is the same power under a different name.

We must therefore not confuse sorcery, which is a religion, with magic, which is a science or an art.

The Hell Fire Caves

Great Britain is still a centre of Celtic tradition and the sorcery that comes from superstition.

At West Wycombe, Buckinghamshire, a vast underground network was once used as an initiation den by a secret society: the Hell Fire Club, which later served as an inspiration for the Hermetic Order of the Golden Dawn.

Little is known about the Hell Fire Club, but Serge Hutin, the great French specialist in occultism, has written that the caves of West Wycombe were a meeting place for a kind of British élite composed of politicians, writers, painters and rich roués who wanted to take erotic vacations in the company of pretty women. The Hell Fire Caves were arranged in such a way that they constituted a place of initiation. They led to an underground river and continued on to the Inner Temple, where rites were performed. These rites were probably much more serious than is commonly believed.

'The Hell Fire Club,' writes Huton, 'was a group with pagan affiliations that may have gone back to mysteries of the pre-Christian era. It practised the rites of what is known as "left" Tantrism, in which exacerbation of sensuality and the imaginative powers is used for the purpose of magic liberation. For each stay in the caves, a male member of the club had to choose a female companion with whom he participated in all the secret rites, up to their culminating point, in the Inner Temple.'

This procedure, common in the eighteenth century, is no longer in use, or so it is thought; but the British have remained faithful to certain practices that are related, on a higher level, to the sorcery of Celtic times.

This was explained to me on the Isle of Man by the Witch Queen, Monique-Mauricette-Marie Wilson.

The Magic Isle of Man

The Isle of Man, between England and Ireland, is one of the sacred places of the world, much older than Benares, Tibet, Rome and Mecca, and also more sacred.

According to traditions, the first god or man created on earth was named Man or Men. Man is pre-eminently magic name: it is the name not only of Manannan, the magician king of the Isle of Man, but also of Mannus, the ancestor of the Aryans; Manu, the first human being according to the Hindus; Mentu or Mont, the Apollo of the Thebans; Mainyu Zend (Ormuzd and Ahriman) and perhaps Mana of the Scandinavians; Maner, the first king of the Egyptians; and the Manitou of the Algonquins.

In magic, in the West as well as in Asia and Polynesia, the word 'mana' designates the immaterial principle of the individual (his soul) and the power it possesses.

It was by mana, says legend, that the giant statues of Easter Island were transported.

The religion of our ancestors may have been born on the Isle of Man. It is an island that has no counterpart anywhere else in the world, with its mountains and its moors strewn with tumuli, cromlechs, magic circles, megaliths and treacherous crevices concealed by a dense growth of thorny bushes and lichens. As in a horror film, mist settles into the valleys, creeps over the hills at knee height and flows into crevices. The landscape seems unreal, with the atmosphere of another age.

Thousands of years ago the Isle of Man was the home of Manannan MacLlyr, a formidable magician who wore impenetrable armour and a flaming helmet. His sword killed at the first blow and he could make himself invisible by wrapping himself in his magic cloak.

No one could follow Manannan on land when he rode his lightning-swift horse, and no one could follow him at sea when he was in his boat that had no sails or oars and took him straight to wherever he wanted to go. This boat was also a flying machine because Manannan, like all sorcerers, was able to travel through the air. He became the king of the island and his gigantic tomb can still be seen at Peel Castle.

Flags bearing Manannan's coat of arms – the three legs of the magician extending from a hub like the spokes of a wheel – float above the monuments of towns and in ports facing the transparent, emerald-green sea.

It is on this consecrated island that the Witch Queen has come to live; it is here that, on ritual dates, she presides over strange ceremonies.

The Witch Queen Is French

Monique-Mauricette-Marie Wilson is a Breton woman with a double nationality, French and British. She is married to a Scotsman, Campbell Crozier Wilson, who is her high priest. She is dark-haired and five feet two inches tall. She wears a black doublet and cloak; the cloak is lined with red velvet, like the one supposedly worn by the devil.

She was brought up in Indochina, came to London in 1954, met Dr Gerald Brousseau Gardner, a fervent adept of witchcraft and acquired the rank of high priestess. She married at this time, founded a large group, organised covens in London and Manchester and was elected queen of the witches in Scotland.

In 1964 Dr Gardner died, leaving her his mill and estate at Castletown, in the southern part of the Isle of Man. On the estate in a museum of witchcraft, the finest in the world. She now lives at Castletown, dividing her time between the museum, which attracts many visitors every day, and her functions as a witch.

She was elected Witch Queen at an assembly of the thirteen covens under her direction. The title gives her the right to wear a crown and a garter with thirteen emeralds. When she officiates she is naked except for this garter, a crescent diadem and a necklace. She has about six hundred adepts. The people of the island, more deeply devoted to Celtism than to the Oriental religions, treat her with respect and friendliness.

The Witch's Religion

The Coven of the Witch's Mill worships a god whose entire name can be known only by third-degree initiates. He is probably the world's oldest god: Cernunos, the mysterious Dis Pater of the Gauls, whose forehead is adorned with a stag's antlers, a symbol of his virility. The ram-headed serpent and the bull are often represented with Cernunos, along with his wife the Great Goddess, who is the Demeter and Cybele of the Greeks.

The worship is phallic; that is, it honours the creative forces of life, without which nothing can exist. It is based on two principles, one male, the other female, which must unite in a communion that is both physical and spiritual.

The devil, Satan and Lucifer seem to be unknown to the coven, and the Witch Queen does not hesitate to say that she does not believe in those entities.

'Our cult is a true religion,' she says, 'earlier than any other. The Druids knew it, but it was already ancient in their time. Our law is to do good by invoking the gods of nature and our Celtic ancestors.

'I sometimes visit sick people, I perform religious marriages and I teach "my people". If an adept misbehaves, it's my duty to punish him. He's whipped, and that also involves a symbol of our religion, since the whip or flail is an attribute of fertility.

'We must always use our right hand; in ceremonies the altar must always be to our right and in the magic circle we must walk clockwise, never counterclockwise.

'Our religion is called Wicca or Witchcraft. In Anglo-Saxon, *wica* means "wisdom".

'Love and eroticism play a part in our rites, but on a high level that can't be explained to the general public.'

Olwen's Sabbath

When she officiates, the Witch Queen bears the name of Olwen. Once a week her adepts gather for ceremonies analogous to those of other religions. The great witches' sabbaths take place on the day before the consecrated dates:

February 1 – Candlemas, or festival of torches.
May 1 – May Eve, worship of the Great Goddess.
August 1 – Beltane, or festival of harvests and the fires of Beltane (Venus).
November 1 – Hallowe'en, the last festival before spring.

Smaller sabbaths take place at the equinoxes and solstices.

I was allowed to attend a sabbath in a room fitted out as a temple, with ancient weapons – daggers, swords, arrows, clubs, etc. – on the walls and a double magic circle painted on the floor. At the centre of the circle stood the altar, with its chalice, a statuette of the Great Goddess, flowers – always roses – amulets, pentacles, candlesticks and several whips.

Olwen officiated, naked except for a diadem, a necklace, a garter on her left thigh and a magic bracelet on her right arm.

On a lectern near the altar, the great sacred book of Witchcraft, the *Book of Shadows*, was closed, since outsiders were present in the room. The high priestess ordinarily reads the rites of worship and comment on its symbols in this book. In the *Book of Shadows* is written, in Olwen's hand, everything concerning the three degrees of initiation.

This lore has been transmitted traditionally since time immemorial.

A dozen barefoot adepts were inside the circle. Most of them were nearly nude, which is how they are expected to participate in a sabbath, so that external evil influences can have no hold on them.

The ceremony consisted of a long, circular movement, interspersed with pauses, inside the magic circle, with each woman between two men and vice versa. Olwen sometimes held a magic wand and sometimes a sword, according to the rite. She spoke incantations in English, with the leit-motive being repeated in unison by the adepts. She filled a chalice with an alcoholic potion and drank it, then adepts came to drink in turn, dancing without ever crossing the inner edge of the magic circle.

It was very hot because the ceremony was being filmed. The naked Witch Queen, the steady stream of spellbound people passing abruptly from darkness into the harsh glare of the spotlights, the smell of incense – everything created a heavy atmosphere favourable to trances and hallucinations.

A young woman was breathing heavily and circling around the altar; I expected to see her fall to the floor and scream. Olwen broke the spell by stopping her with her sword.

The ceremony continued with chants, the admission of a new adept to Wicca and a dagger rite whose esoteric meaning completely escaped me. Then worship of the Great Goddess was celebrated.

The high priest, Scotty Campbell, drank from the chalice, prostrated himself before Olwen, who was identified with the deity, and respectfully gave her seven kisses: on the mouth, the breasts, the navel, the mons veneris and the feet.

The ceremony was over.

Had Olwen altered her usual procedures that night? Probably so, since the veil of Isis is never lifted on the first day of the Mystery.

The Witch's Powers

It would be illusory to judge Witchcraft from what I saw during the ceremony at Castletown. The witch has secrets that she does not reveal; she knows herbs that cure, invocations that drive away 'evil spirits', powerful love potions.

Frances, one of the priestesses of Wicca, told me that her queen had the power to dissolve a cloud and cure by touching.

'We have,' she said, 'an extraordinary method of concentration by which Olwen can psychically "recharge" a sick person. The concentration is so strong that we sometimes have to go into the empty countryside to let out shrill screams that relieve us. In some cases those screams are appeals to powerful entities related to the Central Power.'

There are about eight thousand witches in Great Britain. During World War II they combined their forces to prevent the Germans from landing. Large gatherings were held at cromlechs in the moors.

'They used the Cone of Power to achieve their goal,' Olwen told me. 'There were terrible return shocks. Eight members of Wicca died of them.'

She does not want her sect to be confused with that of the Golden Dawn, which was primarily devoted to a very dangerous kind of erotic worship.

'Some members of the Golden Dawn,' she said, 'had to practise coitus for four or five days. Those who weakened were whipped to make them go on. It was black magic.

'The religion of Wicca is pure and wholesome. Our rites are those of our ancestors. They go back to the time when the "angels" of Azazel came from the sky to impregnate earthly women. Perhaps we still have vestiges of that ancient eroticism, which was necessary to improve the race. I can't tell everything. Witches are still obsessed with the "burning time", when they were burned at the stake. One of my ancestors was burned alive in the Middle Ages – and the Middle Ages aren't as far away in the mind as they are in time!'

Paul Grégor's Magic

The meanings given to magic, sorcery and religion are obviously quite arbitrary. The magic of the ancient Persians was identical with religion, and that of Paul Grégor is close to sorcery as it is understood on the Isle of Man.

'Let us suppose,' writes Grégor, 'that our amorous feelings and the incandescence of our passions are a *degenerated mystical impulse.* Our highest aspirations and our whole transcendent and magic potential would then be imprisoned in matter and sexuality. The impulse would be materialised and therefore absorbed.

'On this assumption – which is plausible if we recall that mystic magic and psychology have a common denominator and that for a good thirty years psychology has been based on sexual behaviour – it is not logical to think that our sexual reactions act as a magic switch which releases almost superhuman energies?'

It is interesting to note the current trend towards freer sexual behaviour. It seems that, in this second half of the twentieth century, there is a reaction against the dictatorship of hypocritical prudery and sexual repression that was instituted, against nature, by bourgeois society and religion.

With the help of this revolution, will the energies postulated by Paul Grégor be manifested in a valid direction, in science and art, for example? Or will they favour the resurrection of ancestral religions under the sign of secrecy?

Black Magic

Black magic still exists but it eludes the law for the simple reason that it is not supposed to exist. At most, judges will accept God and his servants; they totally refuse to believe in the devil and his votaries.

This may be the wisest course, for in 1632, in full accord with the Roman ritual that declares 'speaking or understanding a language one does not know' to be a sign of demonic possession, the University of Montpellier passed judgement on the Loudun case and sent poor Urbain Grandier to his death after he was unjustly accused of practising diabolical sorcery.

Courts are sometimes called on to judge cases in which black magic is undeniably mingled with false sorcery.

In 1966 Hayode Durokaiye Orishagbemi, a Nigerian student in London, killed a Nigerian woman because, he said, she had dangerous magic powers: she changed people into peanuts and took mice, snails and lice from her body.

A sect of Brazilian sorcerers murdered two television technicians in Niteroi, Brazil. Their bodies were found in a forest; their faces had been covered with lead masks, which showed that it had been a ritual murder.

In 1966 the Liberian police arrested Esli Holder, mayor of Kakata, and Amos Nagbe, head of the business college of Monrovia, for having sacrificed women in ritual ceremonies. Nagbe testified that Clarence Simpson, former Vice President of Liberia, had given him a thousand dollars to bring him a woman's eyes, cheeks and lower jaw, to be used in a magic ceremony for the purpose of making him become President.

It is well known that in 1965 Mama Onema was the official sorceress of the Congolese rebels who were hostile to President Tshombe. When she changed sides, she made this statement on the Leopoldville radio: 'I have dug up and destroyed the fetishes I prepared for the victory of General Olenga [leader of the rebels]. They are now worthless.' She then announced to her ex-allies that she was going to turn her magic against them.

A witch from the Okefenokee Swamp in Florida cast a spell on three babies and her predictions came true twenty-two years later.

The Curse of Seals

It is well known in magic that the traits of animals can be transferred to people who wear their skins, which explains the existence in Africa of sects like those of the 'leopard men', 'crocodile men' and 'lion men'.

But the magic properties attributed to skins and furs are different if the animal has been killed cruelly. A fur then becomes a malignant, highly charged fetish. No woman initiated into magic would consent to wear a seal-skin coat, because it would be certain to bring her a tragic destiny. Seals are skinned alive, so that their fur will retain a better quality. This abominable practice is a veritable act of black magic which transfers the unfortunate animal's revolt and curse to the owner of the coat.

A strange case of sorcery occurred in Nyasaland in March, 1963. A 'crocodile man' named Elard Chipandale appeared before a court at Blantyre, accused of murdering a little girl. 'I am a crocodile!' he said repeatedly. Investigation showed that he had disguised himself as a crocodile by covering himself with tree bark. Wearing this disguise, he had waited in a river and pulled in the daughter of a man named Odrick Kasoci, who wanted to get rid of her. When he was told to transform himself into a crocodile, Chipandale answered that he could no longer do it because at the time of his arrest he had lost the talisman that had been given to him by a powerful sorcerer of the region.

Return Shocks

But sorcerers are not always evildoers. They sometimes take up the cause of justice, as a group of them did in France against a diviner of a La Roche-sur-Yon whom they considered to be guilty of misusing her power. She had brought misfortune to an honest family in a La Tardière-en-Vendeé. The magicians of Poitou, justly angry, put a Gypsy curse on her.

In Haiti, sorcerers undertook a struggle against the Catholic clergy. With the approval of President François Duvalier, who wanted to revive the ancient religion of his ancestors, voodoo sorcerers began casting spells on priests, many of whom either died or had to leave the country.

The reaction is sometimes in the opposite direction. At Aron, in the Mayenne district of France, Catholic peasants attacked the local miller, a sorcerer named Robert Brault, and his bearded disciples. Brault, a healer and a delegate of Jehovah, he said, was accused of sacrilege, and strange stories were told about him. According to one of them, he was seen rising into the sky and dancing on the clouds. In February, 1964, at the hour of vespers, nearly a thousand people beseiged his mill and cut off the long hair and beards of his disciples.

The Fréjus Catastrophe

The catastrophic flood in the Fréjus region of France was attributed to chance, but for several years this region has seemed to be doomed to a series of misfortunes. Storms destroy vineyards, there are devastating floods and orchards are ravaged by hail. A group of investigators of occult phenomena believe they have found the reason for this persistent misfortune.

Apollonius of Tyana is said to have founded an initiatic school near Fréjus in the first century. The rest of the account is so strange that I prefer to report it as it was given to me:

> Since there were strong telluric currents with vertical emission in the Fréjus region, Apollonius buried devices similar to batteries that were capable of neutralising the most violent effects.
>
> A short time before the dam burst, releasing a cataclysmic wall of water, practitioners of black magic had settled near the Sudanese mosque of Missri, northwest of Fréjus, where they found and dug up the charge placed by Apollonius. When the protection was abolished, the forces of nature were unleashed. The magicians perished in the titanic torrents that rolled over Fréjus.

It would probably be foolish to believe in this legend, though magicians in the region try to support it; but if legends had to be doubted, would magic exist?

Chapter 9

TIME-TRAVEL DRUGS

The human brain contains billions of little cells, or neurons, which constitute what might be called the library and the seat of human knowledge. Only about a third of them are used; most of them remain passive, like unlighted lamps or closed books.

If we could find a way to put all of them into action, our hardest problems, even those considered insoluble, would easily be solved. A man who could use his entire brain would gain such superiority over others, even those of the calibre of Pascal or Einstein, that he would become a veritable phenomenon and perhaps a god.

Sometimes 40 or 50 per cent of the brain begins functioning and the privileged individual becomes a genius. This was no doubt the case with Pythagoras, Plato, Pico della Mirandola, Pascal, Einstein, etc., and with Rémi Crampe, a shepherd of Ousté in the Hautes-Pyrénées region of France who, when he took the preliminary tests for military service, outscored the engineers and men with PhD degrees who took the tests with him. It was probably also the case with Paolo Z, a Venetian boy who, at the age of five, suffered a head injury from a stone that had been thrown at him. The injury caused a certain anomaly in his brain that made him an exceptionally bright pupil – and a prodigiously brilliant thief.

Is man destined to use all his unknown powers some day? It would be in the natural order of things, for after all, since brain cells exist, are they not meant to be used?

On this hypothesis, mankind would evolve towards a superior stage similar or identical to that of the divinity.

In a hundred or a thousand years, our descendants would be the masters of the cosmos.

This is what certain philosophical and religious schools teach, but, by some sort of intuition, people who consider themselves rational rebels against that eschatology (doctrine of ultimate things) which promises them command of the world and identification with God.

It is possible, however, that our inactive brain cells will play no part in the future because they have already served their function in the past.[41] A man has two breasts, but they do not seem to be meant for feeding babies! Yet they once had a reason for existing.

In primohistoric times, before the Deluge, people seem to have been much more intelligent than we are, since they knew the secrets of levitation, antigravity, divination and interstellar travel. If so, the human race has already reached its peak and we are now in a period of decline.

By a strange perception that may come from their ordinarily inactive brain cells, people now believe that the end of an era is approaching and will be marked by a worldwide cataclysm.

There have always been certain individuals – scientists and initiates – with the ability to make their brains function beyond the usual 30 per cent; that is why they may have knowledge of truths that remain forbidden to the rest of mankind. Yet it is possible for an ordinary person to become a great initiate, a knower, a genius.

The Brain, An Electronic Computer

The activity of the brain is an electrical phenomenon and therefore a form of energy. This phenomenon is fuelled by glucose brought by the blood, and by the oxygenation of cerebral tissue. When these conditions are properly met, the neurons are capable of energetic functioning.

It is essential to know this biological process in order to grasp a mysterious particle of the secret of initiation.

Speaking summarily, it can be said that thought, intelligence, knowledge and initiation are closely related to alimentation, notably the absorption of certain substances which, introduced into the blood through the mouth or by injection, can stimulate neurons in different ways. It is therefore possible to produce artificially not only inspiration and genius, but also stupidity and madness. (There are other ways of stimulating the brain to produce clairvoyance: mirrors, crystal balls, flashes of light, meditation, etc.)

Tranquilisers, barbiturates and other sedatives dull the brain; other products increase alertness, perception and intelligence; still others give rise to clairvoyance, illumination and genuine time-travel. These are the hallucinogenic drugs.

Initiation Drugs

It would be false to say that Moses, Buddha, Pythagoras, Jesus and Einstein were initiates or geniuses because they took miracle drugs. The problem is more complex.

Rationally, it is hard to accept the idea of divine revelation; that is, a direct conversation between God or a god and a human being. In the present state of science there is no way to explain such a miracle, though this does not necessarily mean that it cannot occur.

It may even be said that the reality of the phenomenon is scientifically acceptable if God is defined as a universal intelligence and the gods as initiators who existed physically and may still exist in space-time or in a parallel universe: the Masters of the World. Contacts called miraculous then have the beginning of an explanation, in terms of either an uplifting of human thought or the more mathematical process of time-travel. This, in fact, is what actually seems to happen.

But clinical analysis seems to indicate that the brain of the initiate, the scientist or the prophet receives substances exceptionally rich in glucose and an exceptionally active irrigation of brain tissue, by either alimentary absorption or a mysterious physiochemical alchemy that produces the same effect.

From the most ancient times down to the present, that elevation towards illumination has been practised among all peoples and by various procedures, the most common of which is taking hallucinogenic drugs that have often been called initiatic potions.

Here is a list of the most important of these drugs:

Nauacatl or *teonanacatl.* A hallucinogenic mushroom of the Aztecs (Mexico), called 'flesh of God' by the Indians and 'flesh of the devil' by Catholic Mexicans. This mushroom, the *Stropharia cubensis*, contains an alkaloid (psilosybin) which causes green-coloured visions and intense stimulation of the memory.

In his *Histoire de Mexique* (1574), André Thevet writes as follows about the *curanderos* (healing sorcerers) who ate it raw: 'The devil deceived them, making them eat an herb they call Nauacatl, which made them take leave of their senses and see many visions.'

In his book *Les Plantes Divinatoires*, Alexandre Rouhier, an authority on the subject, writes that since muchamore is very rare in some regions of Asia, it is used as penicillin was used during World War II. When a shaman has drunk the decoction and delivered his oracles, he urinates into a wooden goblet and the muscarine released in this way can be used several times.

Yage. A tropical American vine, taken in an aqueous decoction. Has an amazing ability to make one see and hear at great distances.

Alexandre Rouhier tells how treasure hunters use it in Amazonia. Two pounds of vine are boiled in several quarts of water, at night; when only a cup of liquid is left, a man drinks it, takes a swallow of rum and sinks into semisleep. He is taken in this state to places where treasures are thought to be hidden and made to point out the most likely spots to dig. He sees through walls, rocks and earth. His companions dig where he indicates, and nearly always finds a treasure.

Ayahuasca, or *Banisteria caapi.* Another Amazonian vine. The drink made from it must go back to remote antiquity. Sorcerers add it to yage. It is called 'dream vine' or 'spirit vine' – or 'death vine', when it is used in too large a dose.

Peyote. A small, spineless cactus that grows on high plateaus. It is sold in Mexico under the name of peyote buttons or mescal buttons. Its alkaloid, mescaline, causes visions in constant motion, so prodigiously coloured that they make the subject cry out in surprise. Peyote does not take away consciousness during these visions. It transforms sounds into colours.

Huanta. A solanum with white blossoms, the *Datura arborea* of Ecuador. Extremely toxic. It is used in making a 'trial drink' for sorcerers. They go into a coma for two or three days and come back from their journey to the land of the gods with valuable information on the future.

Huachuma. An arorescent cactus of Peru. Its purgative juice is drunk in order to have the gift of divination. Huachuma is an intermediary between man and the devil, according to Christians. Father Barnabé Cobo, a historian of the Spanish conquest, wrote, 'Intoxicated by this drink, the Indians dream all sorts of fantastic things and believe them as if they were true.'

Tobacco. In South America, initiation and the power to communicate with celestial spirits are sometimes acquired by drinking a decoction of tobacco and smoking in an airtight hut.

Tarasun. The Buriats of Siberia make it by boiling wild

thyme, juniper and fir bark in water, then adding a few drops of goat's blood.

Muchamore, or *Kamchadal boletus.* A poisonous mushroom of the genus Amanita. Used by the shamans of central Asia, probably in a raw state. Its alkaloid, muscarine, is intoxicating in small doses and lethal in large doses. It produces hallucinations similar to those of psilocybin. Divination, memory.

Honda. A mushroom of New Guinea. The Papuans use it in the manner of the *curanderos* of Mexico. Hallucinations, sacred delirium.

LSD. Lysergic acid diethylamide, an alkaloid derived from ergot. Seven thousand times more active than mescaline. Euphoria, or depression, depending on dose and temperament; brightly coloured hallucinations; acceleration of motion and time, as in a film projected at a hundred images per second; distortion of perception; feeling of power; insanity.

These plants and drugs all produce clairvoyance. Such plants were once called 'prophet's herb', and Rousseau, quoted by Alexandre Rouhier, said that they 'free the organs of imagination from matter'. Their use, less simple that it might seem, must be controlled by experience and preceded by fasting.

Initiates have always forbidden certain plants, notably mushrooms, probably for fear that there might be initiations due not to merit, but to chance.

Pythagoras recommended not eating beans because they were composed of the same elements as man and might therefore become the seat of the soul by transmigration. Caesar ridiculed this idea and it must be admitted that it does not seem very rational at first sight. Yet it is inconceivable that such a great initiate as Pythagoras should have made the recommendation to his disciples without an excellent reason. That reason was partially revealed by Cicero: 'Beans are said to prevent divinatory dreams from being manifested.'

I am convinced that deeper investigation into the mysteries of chemical combinations would show that Pythagoras was right, as always.

Besides the hallucinogenic drugs mentioned above, there are many others, such as the kal, yohimbe and iboga of Africa, the pituri of Australia, tea, coffee, mandragora, hashish, opium, wine and Scandinavian mead, made of the juice of the milkweed (a plant of American origin) mixed with milk, barley and honey.[42]

The Wine That Causes Insanity

After the disappearance of the Atlanteans, the Hyperboreans and the ancient Aryans, whose original homeland was North America, the Celts found themselves 'cut off from the land of the gods'; that is, from the source of initiation and knowledge.

But they knew that 'beyond the ocean river, at the limits of the western world,' one could find *greal*, the marvellous drink of their forefathers. This was the origin of the centuries of efforts to return to the source: the prodigious quest for the Grail which, under the influence of Christian ideas, turned away from its true path and lost its whole essence. What was that intoxicating *greal* which brought joy to the heart and ideas to the brain?

Its basic ingredient was probably the juice of the noha grape, which was recently condemned by the French Ministry of Agriculture. The noha has the reputation of producing wine that 'causes insanity', which is a clever pretext for eliminating the initiatic drink of the ancient Aryans, the true Grail!

Drunk in reasonable amounts, noha wine is no more harmful than any other, yet growing noha grapes is forbidden, just as growing marijuana is forbidden.

That banishment is related to secret prohibitions that no one, not even those who believe themselves to be the instigators of them, can explain. The fact is that the noha is the only *natural grape*, the only one that produces *natural wine*. Other species are subject to diseases that must be given three to twenty treatments with sulphur, copper sulphate and other chemicals, all containing poisonous substances.

The wine we drink is therefore mixed with poison, and the intoxication it produces has lost the qualities which, in other times, made it sacred to certain peoples. But the noha grape, and other varieties that have now disappeared gave rise to a delirium of the kind caused by other hallucinogenic plants.

The wines of antiquity were completely different from those of our time; they were aged in the sun and often mixed with sea water, various spices and even opium. Our modern hybridised, drugged wine is no longer a hallucinogenic drink, but the wine of four thousand years ago was undoubtedly different. The Celts, who were jovial and inclined to boast, but very brave nevertheless, must have had a special veneration for wine, which seems to increase strength and courage. Grapes were not ordinarily grown in Gaul, however; they must have been cultivated only by Druids and priests, for the secret needs of their ministry.

Mead was only a substitute; the true *greal* was the drink that the Tuatha De Danann of Ireland brought from the Mag Meld, the Plain of Joy, beyond the Atlantic.

The noha grape, last vestige of the sacred plant of the Atlanteans, is now disappearing, along with old ancestral customs that it is now considered bad form to honour. Only a few initiates, in defiance of the law, continue to cultivate the grape whose wine 'caused insanity' – caused insanity in the same way as dragons devoured men and dolmens were inhabited by the devil!

The Apple

In the myth of the earthly paradise the apple plays a part that is hard to interpret.

'The woman answered the serpent, "We may eat the fruit of any tree in the garden, except for the tree in the middle of the garden; God has forbidden us either to eat or to touch the fruit of that; if we do, we shall die." The serpent said, "Of course you will not die. God knows that as soon as you eat it, your eyes will be opened and you will be like gods knowing both good and evil." ' (Genesis 3.2–5.)

Eve hesitated. Who was giving her the right advice? Who was the evil one in this situation? Was it God, who forbade her to know, to open her eyes; who refused her initiation, access to divinity; who wanted to enclose her in a life of stagnation, without descendants, consciousness or evolution? Or was it Satan, who advocated disobedience to dictatorial orders, who advised her to open her eyes, to know?

Eve did not *know* Adam at that time, but she had the brilliant premonition that she ought to listen to Satan and she ate the fruit, *she drank the cup of initiation.* The story has to be told in this way because it includes everything: obtuse, ignorant people whose eyes were closed; the good initiator who came from the sky; absorption of something that opens one's eyes; the knowledge of hidden things that is an attribute of the gods.

But how can we accept the idea that the apple supplied an initiatic *greal*? There must have been an initial error. Eve did not eat an apple, but another fruit; or else she drank the juice of a vine or a cactus, or ate a mushroom. Otherwise, we must assume that in the time of the earthly paradise the apple did not have the same chemical composition as in our time, which is something that cannot be rejected as a possibility.

The physical appearance of the apple makes it well suited to be a symbol of the womb, love, woman and knowledge under the sign of eroticism (see Chapter 14 of *The Legacy of the Gods*), but I believe that this symbol was born of an erroneous interpretation.

The Bible does not say what the forbidden fruit was,

which indicates that its identity must be kept secret. This is a useful precaution if the fruit is hallucinogenic, but there is no valid reason for it if the fruit is an ordinary apple.

What is the origin of the myth of the apple and traditional quests for the golden apples? Is it reasonable to think that the fruit which became a golden apple was a grape that produced euphoria and stimulated the imagination? Was it even the fruit of a tree?

Sanchuniathon could have told us about it if his book had not been destroyed; it now seems that only botanists can clear up the mystery by discovering the fruit, or the hallucinogenic plant, that took on the colour of gold.

Initiatic Potions

In Celtic mythology there are frequent references to a magic cauldron, endowed with marvellous powers, which the gods covet and try to steal. It must have been a precious object because King Arthur, who carried out an expedition to seize it, lost nearly all his men in the attempt. In this wondrous vessel the Welsh bard Taliesin, inspirer of the Druidic religion, discovered the future, the mysteries of the world and the treasures of knowledge. Its contents revived the dead, but those who came back to life remained silent about what they had seen.

This story undoubtedly refers to an initiatic potion, but we can only make conjectures about its composition.

Ancient texts say that the vessel of Koridwen,[43] the source of universal knowledge, contained a mixture known as *greal* and that Koridwen placed the six effective plants in the brass cauldron surrounded by pearls from the sea. This evokes the six colours of the rainbow: violet, blue, green, yellow, orange and red.[44] Moreover, the mixture known as *greal* seems to be the same thing as the famous Grail, which was both a magic food and the vessel containing the blood of Christ. Christ became involved in it two thousand years ago, but *greal* or the Grail was known several thousand years earlier.

It has been suggested that the six effective plants may have been the violet, the cornflower, lettuce (or fennel), the lotus (or the buttercup or barley), sage and the grape.

Since Celtic tradition and the closely related Persian tradition are the oldest in the world, it is interesting to recall how Korrig the Dwarf, also called Gwyon the Seer, acquired initiation. He was given the task of mixing the six effective plants that the White Fairy had put into a brass cauldron heated over a fire. A few drops of the oiling magic potion flew out of the cauldron and burned Gwyon's hand, which he instinctively put to his mouth. In so doing, he swallowed a little of the liquid and immediately had knowledge of all things.

That is the basis of the Celtic mysteries, from which were derived the mysteries of Samothrace (Greece), Phoenicia and Assyria. The Casmil of the Pelasgians, the Gigon of the Phoenicians and the Apollo and Prometheus of the Greeks were avatars of the Gwyon of the Celtic West. Similarly, Koridwen was the Great Goddess (Demeter, Cybele) of the Cabiric rites of Thrace and Phrygia. Since the advent of the Catholic religion, borrowings from the Celtic West have been implacably denied. It is worth noting, for example, that the Island of Gwyon, or Avalon, or the White Island, has been mysteriously transported into the Gobi Desert!

In its original essence, the great tradition of mankind can be rediscovered only through the Celtic myths. Rediscovering something implies that it has been lost, and that is the main theme of Celtic tradition: something that has been lost must be found again. It is the meaning of all the traditional quests: to go and conquer the Grail, the cup or bowl of the Atlanteans, the vessels of Dagda, Bran and Medea.

The Lost Potion

The soma of the Hindus (the Avestan hoama or amrita) is a juice obtained by pressing a plant between two millstones, but it is also golden nectar, the potion of immortality for the gods and inspiration for mortals.

An Oriental tradition states that at a certain time the secret of making soma was lost, which is a variant of the old Celtic myth. Another potion was substituted for the true soma, but Hindu sages were unable to regain the illumination their ancestors had experienced.

The haoma of the Avesta was both a potion and a sacred plant. The plant was pressed through a sieve and its fermented juice enhanced spiritual powers. We read in the Avesta: 'Vivanhvat was the first mortal of the corporeal world who prepared me. He had the privilege of having as his son Yima the Splendid, the good shepherd, the most glorious of those who were born, the only mortal who possessed the solar eye[45] and, by means of his power, was able to make men and animals immortal.'

The Persians lost the secret of haoma, just as the Hindus lost the secret of soma. The original haoma was white and was gathered on the Alborj or Sacred Mountain. The potion substituted for it was yellow and its secret was later lost also, which clearly indicates that transmission of the secret deteriorated in the course of time.

The Third Eye

Besides the initiatic potions discussed above, there were also the ambrosia and wine of the Greeks, the wine of the Hebrews and Christians, the plant decoctions of the Egyptians, the mushrooms of the Mexicans, and so on.

Whether it is a potion or a plant, the magic substance always serves the same purpose: to give knowledge of all things. In other words, initiatic potions must give the Third Eye, the one that sees hidden things in the past as well as in the present, and penetrates the Mysterious Unknown.

This Third Eye is also an attribute of the true Master of the World, who is given different names in different countries: Viracocha, Kukulkan, Quetzalcoatl, Baal, Marduk, Prometheus – and Lucifer. Lucifer is the god who befriended and initiated man and brought him wisdom and knowledge; who, in the disguise of the serpent, gave to Eve, the first initiated mortal, the good advice that led to the appearance of *Homo sapiens* and all civilisations. Lucifer came with a third eye in his forehead: a green emerald, colour of the planet Venus. And from that emerald the 'angels' made the Grail.

Lucifer lost his paradise out of love for man, yet by a scandalous injustice he has been slandered, vilified, debased and turned into a kind of demon! But the knowledge he brought from another planet will be miraculously regained through the magic of hallucinagenic drugs. Initiation, the first fathers' journey into the sky, ritual climbing in initiatic sessions, disclosure of the past and future by planetary knowers – everything will be related logically and clearly to the planet Venus. Everything will be placed under the sign of Quetzalcoatl and Lucifer and their sacred symbols: the jade Third Eye for Quetzalcoatl, the emerald Third Eye for Lucifer.

And, masked by the deterioration of time, it will be the Third Eye of Shiva, prince of the Asuras (Ases), prince of the lingam (phallus), the engendering god whose passionate lovemaking with the beautiful Parvati (Venus-Astarte) shook the world.

It will also be the Third Eye of Horus, whose symbolic colour is green. Horus was the Apollo of the Egyptians and the husband of Hathor, Queen of the West, identified with Venus and Astarte. Always the planet Venus, always the green of the ancient Masters of the World.

Chapter 10

THE PALENQUE SLAB

Huantla de Jiminez is a village in the Sierra Mazateca, in the north-central part of the State of Oaxaca, Mexico. In 1953 a wealthy New York banker and his wife, Gordon and Valentina Wasson, went there with the ethnologist Weitlaner to consult a *curandero* (healing sorcerer) named Aurelio.

Their main purpose was to study a mystery that was beginning to filter through to the outside world: the mystery of 'sacred mushrooms'. These mushrooms were said to give a number of powers, including the ability to tell in a vision whether a sick person was going to recover or die, and the ability to locate missing persons and objects.

The Catholic authorities persecuted the poor *curanderos*, accusing them of sorcery, black magic and even cannibalism, but after having vainly addressed themselves to Saint Anthony, the patron saint of lost objects, the Indians always came back to the *curandero*, who had the advantage over the good saint of always telling the truth and finding whatever had been lost.

In 1955 Mr and Mrs Wasson tried *kisos*, sacred mushrooms, for themselves, and then one day witnessed what can be called a demonstration of initiation by the famous *curandera* Maria Sabina, of Huantla de Jiminez.

The Fantastic Powers of Maria Sabina

After eating nine or thirteen pairs of *kisos* purified by a fire of copal resin, Maria Sabina said a kind of prayer, then went into a trance twenty minutes later, violently clapping her hands, uttering unintelligible words and making magic signs with her fingers as if she were calling spirits. Then she began speaking . . .

The Wassons had already become convinced that her clairvoyance was accurate. She had clearly seen their son in New York at a time when they had thought he was in Boston, and she had announced his enlistment in the army and the death of one of his cousins.

She gave an even more convincing demonstration to the archaeologist Frank Snell. She told him that when he reached Mexico City his plane would land near a red car and that he must stay away from it to avoid being burned. She also predicted that he would find a great deal of money and build a beautiful house beside a river.

Snell may not have believed her at the time but, if so, he soon changed his mind. After leaving her, when his plane landed at Mexico City he saw a little red car belonging to the airport fire department. It stopped a hundred feet away from the passengers getting out of the plane. Snell remembered the prediction but, out of curiosity or bravado, he left the other passengers and walked toward the car. Suddenly it exploded and burst into flame. A fragment of metal struck him on the right arm but he escaped uninjured, with only a scorched sleeve.

A few months later, in the State of Sonora, he discovered a lode of silver that made him rich, and in 1960 he fulfilled the rest of the prediction by building a beautiful house on the bank of the San Antonio River.

In 1966 Roger Heim, director of the Paris Museum of Natural History, gave a televised lecture followed by a projection of a film that presented a scientific report on the mystery of sacred mushrooms. At the Museum of Man he had experimented with the effects of the mushrooms (*Psilocibe mexicana*), using volunteer subjects. Films of the experiments were shown on television.

The subjects sank into a kind of trance and, according to their temperament and the dose they had taken, they had visions, hallucinations, states of euphoria or depressions. Three salient facts were observed:

– Memory acquired a prodigious power to bring back things that seemed to have been forgotten forever.

– The sacred delirium often prompted the subject to make drawings.

– The coloured universe created by the mushrooms was predominantly green.

The drawings made by one subject represented a rooster and a geometric design placed behind an eye. They recalled the fluid writing of Jean Cocteau, with its light, almost feminine lines, probably linked to the subtleties of his inner world.

In 1963 Roger Heim and several botanists went to Huantla de Jiminez to see Maria Sabina. She made predictions for them which seemed implausible at first, but proved to be accurate.

'Although my mind is inclined toward rationalism,' said Heim, 'I am forced to conclude that those mushrooms gave rise to a puzzling phenomenon that goes beyond normal phenomena.'

It would have been hard for him to say, 'Maria Sabina proved to me that the phenomenon known as clairvoyance is real. In her trances she undeniably has the ability to travel into the past (memory) and into the future (divination).' No, Heim did not say that, but what he did say clearly implies that he thought it.

In my opinion, however, the important point was one that did not make a strong impression on the experimenters: the visions created by the sacred mushroom were *green*.

Life in Green

On January 19, 1966, the French newspaper *Nice-Matin*, and later the whole French press, reported a strange incident that occurred at Menton. The article described the experience of Madame Vial and her two children after they had inadvertently eaten hallucinogenic mushrooms.

'For some unknown reason,' wrote Roland Moreau, 'those Copelandia mushrooms, indistinguishable in appearance from edible mushrooms, began growing in the lawn of La Pinella, the house that Madame Vial and her husband own in the hamlet of Roquebrune.' She picked some of them and cooked them, then she and her children ate them. 'Within ten minutes, all three of them were no longer in their normal state. Sylvie had violent convulsions and jumped up and down; her brother saw everything coloured green, and objects took on geometric shapes; their mother saw hideous forms . . . surrealistic compositions. To put the finishing touch to those bright-green visions, everything was moving . . . the horizontal and the vertical had lost all meaning.'

Determined to put an end to her nightmarish visions, Madame Vial succeeded in picking up the telephone even though it seemed to be whirling and green. At the Menton hospital, 'the three patients reacted according to their ages in the midst of their green hell.' Fortunately their disorders ended as soon as they came out of their 'life in green', to use Madame Vial's expression.

This takes us to the heart of the enigma. Hallucinogenic mushrooms, whether they be the Copelandia of Peru, the *Stropharia cubensis*, the *Psilocybe mexicana* or the *Psilocybe zapotecorum*, have the miraculous power of creating visions in a green universe. And the colour green is of primordial importance:

– It is the symbolic colour of the planet Venus and the sacred art of the Mayas, Incas and Hindus.

– Lucifer is the name of Venus, the morning star. Lucifer is an 'angel' who came from the bright planet to give life, knowledge and love to mankind. He bore a green emerald[46] on his forehead.

– According to theosophists the four Masters of the World, who are Venusians, live in Chamballah (the Gobi Desert) in the Jade Palace (jade is green).

– The Pillar of the World at the temple of Chavin, in Peru, was consecrated to the great King Naymlap, who flew off into space after bringing knowledge and progress. This pillar is a monolith of green serpentine marble.

– Among the ancient Indians, jade was regarded as a gift from the gods who came from the planet Venus.

– In China and India, jade is a substance reserved above all for the gods.

– The Cathari claimed to be in possession of the 'green stone', or Grail of eternal truth, and that stone had 'fallen from the sky'.

– Kukulkan and Quetzalcoatl, the great gods of the ancient Mexicans, had come from the planet Venus. They are traditionally depicted with jade set into their eyes and navel.

– Minerva, a Pelasgian goddess, was Aurora, the morning star (Venus), called Athana in Sanskrit. She traditionally had green eyes (Minerva Glaucopis).

Callais, Jade and Serpentine Marble

Maurice Magre writes in *La Clef des Choses Cachées*, 'M. Chaboseau (*Histoire de la Bretagne Avant le Douzième Siècle*) points out a curious fact: there is a sea-green precious stone called callais, similar to turquoise, of which only 830 specimens are known, and all of them have been found in dolmens. What virtue did that rare stone have, what powers related to mortuary use, and what possibilities concerning the future life were hidden in it?'

At La Venta, Mexico, north of the pyramid, the archaeologist Matthew W. Stirling found a mosaic of little green serpentine marble cubes and thirty-seven axes of the same stone arranged in a cross.

In *L'Enigme du Dieu Blanc Précolombien*, Pierre Honoré notes that the ancient Mexicans had a mysterious devotion to jade above all other precious substances, even diamonds and gold, and that they made their most highly venerated figurines of it.

Among the Olmecs of La Venta, the giant sculpted heads are made of green serpentine marble and it is interesting to note that these bulldog-faced giants wear helmets like those of our modern astronauts.

The Olmecs also made carved jade effigies of the gods,

and the Aztecs used jade as their currency.

The same devotion to jade was found in ancient China and India.

Lao-tse went off toward 'the land of the west' riding a green ox and the scene is often depicted by a green figurine.

The Cretans and Phoenicians made jade jewellery. Some historians believe that the search for jade brought Asians to the shores of the New World, specifically to Guatemala and Mexico.

A jade statue found at Tres Zapotes represents a winged being with a duck's beak but an otherwise human face.

Finally, it should be noted that Asian and Amerindian jade is related to amber, the precious substance of the ancient Nordic peoples. Their only source for it was the shore of the Baltic, adjacent to the land of the Hyperboreans.

The Extraterrestrial Plant

We thus find ourselves in a maelstrom of green and Venus, bound up with each other in an indissoluble whole. For as soon as we approach the subject of Venus, the colour green arises, just as it does when we consider the most ancient civilisations: Greenland, the Green Land of the Egyptians, the Green Knight of the Arthurian stories, the symbolic green of Thule, the Emerald Isle of Erin.

How can we fail to establish a logical connection between Mexico – the country most closely associated with hallucinogenic mushrooms and gods identified with Venus – and the green universe created by sacred mushrooms? Is it not their function, through clairvoyant penetration of the past and the future, to make it possible to travel in time and space to the universe inhabited by the Great Ancestors?

It seems that the Masters of the World who came to Mexico five thousand years ago brought with them the plant that was easiest to acclimatise: the mushroom. They chose a hallucinogenic variety to enable priests to raise themselves artificially to their level of understanding. Without hallucinogenic mushrooms, the ancient Mexicans would never have been able to understand the language and knowledge of the Venusian initiators.

These mushrooms, as well as initiatic potions, in Mexico and elsewhere, must have been quick and convenient means of establishing communication between extraterrestrials and earthlings – between superior men and inferior men.

One day the last initiators disappeared – this was the end of the gods – and all over the world pythonesses, sibyls, witches, diviners, priests (for the ancient priests were diviners and prophets) and all other scholars and knowers were cut off from the source of initiation. But they continued the use of initiate potions or smoke.[47]

'According to Buriat tradition (Siberia, the Lake Baikal region), in ancient times shamans received their *ucha* (gift) directly from the celestial spirits; only in our time do they receive it solely from their ancestors . . . The first shamans really flew.' (Mircea Eliade, *Le Chamanisme.*)

That is why the secret of soma and haoma was forgotten, and men all over the world set off in search of something that had been lost. Substitute potions, made with plants that had no doubt degenerated,[48] were no longer effective. But the more tenacious ones kept part of their power; or so we must assume, since Maria Sabina predicts the future.

From the remote times when the Masters of the World came to Earth and a few privileged human beings (priests and shamans) may have been able to go to another planet, there still remain rites preserved by tradition. During initiations in South America, Polynesia, Africa and Asia, candidates must drink a potion, then climb up a tree, a pole, a rope or a ladder, as their ancestors went up into the sky with divine spirits. And it is only when they have come back down – that is, after their symbolic return from an interplanetary journey – that their initiation becomes effective.

Clairvoyance for Rationalists

Through the experiments of Wasson, Snell and Heim,

clairvoyance and divination have become officially accredited.

The Mysterious Unknown is not a fantasy, but a supranormal reality evidenced by facts whose explanation is still all but unknown.

Certain 'rationalists', more sectarian than rational, have nevertheless tried to give an explanation. They maintain that the images produced by hallucinogenic drugs are created entirely by the subject, who somehow exudes them, then believes he sees them *from outside* by means of his double.

This view might possibly be accepted with regard to clairvoyant visions of the past: there is a doubling of the subject, whose double, separated from his physical body, can externally perceive images created by his enhanced memory. We must then assume that chromosomes preserve, perhaps by induction, a hereditary memory that may go back to the earliest days of mankind. Pythagoras and Einstein, for example, recovered the genius and hereditary traits of their remote ancestors. It still remains to be proved, however, that the subject's ancestors knew or could have known the answers to such questions as where a certain person or object is hidden. In most cases this would be impossible.

The view breaks down completely with regard to travelling in the present and the future.

However great man's mnemonic powers may be, it seems unlikely that he could have knowledge of the whole universe within himself, unless the microcosmic universe in his brain receives knowledge of the macrocosm by induction, for we cannot reject the hypothesis of an identity between the two universes.

But the idea of projection in space-time seems more plausible to me. To explain Maria Sabina's powers on this basis, we must assume travel in the present and the future. I have studied this problem in terms of parallel universes in *The Legacy of the Gods*, Chapter 12.

It seems rather likely to me that the power of clairvoyance was taught to us by the ancient 'gods' (extra-terrestrial initiators), especially when we consider that our own astronauts, if they succeed some day in landing on another planet, will need to bring with them a means of communicating with the conscious beings they hope to find there. And the idea of hallucinogenic drugs or mushrooms immediately suggests itself. Furthermore it is important to note that efforts to acclimatise plants have the greatest chance of success with fast-growing mosses, lichens and mushrooms.

The Man in the Jade Mask

Mushrooms were held in such high honour in Yucatan and Guatemala that many representations of them, carved out of green stone, have been found there.

The Rietberg Museum in Zurich has several types of stone mushrooms, some of them in human form or with human features.

No other plant has been honoured in that way, and this clue takes on a singular value in a country where all the gods are associated with Venus and where the subtle art seems to be a direct expression of inspiration imparted by hallucinogenic mushrooms.[49]

In the pyramid at Palenque, in Yucatan, is a mysterious sepulchre, the only one of its kind in all of Mexico, whose tombstone poses a great enigma.

On June 15, 1952, Alberto Ruz Lhuillier, of the Mexican National Institute of Anthropology, one of the most eminent archaeologists of our time, entered a crypt that had previously been unknown. He had discovered it inside the pyramid supporting the temple of Palenque. On the wall, tall figures moulded into the stucco seemed to be standing guard. Each of them wore a headdress adorned with the beak and long feathers of the quetzal bird dear to the great god of Mexico, representing the planet Venus: Quetzalcoatl.

'What surprised me most in that crypt,' Alberto Ruz Lhuilliers wrote in the November, 1964, issue of *Arche-*

ologia, 'was the enormous monument that occupies most of it. Imagine a horizontal stone seven feet wide and twelve feet long, sculpted on its sides and its upper surface. It rests on a monolithic block whose sides are also sculpted.'

The slab covered a sarcophagus containing the bones of a man in his forties, five feet eight inches tall, who had probably held a very high position. He wore a jade mask and was surrounded by many jewels. He held a large cubical gem in his right hand and a spherical one in his left. At his feet was a magnificent jade figurine.

All this was an extremely valuable find and the round and cubical gems represented an unusual mystery. But the most important part of it was the cover of the tomb or, more exactly, what was carved on it. Alberto Ruz Lhuillier saw it as a symbolic representation of the buried man.

The Space Rocket of Palenque

I have meditated a long time on the strange carving of Palenque. To anyone who examines it without preconceived ideas, the eminent Mexican professor's interpretation is unsatisfactory.

If such a picture (reproduced on the next page) had been found in a cave in France, or even on a Merovingian sarcophagus, it could not have failed to arouse intense curiosity!

Even more than the Puerta del Sol of Tiahuanaco, in Bolivia, on which strange space machines appear, the Palenque slab presents an enigma that is obviously related to space rockets.

It was carved in the time of Mayan prehistory, yet the person – man or woman – seated in the elaborate machine irresistibly reminds me of a modern astronaut. My opinion is shared by Guy Tarade and André Millou, from whom I borrow the following interpretation:

> The person at the centre of the carving, whom we will call the pilot, is wearing a helmet and looking towards

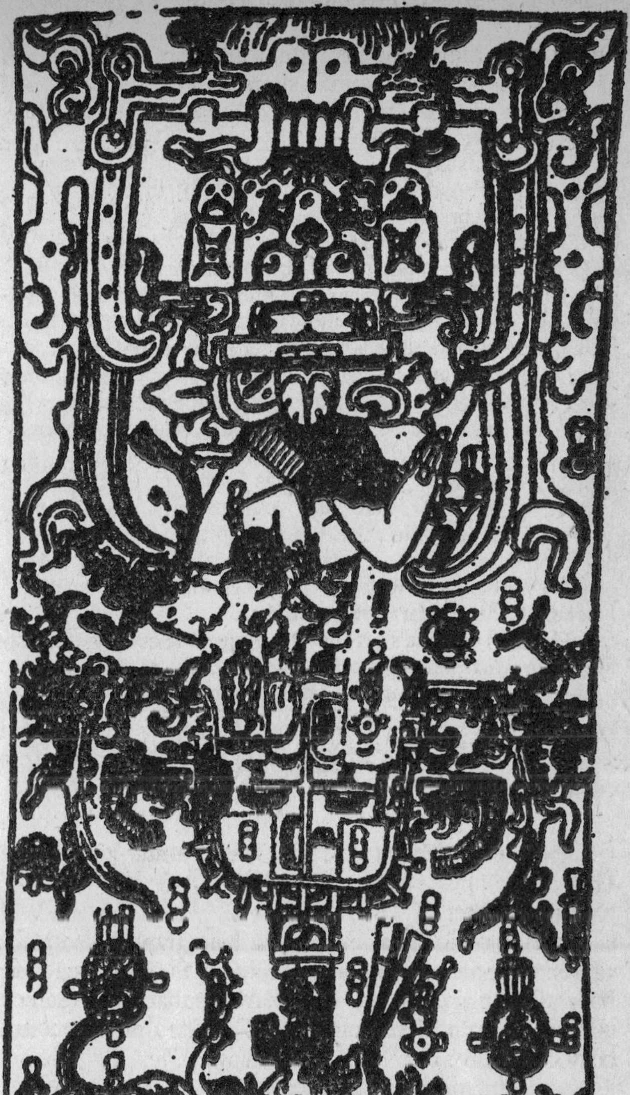

the front of the machine. His hands are manipulating levers. There is a support behind his head and an inhalator in his nose, which clearly indicates the principle of stratospheric flight.

The craft, shaped like a rocket, seems to be a cosmic vessel using solar energy. At the front of it is a parrot, a bird that represents the flying god in Mayan symbolism. The word 'energy' would be more appropriate than 'god', since in the decomposition of light by a prism we find the range of colours of a parrot's plumage. The dominant colour of that bird is usually green, the colour of the Venusian gods, and it is interesting to note that, according to the reports of certain witnesses, appearances of 'unidentified flying objects' tinge the sky with green.

In the front part of the rocket, just behind the nose, are ten storage cells, and other devices for accumulating energy are visible. The motor has four compartments in front; at the rear, cells and complex organs are connected by pipes to an exhaust nozzle spitting fire.

Propulsion in space is clearly indicated, and seems to result from a mixture of two antagonistic forces: one solar, the other extraterrestrial.

There were once sites for launching such craft, notably on the vast platform of Monte Alban, which is the Mexican counterpart of the terrace of Baalbek in Lebanon. (Baalbek was the temple of Baal the Venusian.) These sites still remain in the form of what seems to be giant runways made of immense stone blocks put in place by some powerful means now unknown to us.

Such is the account given by Guy Tarade and André Millou. I will make a necessary addition to it.

The alphabet of Diego de Landa, which has made it possible to decipher a few Mayan hieroglyphs, also gives an approximate but edifying meaning to the Palenque slab. Along its top and bottom are two friezes that are actually a text in ideograms, composed of eighteen drawings (rectangles): nine above and nine below. *They all have an astronomical meaning.*

The drawing with four balls connected to a central globe is the sign of the starry sky. The three ideograms with crossbars have the meaning of force of the arm and brain, and command of force (motor).

Since Mayan writing has not been translated, the text cannot be deciphered literally, but there can be no doubt of the general idea it expresses: an astronaut piloting a spacecraft toward a planet.

We can even say with certainty which planet is involved: Venus. The drawing between the two friezes contains only two correctly drawn symbols; these symbols, behind the astronaut, consist of a rectangle enclosing a square or lozenge with a circle in the middle. They are particularly apparent, well drawn and placed on both sides of the motor.

This symbol is one of the major signs of the Mayan alphabet. Its name is *ik* and is signifies 'wind', 'breath', 'spirit', 'nineteenth day' and 'Venus'.

The Mayan *ik* is also represented by a bull's head in a rectangle, and by a trident with two eyes. It is extremely interesting to note that the first of these two signs is that of Baal and Astarte, the Venusian gods of Asia Minor, and that the second, in the hieroglyphs of Asia and Siberia, also designates the planet Venus. There is thus reason to believe that the astronaut-initiators who came from the sky five thousand years ago introduced the sign of the bull and the trident in all parts of the globe, which shows that they were true Masters of the World. It also supports the idea that there was once a single language spoken by the learned classes all over the world.

As will be seen in Chapter 12, plates XXII and XXVI of the Troano Manuscript contain ideograms identical to those of the Palenque slab. And the Troano Manuscript unmistakably deals with flight in a craft with a rocket engine.

The figure on the Palenque slab may be a portrait of the dead man buried in the pyramid, as Alberto Ruz Lhuillier maintains, but I can state with confidence that it also represents an astronaut piloting a spacecraft to or from Venus.

The body may be that of Quetzalcoatl or a Master of the World who came from Venus.

Visionary Art

When was the pyramidal temple of Palenque built? In the seventh century, say historians. But the crypt is certainly much older. The pyramids of Mexico, like those of Autun, are formed of successive structures, one built over another, and the outer ones are the most recent.

Historians like to pontificate, but I recall the mishap they encountered after they had assigned a date of 450 B.C. to the Cuicuilco pyramid, between Mexico City and Tlalpan. It had been covered with lava from the volcano Xitle, and when geologists analysed that lava they fixed the time of its ejection at eight thousand years ago!

We may therefore assume that the pyramidal temple of Palenque is considerably older than historians have officially stated.

But the real mystery still has to be elucidated. What is that astronaut doing there? How did the Mayas know about spacecraft with an inhalator for the pilot?

The case of Maria Sabina makes it possible to give a rational answer – the word 'rational' can now be used in connection with clairvoyance – in terms of hallucinogenic drugs.

Had the sculptor of the Palenque slab seen a spacecraft? It is possible, but rather unlikely. I believe he must have worked under the influence of sacred mushrooms and seen, in the images they created, the amazing spacecraft that had brought to our planet the Venusian gods or the eminent personage buried in the crypt. He was unable, of course, to carve an exact reproduction of the machine he had seen in his vision, but he conveyed its essential features: its form, means of propulsion and particularly striking details.

He invented nothing, just as there is no invention in the helmeted Olmec giants of the Yucatan forest, the flying saucer reproduced in the Magliabecchiano Codex and the flying gods and monsters of the Troano Manuscript,

It is also probable that the sculptors of the motors and space suits of the Puerta del Sol of Tiahuanaco, in Bolivia, copied visions that they had after drinking ayahuascar, a decoction of hallucinagenic herbs that is still sold in the mountains, particularly at Pisac.

Chapter 11

THE INVISIBLE MASTERS

The genesis of civilisation, which historians, archaeologists and geologists try to discover empirically, is known to initiates through the teaching given to them in certain sanctuaries: among the Rosicrucians in France and America; in the Hawaiian Islands; in the Agartha and the monasteries of lamas in Tibet; at Chamballah (Gobi Desert), according to theosophists; in the sanctuaries of Persia and Ethiopia; and finally in Mexico, where the tradition was transmitted by the Mayan bas-reliefs and manuscripts.

There is a strong probability that revealing documents also exist in the Moslem libraries of Fez and Rabat, and in the Vatican Library. These documents, some of which have been partially divulged, are known as the Books of the Masters of the World.

Who are or were those Masters? Initiated mortals, either earthly or extraterrestrial, or beings of 'divine' origin?

The Metatron and the Agartha

According to René Guénon, who has written a great deal on this subject without ever basing his views on any conclusive documents, there is a King of the World, or Metatron, a special representative who mediates between divine forces and mankind and can be identified with the Azazel of the Book of Enoch and the Saint Michael of the Christians. The shadow of Metatron, or dark force of Mikael, is represented by Samael or Sar Ha-Olam (Satan), the spirit of this world in the inferior sense. The mysterious Melchizedek was also, or still is, the Master of the World.

In 1890, according to statements by Hindus, the King of

the World made a prophecy when he appeared at the Narabanchi monastery: 'The peoples of the Agartha will come out of their caverns and appear on the surface of the earth.'

For theosophists, there are four Masters of the World who reside at Chamballah in the Jade Palace. They are Venusians and their 'aerial' sanctuary is in opposition to the underground sanctuary of the Agartha, which is inhabited by dark forces.

Yet underground sanctuaries, under the sign of white magic, have their supporters, who relate cave worship to the idea of the cavern of the heart, the 'inner places' similar to that of the Egyptians, formed by the serpent and the ring, to which adepts symbolically withdraw to meditate.

Ossendowsky says that the Agartha was not always underground; it became so six thousand years ago, to protect the sages from the curiosity of the perverted world.

With regard to the *firdos* of Hawaii, Swami Matkormano told me that the sanctuary was hidden and that occult forces formed a kind of magnetic barrier around its entrance.

These various stories are unconvincing because they are not supported by documents or any kind of evidence.

The concept of a Master of the World is attractive, but it must be based on something more solid than a 'revelation' given by God or angels, an underground kingdom that cannot be found, or a palace located at Lob Nor, from where the Chinese launch their rockets!

There are no longer many believers in 'revelations'. Those of the Mormons are opposed to those of the Christians, which in turn are opposed to those of the Hindus, and so on down to the countless 'revelations' that still haunt the minds of people with a need to believe in the fantastic.

Yet the Masters of the World existed, since they left their mark on societies and religions all over the world and imposed a universal language and symbols that are found in America, Europe and Asia.[50] They were called gods, watchers and heroes, and they had the power given to them by their scientific knowledge and their ability to move through space in flying machines.

Yet despite the many good reasons for believing in the reality of those Masters of the World, they have been ignored by spiritualistic writers, who have preferred to invent pseudo-demiurges holed up in sanctuaries unknown to everyone, including themselves!

Pherecydes the Initiate

Ossendowsky and René Guénon sinned by lack of caution. I vastly prefer those great initiates, those men superior to all others (and to all the gods we invent), whose names radiate pure light: Sanchuniathon, Pherecydes, Pythagoras.

Sanchuniathon was the first champion of truth, the first freethinker, which is the main reason why he is banished from classical culture and ignored even by many people who pride themselves on being cultured.

Pherecydes? He lived in the seventh century B.C. and is known chiefly for having been Pythagoras's teacher. What is less well known is that Pythagoras, the greatest of the great, said that he was supremely honoured to be the disciple of such a great teacher.

According to the historians Josephus, Suidas, Eusebius and Hesychius, who spoke of him, Pherecydes was a self-taught man who took his erudition from Phoenician manuscripts written in a mysterious language. Like Sanchuniathon! And probably from the same course: the Masters of the World.

Those Masters said that God was a mysterious concept about which nothing could really be said, and that the gods of *all* religions were impostors. Pherecydes categorically denied being a 'messenger from the gods', as others tried to depict him, and stayed within the limits of his knowledge. His example and high authority brought about a revolution in the Greek mind.

'Until his time,' says the *Encyclopédie*, 'philosophers prophesied like Hebrew prophets, taught a few desciples in seclusion and refrained from writing their thoughts, which is typical of false prophets, false messiahs and false initiates. In his school, Greek philosophers began speaking like ordinary mortals; they abjured mystery, openly professed their ideas and were no longer afraid to put the secrets of their minds in writing.'

He was the first of the Greeks to discourse on the immortality of the soul.

At the end of his old teacher's life, Pythagoras illustrated by example one of the noblest human sentiments: love of one's fellow man. The story below was given by the historians Diodorus Siculus, Porphyry, Iamblichus and Apuleius.

Pythagoras: A Lesson in Love

Old, sick, disabled, covered with vermin and festering sores, Pherecydes had become a veritable piece of human refuse. Despite his great renown, he was so contagious and repulsive that no one was willing to come near him.

When Pythagoras was informed of this, he immediately left Italy and went to help Pherecydes.

To avoid being seen, Pherecydes had ordered that no one be allowed to come into his bedroom. Pythagoras opened the door and asked him how he was. Pherecydes had covered himself in his bed, but when he heard his disciple's voice he put out a finger from which the flesh had been eaten away and said, 'My whole body is in that condition.'

Pythagoras took care of him until he died, then buried him with his own hands and conducted a funeral service.

Pherecydes's pitiful end and the menial tasks performed by Pythagoras – bandaging sores, washing clothes stained with blood, pus and excrement – do not diminish the glory of the two philosophers. On the contrary, Pythagoras's behaviour was the mark of the true initiate. Many 'gods' do not have such edifying acts to their credit.

It is easy to give money to the poor, it is easy to preach, it is even easy to die for an idea, as is shown by millions of deaths in every century; it is much more difficult to be a prince of the mind and pass a basin to a suppurating, contagious invalid.

And yet, in the meaning given to the word by religious minds, Pythagoras and Pherecydes were atheists!

The inhabitants of Delos accused Pherecydes of impiety because he did not sacrifice to the gods and advised his disciples not to do so. But they tried to deify him during his lifetime. He refused that honour with as much determination as Pythagoras later refused the title of sage.

Guy Tarade's Master of the World

Like André Bouguenec, the father of French Cabalism, Guy Tarade, director of the Centre d'Etude et de Recherche d'Eléments Inconnus de Civilisations, believes that 'we are acted on'; that is, our destiny is governed by mysterious forces brought forth by the Masters of the World.

Tarade feels that extraterrestrial civilisations at war with each other might covet the earth and struggle for possession of it.

> In that case [he writes] our planet would become a great chessboard on which a vital game would be played by superconscious space beings whom I call the Cosmic Masters.
>
> The first earthly human race was taught by guides who came from the sky, as is related by the Hebrews, Christians and Moslems. Moreover, Madame Blavatsky and the sages of India have stated that those initiators were Venusians, which is the mysterious key to the past . . .
>
> For five thousand years the world has been secretly under the sway of a Martian-Venusian religion (Mars being the wrathful, warlike Jehovah of Moses, and Venus the initiating mother, the Astarte of the Phoenicians). Even the layout of cathedrals – nave, transept, chancel, apse – reproduces the ansate cross that is the symbol of Venus. Their architecture usually borrows from the letter H, the Cabalistic sign of femininity, and the altar is dedicated to Jehovah-Mars.

And Tarade concludes as follows:

> Here is how the war of the mythological gods might be explained in the light of the present conquest of space. Two planets fight over a third, conquer it and destroy pockets of resistance here and there (Atlantis and Mu); the colonisers make an alliance with a few superior earthlings – the Masters – and the whole hive supplies honey to *living gods* from another world.

What would be the nature of that 'honey'? It might be a psychic force that nourishes vampire-gods. After all, man is the vampire-master of the cattle he carefully raises for the purpose of feeding on their flesh. Are we, as the philosopher Michel Simkine speculates, a herd incapable of knowing the designs of its herdsman?

All sorts of suppositions are permissible but, considering the cosmic adventure we are now attempting and the frequent appearances of mysterious unidentified craft in our skies, it is important to study Guy Tarade's hypothesis. If it is correct, the Masters of the World might be the Venusians of the theosophists.[51]

Peter Deunov's Masters

In several books in which his statements have been collected, Peter Deunov gives a quite different version of the Masters of the World. Deunov, who is Bulgarian, is said to be an initiate; he too has had revelations, but he has never been able to give the slightest evidence for his 'truths'.

And that is the stumbling block for any rational and honest man. The Christians speak of heaven, the theosophists of the Gobi Desert, others of the Agartha, Peter Deunov of the sun. All this is rather irreconcilable; on the most favourable hypothesis, there is error, hallucination or deceit in all those views except one.

The idea of a God or a universal intelligence is so inherent in the human mind, and so logical, that the atheistic theory can never prevail over religious belief, but that only increases our admiration of men like Pherecydes, Pythagoras and Plato, who were wise enough to suspend judgement.

Peter Deunov has made the following revelation with great seriousness:

> There is on earth a lodge of scientists who meet once a year to deliberate on various scientific matters. With regard to the past and present state of our planet, these initiates know much more than contemporary scientists who represent official science. But they too have no positive knowledge of the future of the earth; they can only make suppositions.
>
> Besides this earthly lodge of initiates, there is on the sun [*sic*] another lodge of Great Initiates who have positive knowledge not only of the earth's past, but also of its future. But both lodges are only organs of the sublime universal organism of perfectly, supremely advanced beings who form the August Universal Brotherhood. These perfect beings are incomparably more advanced than the greatest earthly geniuses because they came out of the First Principle much earlier than mankind.

Once again, if this is the truth we can only deplore the lack of wisdom, love and efficiency of those sublime 'scientists' who tolerate so many monstrosities in our poor human life!

God: Two Arms, Two Legs . . .

Another concept of the Master of the World is presented by the engineer R. J. Mouton, who is now formulating his views in a book whose title will be *La Révélation Scientifique du Saint-Esprit.*

Mouton has reached the conclusion that certain Biblical texts have a precisely verifiable accuracy which demonstrates their purely divine nature. Despite all theological affirmations, he does not doubt that God is really in man's image and resides in the sky. The Master of the Universe is thus God himself; he is a divine entity, but he is made like us, with a body, a head and four limbs.

Mouton's concept of the deity may make some people smile, but certain theologians are not afraid to venture along that path and it is not impossible that in a thousand years, or much sooner, men will accept that God in their image as the most plausible and scientific representation of the Master of the Universe.

That Master, totally different in essence from R. J. Mouton's God, would not be the creator; he would only have substituted himself for the creator.

On the mathematical level, it is possible to explain that the creature can go back in an alternate time and become his creator. On this hypothesis it is clear that mankind once knew high civilisation, not only on Earth but also on other planets.

Becoming God

I am personally convinced that man in his present physical form is only a link in his own evolution and in universal evolution, but that is only a hypothesis, almost an impression; the truth is no doubt more fantastic.

If we assume that no end of the world threatens the human adventure in the next few thousand years, we must also assume that the geometric progression of discovery will provide the human race with vast, terrifying power before the year 3000.

By that time, if man continues his evolution, he will be able to solve any problem, create or destroy matter solely by the power of his speech or thought waves, either directly or by means of a machine. He will be able to create planets and mould the universe; in short, he will substitute himself for God by becoming his thinking, acting and creative form.

The very essence and potential of God will pass into his creature. It will be concretised in men, who will thus become incarnations of the deity. The total mass of God will diminish as man amasses essential energies. The initial God will tend towards zero as he is transmuted into increasingly subtle men who will become the expression of the final God.

When men have become gods and God himself, it is likely that one of them will be charged with more and better energy than any of the others. He will then become the guide and leader of other men and assume the functions of the Master of the World.

That great culmination belongs to our destiny, as it belonged to the destiny of our ancestors in the remote past, on the planet where they achieved their transmutation. From that unknown planet, the Master of the World acts on us as he sees fit, according to his plans, awaiting the time when he will be dethroned by one of us.

Do the mysterious 'flying saucers' come from the universal control centre?

Are our impressions and premonitions, and even our beliefs and psychic powers, privileges granted by that human God? Or are they secret, perhaps forbidden indications stolen from the 'Lord' by a good Lucifer who is a friend of earthlings?

All these speculations, as the philosopher Jean Fourastié would say, are only games for adults, since 'the human mind manufactures whatever gods please it, without concerning itself with their reality.'

Are the Masters of the World, like the gods, only phantasms of an unknown that defies human sagacity?

Whether it is soluble or not, the problem will always be tempting to curious minds, but they must avoid the facile imaginings and inventions of certain occultists. It is, of course, much harder to *prove* something than to have 'revelations'.

Chapter 12

THE BOOKS OF THE MASTERS OF THE WORLD

The monuments and manuscripts of ancient civilisations relate the great events that mark the history of mankind: the creation of the world, the coming of celestial initiators, the Deluge, wars against monsters or gods, the discovery of agriculture, fire and the smelting of metals, and so on.

The oldest of these documents seem to be the Popul Vuh of the Mayan Quiches, the Book of Enoch, the Avesta of the Persians, the Vedas of the Hindus, the manuscripts of Egypt, Phoenicia, Tibet and Ethiopia, the Edda of the Scandinavians and the clay tablets of Glozel (France).

Then come the Bible, the manuscripts and tablets of Asia Minor and, under another aspect, the engraved stones of the Celts, Incas, Hittites and Egyptians, the Inscriptions on temples in Mexico and the Mayan manuscripts.

It is difficult to date stone documents.

The cave paintings at Lascaux (France), the prehistoric library at Lussac-les-Châteaux (France) and the inscriptions on objects found in caves are unquestionably earlier than the Deluge.

The same may be true of the monuments in Peru and Bolivia (the famous Puerta del Sol), the Egyptian pyramids and the Celtic megaliths, but it would be hazardous to assign precise dates to them.

The manuscripts found in Mexico are numerous and particularly interesting because they give vivid reports of events that are often twelve thousand years old. Among the most famous of them are the Troano Manuscript, the Barbonicus, Cortesianus and Vaticanus Codices, the Chilam Balam, the Dresden Codex and the Perez Codex.

They are written in ideograms, though some historians wrongly use the word 'alphabet' in relation to them. They have so far been translated only approximately, but they have never been falsified, which gives them an inestimable value and authenticity.

They are said to be composed in the form of calendars, using a kind of time that eludes our Western concepts. For the Mayas, sacred time annulled profane time in a mythological world that was always more present than the real world.

Translating the Writing of the Mayas

The numerical system that appears in the Codices is at first sight almost childishly simple: the figure 1 is indicated by a dot, 2 by two dots, 3 by three dots, 4 by four dots, 5 by a line, 6 by a dot over a line, 7 by two dots over a line, and so on. Multiplication, whose sign is an eye, was performed by means of these elements, but the system could not be used for large calculations. Since the Mayas showed remarkable astronomical knowledge, however, we must assume that they did not use that rather primitive system for their mathematical operations. It should be noted that their whole civilisation was impregnated with psychic powers, from art and science to everyday life.

From these considerations it follows that interpretation of their writing and mathematics must have been done by means of the Third Eye, designated by the sign for multiplication, which indicates a state of superconsciousness under the influence of hallucinogenic mushroom. Under that influence, everything became clear and easy: deciphering of ideograms, multiplication of astronomical numbers, algebra problems.

We can form an idea of that kind of miracle by thinking of the marvellous understanding that exists between lovers, between drunks, or between a person and a dog he loves; it is an understanding that takes place on the psychic level.

Since the bas-reliefs and manuscripts of ancient Mexico

could be wholly understood only by initiatic vision, the alphabet discovered by Diego de Landa must be considered incomplete and inconclusive.

For four centuries archaeologists and historians have laboured without grasping the meaning or essence of Mayan writing, even though one of its characteristics is obvious: it is not rational in the sense we give to that word.

In all the manuscripts and Codices, along with writing in the form of ideograms there are purely graphic drawings which comprehensively represent things that are either inexpressible by means of ideograms or easily expressible by direct representation.

In their visions, Mayan priests saw images of flying machines, motors, exhaust pipes and various forms of energy that could not be designated by ordinary language. They had no choice but to draw, in their fashion, those unwonted images. To make them intelligible to their contemporaries they associated them with the known alphabet or ideograms, thus giving the *idea*, but they also reproduced, as accurately as they could, details that depicted the *form* of the real object.

In hundreds of drawings we clearly recognise rites, scenes from everyday life and symbolic explanations of divine events, but in a few there are strange, completely anomalous objects. These mysterious representations all have traits that link them directly to flight and space travel by means of machines with exhaust pipes from which propulsive gases are ejected. Known symbols – fire, bird, serpent, sky, upheaval of the earth – reinforce the idea and description of aerial travel.

Seen in this light, the Troano Manuscript and the Dresden, Cortesianus and Perez Codices reveal a singular past, marked by extraterrestrial adventure.

Several important points should be stressed:

– No one knows how to translate the Mexican manuscripts, except perhaps for Maria Sabina and the Mexican *curanderos.*

– A few of the ideograms, however, have meanings

accepted by most specialists in the field.

– These ideograms always have several meanings and are seldom drawn in exactly the same way each time.

The Troano Manuscript

The first leaf of this manuscript tells of the Deluge. It was translated by Abbé Brasseur de Bourbourg, using the code or alphabet of Diego de Landa. The literal translation begins as follows: 'The master of the upheaved earth in the basin of water [is] fire; lava thrust from the deep centre entered nine [nine times or in nine places]. He of the upheaved earth . . .'

Paul Schliemann, grandson of Heinrich Schliemann, gave a translation that is quite different, because it borrows from the chronological sense of the Mayan calendar:

> In the year of 6 Kan, on the 11 Muluc, in the Month Zac, there occurred terrific earthquakes which continued without interruption until the 13 Chuen. The country of the hills of mud, the Land of Mu, was sacrificed. Being twice upheaved it disappeared during the night, being continually shaken by the fires of the under earth. Being confined these caused the land to sink and to rise several times and in various places.

This translation is arbitrary with regard to the designation of Mu. Schliemann related the cataclysm of the Deluge to the disappearance of Atlantis and Mu, the latter being traditionally located in what is now the Gobi Desert and the Pacific Ocean. He was probably right, but he deliberately introduced a place name that does not appear in the Mayan text.

Abbé Brasseur de Bourbourg's translation seems to me closer to the truth. It is controverted, however, not because of the ideas it expresses, but because of its arrangement and choice of words. This is essentially a linguistic dispute with no great importance as far as the actual content of the text is concerned, but it is good to point out that there are as many interpretations as interpreters. I will stress again that Mayan writing has not yet been translated.

The theme remains the same, with images of earthquakes, volcanic eruptions and engulfed continents, which well represent a universal Deluge. Only the details differ and show that a translation of ideograms is valuable chiefly for the general idea it suggests.

I have therefore considered it advisable to limit my own interpretation to analysis of graphic images supported by enclosed symbols, or 'tablets', whose meanings are relatively well known.

Eight symbols, most of them belonging to the accepted alphabet, will serve as keys.

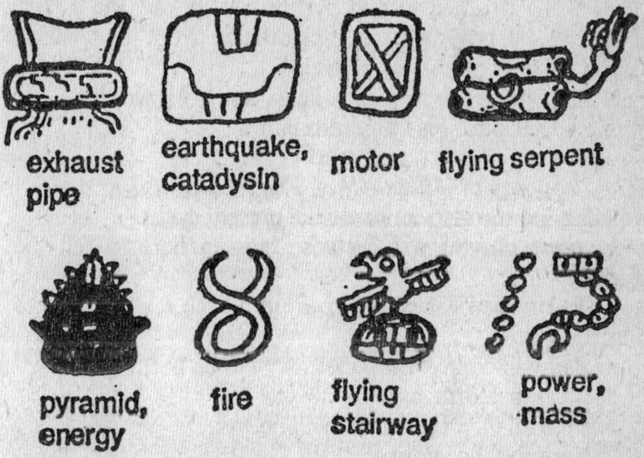

The designation of 'exhaust pipe' was suggested to me by obvious visual identification, and that of 'motor' by the commanding position occupied by the symbol in all images where it appears.

Two Revelations of the Mayas

Here are the prophecies of two Mayan initiates translated from hieroglyphic documents, closely related to the

Troano Manuscript, which tells of the Universal Deluge, and the Lhasa Manuscript, which describes a cataclysm caused by the fall of 'the star of Baal'.

The Prophecies of Napuctum

(Sibylline prophecies published in *Lizana Devocionario de Nuestra Señora de Itzmal*, Mexico City.)

1. When this peninsula ends by fire, he who dominates above the foam.

2. will arise triple divinity [the volcano that will become triple], no doubt in the presence of days to come.

3. Being doomed to end by fire here below, the superb one will be consumed in accordance with the cyclical laws engraved on the old palace.

4. He who sees him will be he who says his words

5. will weep for his numerous pains.

The Prophecy of Ahkuil-Chel, The Idolatrous Priest

1. Ended the inscription of the present cycle.

2. none of you will be wise enough here to tell the future.

3. To none will it be given to unroll the mat of cyclical inscriptions.

4. Pail will come, will penetrate, will be in the throat.

5. As in the north, as in the west

6. from all directions there will be, yes.

7. No priest, no prophet

8. will be there to say the words of the sacred writing

9. among so many princes;

10. none of you [will be] intelligent enough in so many different countries.

The Tablets of the Gobi Desert

In the nineteenth century, archaeologists discovered in the Gobi Desert a number of gold tablets which related the history of mankind. These tablets, written in an unknown language from which Zend was derived, were deposited in several sanctuaries, where they were transmuted into copper.

Here is what we know of their contents.

At the time of the Universal Deluge a leader of the kingdom of the Land of Mu, in Asia, left to his wife, who proved to be the only survival, some gold tablets on which the history of mankind before the cataclysm was engraved. They revealed the existence of 'Masters of the World who came from the sky' and identified them as astronauts from Venus and the star Sirius. They also gave precepts concerning a rational system of eating and breathing, and the secret of regaining youth. Their most secret and therefore most initiatic part will not be made public until a certain date inscribed in the Akashic Archives.

At the age of nine, Anahita, daughter of the Queen of Mu, acquired the faculty known as 'double memory'. Following instructions from her parents, she transcribed the ancestral documents and added her personal message, written on a hundred thousand little gold tablets. Some of them were discovered in the Gobi Desert; others are said to be still buried in high places, notably Mount Mano in Tibet.

According to Swami Matkormano, who saw and translated the tablets deposited in the *firdos*[52] of Hawaii, in the time of Anahita the white race was divided into two branches, one of which followed the course of the sun (towards the west) while the other remained in India. The branch to which Anahita belonged invented the Zend language, which directly gave rise to Sanskrit.

Twelve thousand years ago Sirius, the brightest star in the sky, was very near the earth.

'It is on Sirius,' said Jérôme Gheibardlt, 'that "adepts with awakened consciousness" are reincarnated.'

Chapter 13

SCHLIEMANN'S SECRET WILL

Troy, or Ilion, in Asia Minor, is said to have been founded by the Pelasgian Celts, and its mighty walls are said to have been built by Poseidon and Apollo and Hyperborean.

This legend clearly links the ancient history of Asia Minor to that of the Celtic West and also, through Poseidon, the god of the Atlanteans, to Atlantis.

In the *Iliad* and the *Odyssey*, Homer immortalised the siege of Troy in which the Greek leaders Agamemnon, Achilles, Ulysses, Ajax, etc., fought against the sons of King Priam, Hector and Paris, the latter having been rash enough to carry off the beautiful Helen, wife of Menelaus, King of Sparta. The city was taken by means of Ulysses' stratagem (the famous Trojan horse), then pillaged and burned.

In 1871 the German archaeologist and Hellenist Heinrich Schliemann, scorning the claims of conventional archaeologists, took Homer and Plato at their word and discovered the ruins of the ancient city.

Below the Troy of Priam he uncovered the foundations of the original city, which was Aryan, as was proved by the many potsherds and small pieces of pottery bearing Aryan religious symbols, including the swastika of the Hindus. Most of the bases were in the form of an owl, the bird dear to Minerva Glaucopis, the protector of Troy,[53] and engraved on their sides were the hooked nose, eyes, breasts and navel of the goddess. Schliemann also found objects and weapons of flint, silver, gold and copper,

The copper weapons of Troy are identical to the bronze weapons of prehistoric Denmark and the lake towns of Switzerland.

These correlations convinced Schliemann that there was a close connection between the Aryan prehistory of Troy, denied by archaeologists, and another prehistory that was also called a myth:[54] that of Atlantis.

Schliemann Would Have Been Murdered . . .

Was Heinrich Schliemann really aware of having made one of the greatest discoveries of all time: that of the true history of the world? Yes, since like all initiators he realised that if he spoke he would be mercilessly murdered, as were the dragon and Jesus. Being a prudent initiate, he decided not to reveal the most important part of his discoveries until after his death, when time had accredited his historical views.

He took precautions to save his life, his work and the truth he was going to launch into the world: he hid the most valuable finds from his excavations, wrote his message and bequeathed all this to his family, along with a large sum of money for the specific purpose of assuring that his last wishes would be carried out. This, at least, is what his grandson reported.

In spite of all these precautions, the revelations were smothered as soon as they appeared. An eminent supporter of Atlantis, the writer A. Bessmertny, even gave a certain credence (though he may have had good reasons for being reticent) to a letter sent to him by Wilhelm Doerpfeld, Schliemann's collaborator from 1882 till his death in 1890.

'To the best of my knowledge,' wrote Doerpfeld, 'Heinrich Schliemann never made a thorough inquiry into the question of Atlantis, but I consider it possible that he may have gathered notes on it. I do not, however, believe in the existence of an original work by him on that subject.'

But the documentation I will give below shows, if it is authentic, that Schliemann considered the subject of Atlantis to be of major importance.

On October 20, 1912, his grandson, Paul Schliemann, published in the New York *American* an article entitled 'How I Found the Lost Atlantis, the Source of all Civilisation.'

Here are extensive quotations from that article (passages in italics are my own insertions):

> Some days before my grandfather, Dr Heinrich Schliemann, the real discoverer of the great Mycenean civilisation whose history is preserved in the books in Homer, died in Naples in 1890, he left a sealed envelope in care of one of his closest friends. The envelope bore the following inscription: 'This can be opened only by a member of my family who solemnly vows to devote his life to the researches outlined therein.'
>
> Just an hour before my grandfather died he asked for a piece of paper and asked for a pencil. He wrote with a trembling hand: 'Confidential addition to the sealed envelope. Break the owl-headed vase. Pay attention to the contents. It concerns Atlantis. Investigate the east of the ruins of Sais and the cemetery in Chacuna Valley. Important. It proves the system. Night approaches – *Lebewohl*.'
>
> He closed it in an envelope and directed the nurse to send it to the friend whom he had entrusted with the other package. This was done. [. . .] The envelopes were deposited in one of the banks of France.
>
> After I had studied for some years in Russia, Germany and the Orient, I decided to take up the work of my illustrious grandfather. I felt that what he had felt so important that he had so safeguarded it must be important enough to devote one's life to. In 1906 I took the vow and broke the seals. Within were a number of documents and photographs. The first paper said:
>
> 'Whoever opens this must solemnly swear to carry out the work which I have left unfinished. I have come to the conclusion that Atlantis was not only a great territory between America and the west coast of Africa and Europe, but the cradle of all our civilisation as well. There has been much dispute among scientists on this

matter. According to one group the traditions of Atlantis is purely fictional, founded upon fragmentary accounts of a Deluge some thousands of years before the Christian era. Others declare the tradition wholly historical, but incapable of absolute proof.

'In the included material records, notes and explanations are to be found the proofs that exist in my mind of the matter. Whoever takes charge of this mission is solemnly obligated to continue my researches and to form a definite statement using as well the matter I leave with this and crediting me with my just dues in the discovery. A special fund is deposited in the Bank of France to be paid to the bearer of the enclosed receipt, and this should pay the expenses of the research. The Almighty be with this great effort.

Heinrich Schliemann.'[3]

I cannot in this limited space give all the papers – nor do I care to. But one of the most important from the narrative's standpoint read:

'When, in 1873, I made the excavation of the ruins of Troy at Hissarlik and discovered in the Second City the famous "Treasure of Priam", I found among that treasure a peculiar bronze vase, of great size. Within it were several pieces of pottery, various small images of peculiar metal coins of the same metal and objects made of fossilised bone. Some of these objects and the bronze vase were engraved with a sentence in Phoenician hieroglyphics. The sentence read, *From the King Chronos of Atlantis.*

'You who read can imagine my excitement! Here was the first, the very first material evidence of that great continent whose legend has lived for ages throughout the world. This material I kept secret, eager to make it the basis of investigations which I felt would prove of infinitely more importance than the discovery of a hundred Troys. But first I had to finish the work in which I was engaged, and I was the more eager to do this because I felt that I was sure to find other objects which would bear directly upon the lost continent. I was rewarded for my faith as you will see in the document marked B.

'In 1883 I found in the Louvre a collection of objects excavated from Tiahuanaca, in Central America. And among these I discovered pieces of pottery of exactly the same shape and material and objects of fossilised bone which reproduced line for line those that I had found in the bronze vase of the "Treasure of Priam"! The similarity could not be a coincidence. [. . .] The Central American vases had no Phoenician characters upon them nor writing of any kind. I hurried away to examine again my own objects and by tests and exhaustive examinations became convinced that the inscriptions had been made by other hands after the objects themselves had been manufactured.

'I secured pieces of these simulacrums from Tiahuanaca and subjected them to chemical and microscopic analysis. These tests proved conclusively that both the Central American vases and those from Troy had been made from the same peculiar clay, and I learned later, further and definitively, that this clay does not exist either in old Phoenicia nor in Central America!

'The metal objects I had analysed, because I could not recognise what they were made of. The metal was unlike any I had ever seen. The chemical analysis showed the material to be platinum, aluminium and copper – a combination never before found in the remains of the ancients and unknown today.

'Objects, then, perfectly similar and having unquestionably a common source were found in such widely separated countries as these. The objects themselves are not Phoenician, Mycenean nor Central American. What is the conclusion? That they came to both places from a common centre. The inscription on my objects gave that centre – it was Atlantis! [. . .]

'This extraordinary discovery and my failing health induced me to push more rapidly my investigations. I found in the Museum of St Petersburg one of the oldest papyrus rolls in existence. It was written in the reign of Pharaoh Sent, of the Second Dynasty, or 4571 years B.C. It contains a description of how the Pharaoh, named sent out an expedition "to the West" in search of traces of the "Land of Atlantis", whence "3,350 years ago the ancestors of the Egyptians arrived carrying with themselves all the wisdoms of their native lands." The expedition returned after five years with the report that they had found neither people nor objects which could give them a clue to the vanished land. Another papyrus, in the same museum, written by Manetho, the Egyptian historian, gives a reference to a period of "13,900 years as the reign of the sages of Atlantis". This papyrus places this at the very beginning of Egyptian history; it approximates 16,000 years ago.

'An inscription which I excavated at the Lion Gate at Mycenae in Crete recites that Misor, from whom, according to the inscription, the Egyptians were descended, was the child of Taaut or Thoth, the God of History, and that Taaut was the emigrated son of a "priest of Atlantis, who, having fallen in love with a daughter of King Chronos, escaped and landed after many wanderings in Egypt". He built the first temple at Sais and there taught the wisdom of his native land. This full inscription is most important, and I have kept it secret. You will find it among the papers marked D.'

I cannot go further here into more than a small part of the enormous mass of evidence, and it is material evidence of this continent of Atlantis that my grandfather had collected. I must pass to the end of this remarkable document:

'One of the tables of my Trojan excavation gives also a medical treatise of the Egyptian priests – for there was communication between Crete and Egypt for many centuries – for the removal of cataract from the eye and ulcer from the intestines by means of surgery. I have read almost a similar formula in a Spanish manuscript in Berlin whose writer took it from an Aztec priest in Mexico. That priest had gotten it from an ancient Mayan manuscript.

'In coming to my conclusion I must say that neither the Egyptians nor the Mayan race that made the civilisation of Central America before the Aztecs were great navigators. They had no ships to cross the Atlantic. Nor did they. We can dismiss the agency of the Phoenicians as a real link between the two hemispheres. Yet the similarity of Egyptian and Mayan life is so perfect that it is impossible to think of it as an accident. We find no such accidents in nature or history. The only possibility is that there was, as the legend says, a great continent that connected what we now call the New World with what we call the old [. . .] It was Atlantis. From Atlantis came the colonies that settled Egypt and Central America.'

Following his grandfather's instructions, Paul Schliemann began the necessary travelling and research.

I at once proceeded to investigate the hidden collection in Paris. The owl-headed vase was unique, of obviously extraordinarily ancient origin and on it I read the inscription in Phoenician characters: 'From the King Chronos of Atlantis.' I hesitated for days to break it for I still thought that last letter of my grandfather might have been the result of a mind weakened by the approach of death. [. . .]

Finally I broke it. I was not a little startled when out of the bottom of the vase slipped a square of white, silverlike metal upon which were drawn strange figures and an inscription which were not like any hieroglyphs or writings I had ever seen. These were on the head side of the coin or metal. On the obverse side was engraved in ancient Phoenician: *Issued in the Temple of Transparent Walls.* How did the medal get in the base? I do not know. The neck was too small for its insertion, but there it was and it had been imbedded in the clay of the bottom and my grandfather had evidently known it was there. [. . .]

Besides this I found in the collection the other material objects which my grandfather had said came from Atlantis. One was a ring of the same peculiar metal as the coins or medals. There was a strange-looking elephant of fossilised bone, an extremely archaic vase and some other objects which I will not discuss now. The map by which the Egyptian captain had sought for Atlantis was there too. I prefer to save these other objects for my extended work – nor could I, under the instructions of my grandfather, tell of them. It is sufficient to say that no scientist can controvert them. The owl vase, the archaic vase, the bronze vase and the ring have the Phoenician inscription. The elephant and coins did not.

My grandfather had written that I should first pay attention to the ruins of the Temple of Sais and the Chacuna Valley in America. I arrived first in Egypt and started to excavate around the ruins of Sais. I worked a long time in vain. I found interesting pieces of antique ceremonial uses, but no trace of what I wanted.

But one day I made the acquaintance of an Egyptian hunter who showed me a collection of old medals he had found in a sarcophagus in one of the tombs near by. Who can describe my surprise in finding among his collection two of the same design and size of the whole medal I had found in the vase of Troy?

Paul Schliemann continued his investigations on the west coast of Africa, then returned to Europe.

I went to Paris and sought the owner of the Central American collection which my grandfather had alluded to. He consented that I break his owl-headed vase for the purpose of investigation. I broke the vase.

And out of it slipped a medal exactly the same size and material as the three I had! The only difference was in the arrangement of the hieroglyphs!

Here there were five links: The coins in my grandfather's secret collection. The coin in the Atlantis vase. The coins in the Egyptian sarcophagus. The coin in the vase from Central America. The head from the Moroccan Coast.

I at once went to Central America, to Mexico and Peru. I have dug up graveyards and excavated in the cities. The cemetery of the Chacuna Valley, where the ancient Chimus are buried, gave me immense material for other clues. I will say that although I found fragments of the owl-headed vases, I found no more medals there. But what I did find was just as important. These are inscriptions which will startle the world. And I found other medals at the Pyramid of Teohuatican in Mexico of the same alloy, but with different script! [. . .]

I pass on the translation of a Mayan manuscript which is part of the famous collection of Le Plongeon, the Troano manuscripts. It can be seen in the British Museum. It reads:

'In the year of Kan, on the 11 Muluc, in the Month Zac, there occurred terrific earthquakes which continued without interruption until the 13 Chuen. The country of the hills of mud, the Land of Mu, was sacrificed. Being twice upheaved it disappeared during the night, being continually shaken by the fires of the under earth. Being confined, these caused the land to sink and to rise several times and in various places. At last the surface gave way, and then ten countries were torn asunder and scattered. They sank with their 64,000,000 of inhabitants 8,000 years before the writing of this book.'

In the records of the old Buddhistic Temple at Lhassa there is to be seen an ancient Chaldaic inscription written about 2,000 years B.C. It reads:

'When the star Bal fell on the place where is now only sea and sky the Seven Cities with their Golden Gates and Transparent Temples quivered and shook like the leaves of a tree in a storm. And behold a flood of fire and smoke arose from the palaces. Agony and cries of the multitude filled the air. They sought refuge in their temples and citadels. And the wise Mu, the hieratic of Ra-Mu, arose and said to them: "Did I not predict all this?" And the women and the men in their precious stones and shining garments lamented: "Mu, save us." And Mu replied: "You shall die together with your slaves and your riches and from your ashes shall rise new nations. If they forget they are superior, not because of what they put on, but of what they put out, the same lot will befall them!" Flame and smoke choked the words of Mu. The land and its inhabitants were torn to pieces and swallowed by the depths in a few months.'

How to account for these two stories – one from Tibet, the other from Central America, each mentioning the same cataclysm and each referring to the land of Mu?

When I throw open the facts I have, there will be no mystery about it.

(End of quotations from Paul Schliemann's article.)

Forbidden Revelations

Such are the revelations made by Paul Schliemann in 1912. His article aroused great curiosity in archaeological circles but for some reason he refused to add anything to what he had said.

What had happened? Had he simply wanted to hoax his contemporaries, as Wilhelm Doerpfeld wrote? Did he suffer from an inferiority complex that made him want to create a scientific reputation in keeping with the prestigious name he bore? We can only conjecture about the value of the documents he referred to.

Two points tend to support the idea of a hoax:

1. The papyrus 'written in the reign of Pharaoh Sent, of the Second Dynasty, or 4571 years B.C.' that Paul Schliemann claimed to have seen in the museum of St Petersburg (now Leningrad). There is no papyrus known to be that old.

2. The papyrus written by Manetho that he claimed to have seen in the same museum. We have no part of Manetho's history of Egypt, the only work he is known to have written, except for borrowings from it made by ancient authors.[55]

Another point may also seem suspicious: the alleged translation of the Troano Manuscript, whose ideograms or hieroglyphs still pose enormously difficult problems to those who try to decipher them.[56]

And why did Paul Schliemann suddenly disappear from the stage on which he had wanted to present a spectacle?

There are undeniably some very strange things in the whole affair, but it is equally undeniable that certain things tend to support the authenticity of the documents and discoveries.

If Paul Schliemann was a hoaxer, he showed incredible

naïveté and awkwardness in launching an attack, then immediately stopping it. What could he have hoped to gain from such an indecisive effort?

And could a man so awkward have invented a text that subtly reveals a deadly threat of which Heinrich Schliemann was clearly aware? For if Heinrich Schliemann wanted half a century to pass before someone else continued his work, he must have known that in his own time there were powerful, implacable enemies – those who sabotaged his excavations, denigrated his discoveries and made France lose King Priam's treasure – who would either kill him or ruin his efforts. This aspect of the problem deserves to be taken into consideration.

Furthermore, the documents, true or false, published in the New York *American* give evidence of extraordinary knowledge that I would even call initiatic. It implies the existence of centres of secrecy in Phoenicia. This idea is supported by Sanchuniathon: he also found in Phoenician temples a history of the world in mysterious writing which gave rise to the same prohibitions, censorship and blackout as the documents of 1912.

What Sanchuniathon wrote is in complete harmony with what Heinrich Schliemann is said to have written. It would seem that either Schliemann was inspired by Sanchuniathon or they both drew on the same sources.

As for the coins of an unknown white metal composed of platinum, aluminium and copper – perhaps the famous orichalcum of the Atlanteans – their existence can scarcely be placed in doubt, since Christos Mavrothalassitis, an archaeologist of the kind called 'amateurs', has found others like them in North Africa, particularly on the island of Jerba.

And the connection between Tiahuanaco[67] and Phoenicia-Egypt fits in exactly with my views and the new ideas expressed by unconventional archaeologists.

One final point also deserves attention: Heinrich Schliemann, Paul Schliemann and Christos Mavrothalassitis all make their discoveries converge on a single, hidden truth: Atlantis, the cradle of our civilisation.

The Strange Christos Mavrothalassitis

Heinrich Schliemann believed in Homer and discovered Troy. Christos Mavrothalassitis believed in what was told to him by his father, a Mediterranean sailor, and he now has one of the world's finest collections not only of Etruscan pottery dating from three thousand years ago and more, but also of Atlantean coins from before the Deluge. He may even have discovered ancient Poseidonis.

In 1922, while cruising off the Tunisian coast south of the Gulf of Gabès, Christos's father stopped his 280-ton, two-masted ship and had a long discussion with the men aboard, who were divers like himself. Christos was twelve years old. He listened to his father speaking of Plato and a submerged city that he and his divers had seen just below the ship.

'That's where Poseidonis is!' the old sailor said forcefully.

For twenty-five years Christos sailed all over the Mediterranean, which means that he knows it as well as anyone in the world, and his awakened curiosity was always on the lookout for anything related to the fabulous continent described by Plato.

In 1947 he found an ancient document showing the island of Jerba set into the African mainland but surrounded by a channel that extended into the desert. He remembered that his father maintained that Jerba had been the end of the route leading from Atlantis to the Mediterranean, which was then closed off at what is now the Strait of Gibraltar. Finally, the marvellous accident that had put Heinrich Schliemann on the trail of the Atlanteans and their orichalcum coins was reproduced with Christos on Jerba.

One day an old Berber hermit became friends with him and told him the location of the cemetery of 'the first ancestors of our race'. It was in Tripolitania; the information was precise, marked on a map. After a night and a day at sea, Christos reached the site. He found the landmarks described by the Berber and began digging in the sand.

Two days later he uncovered graves containing pottery similar to that of Tiahuanaco and the Schliemann collection. But he also found something of much greater value: coins made of an unknown white metal.

The miracle of Troy was repeated, as though Christos Mavrothalassitis, by a mysterious decree of destiny, had become Heinrich Schliemann's successor and spiritual heir.

Orichalcum Coins

When the Berber had learned of the successful outcome of the expedition – and received his share of coins and pottery – he revealed the location of Atlantean temples and more graves. For his part, Christos had gathered enough information to reconstruct the history of the whole Mediterranean region before the Deluge.

Despite his friendship for me, he could not tell me everything about the secret that binds him to the Berber hermit. I do know, however, that the Atlantean cemetery is in Tripolitania. That is where Christos found the pottery and white metal coins, which are now safely stored in a Marseilles bank. But he also made fruitful excavations in Benghazi and Egypt, and even on Jerba.

'The documents I have in Marseilles,' he told me, 'have given me a few certainties. For example, I know that the level of the Mediterranean rose a hundred and thirty-five feet after the Deluge. I know the exact course of the Atlantean maritime route that connected the Atlantic and the Mediterranean through Africa. I have a map of Atlantis that was made before the destruction of the continent.'

'Do you mean,' I asked in surprise, 'that you have written documents twelve thousand years old?'

'Yes, and you've seen them: my orichalcum coins!'

It is true: those rare, unique coins are actually engraved documents depicting scenes from the life of the Atlanteans and, to some extent, the history of the ancient world. They have suffered from their long stay in the desert sand, but they are not oxidised. Their relief has been diminished, however, and the details must be seen through a magnifying glass.

Hèlène and the Atlantean Space Rocket

One of the coins bears a picture of horses, and it is well known that those animals were venerated by the Atlanteans and their last survivors, the Celts. On one horseshoe-shaped coin, the head of a horse can be distinctly seen, wearing a bridle and a bit, which overturns our previous knowledge on the subject. On others, my friend Christos has identified fantastic drawings related to atomic energy and the conquest of space.

One coin, found on Jerba by his granddaughter Hélène, shows on one side what can only be described as a space rocket, with a splayed base and a nose equipped with a kind of radar. On the other side is an astronaut's cockpit with two antennae. The astronaut's head is clearly shown inside the cockpit.

Since Christos Mavrothalassitis is now writing a book on Atlantis as seen through images left by the Atlanteans, it would not be fair for me to say much more on the subject at this time, but it is undeniable that he seems to have cleared up a great mystery. His coins, made of a white, rustproof metal, which there is good reason to identify as the Atlantean orichalcum, tell of a civilisation which at the very least knew the horse, the bridle, the bit and spacecraft like our own rockets. The civilisation developed in a vast land situated in the Atlantic, between Africa, Europe and America.

My friend Christos may be mistaken in his interpretation, of course, but he can produce strong evidence in his favour. One coin showing the geographical image of Atlantis is made of two metals: a white one for the sea, a copper-coloured one for the land. Strange . . .

Conventional French archaeologists have shown no interest in Christos's discoveries; but German archaeologists are urging him to sell his precious collection,[58] just as Americans are urging Emile Fradin to sell (at an incredibly high price!) the even more precious collection of the Glozel Museum. France has already lost the treasure of Troy; how much longer can we expect the patriotism of Christos Mavothalassitis and Emile Fradin to hold out?

The treasure of the Atlanteans is at Marseilles, in a safe place. It could be the subject of a wonderful exhibition, but Christos, even though he has risked his life a hundred times to gather his collection, is afraid! Afraid of being robbed, dishonoured, perhaps even killed!

That same fear has gripped Sanchuniathon, Heinrich Schliemann, Paul Schliemann, Emile Fradin and all the other great discoverers, and it is justified because there are those who will stop at nothing to make sure that the historical truth of mankind is not made public. For that purpose millions of people have already been slaughtered, tons of manuscripts have been burned, acres of parchments have been erased . . . What is a man's life worth when he becomes a troublemaker?

Even so, Christos Mavrothalassitis is now preparing his book, just as Paul Schliemann prepared to divulge his discoveries . . .

Chapter 14

ODDITIES

There are anomalies that puzzle those who study the history of civilisations. People who lived four thousand years ago did not have the wheelbarrow or the steam engine, yet their scientific knowledge sometimes surpassed that of the twentieth century. Did they study a science parallel to ours? Did they operate by magic? Were they aware of secrets known to our Superior Ancestors? These questions remain shrouded in mystery.

Needles, hooks and scrapers made of cold-hammered copper were recently discovered at the archaeological site of Cayonu in southeastern Turkey. They are said to be about nine thousand years old.

The Athens Museum has an astronomical clock fifty-five hundred years old which some fishermen took out of their nets in 1955. It is wound with a key and it indicates the months, the times of the rising and setting of the sun and stars, the phases of the moon and the movement of the planets.

In *Moeurs et Coutumes des Musulmans*, Professor E. F. Gautier notes that in Bourlet's algebra textbook, still used in French schools, there are little problems borrowed from a Chinese manual from the second millennium B.C. These problems presuppose knowledge of the theorem of the square of the hypotenuse, whose discovery is generally attributed to Pythagoras.

The Mayas Invented Soccer

The siphon, which was not known in Europe until the

sixteenth century, was used by the Incas in their irrigation systems.

In one of his books on ancient South America, Abbé Brasseur de Bourbourg reproduced a letter from an archaeologist who wondered at 'the slender gold and silver statues, empty inside' that were made by the Indians. 'I held one of them,' he wrote, 'that was a kind of mummy. I could see no solder on it. We also admired dishes with eight faces, alternately gold and silver, without any solder, and cast-iron fish whose scales were mixed with gold and silver. The Indians were also well versed in the art of enamelling that was sought so long by Bernard Palissy.'

Practically speaking, rubber has been used in Europe only since 1736, but the sixteenth-century conquerors of Peru saw objects that the natives had made of rubber: balls, syringes, sandals, bracelets.

In his book *Histoire de Saint-Domingue* (1730), Charlevoix speaks of the *batos*, or ball made of a strong, light and elastic material, which the Mayan Indians used in their games several centuries before the English 'invented' soccer (which was actually the French *soule*).

My friend Gregori B, restorer of the religion of the Incan sun, writing in *Le Soleil Inca*, the fascinating bulletin he publishes, reveals that in the ancient Peruvian empire scientists had more advanced knowledge than those in Europe. They used a device called the *quilpi*, which is translated as 'mirror with concave and convex glasses' or 'optical instrument for seeing far away'.

Cuyo Lamps

Incan surgeons performed operations – on the skull, for example – with perfectly precise stitches. It is now known that they lighted the inside of human tissues by means of a penetrating light produced by an insect called the cuyo.

The cuyo is a glowworm that emits a kind of harmless X-ray. The light it gives off is green, and Gregori B writes, referring to the legends of Tiahuanaco, that 'the luminous cuyo was brought by our mother Orejona when she came from the planet Venus in a spacecraft brighter than the sun.'

It is interesting to note that the glowworms, about two inches long, secrete substances called luciferin and luciferase. Again the planet Venus, personified in the West by Lucifer!

For two thousand years alchemists and occultists have vainly sought the secret of the mysterious eternal lamps mentioned by Maspero, but the Incas had something even better: their lamps with domesticated cuyos gave a light that was not only permanent but was also able to pass through opaque bodies. These lamps were so bright that they made it possible to see at a distance of sixty yards.

The Mystery of the Kneaded Stones

At Amélie-les-Bains, in the Pyrénées-Orientales district of France, an enigma is posed by some hard sandstone rocks in a public park. They bear imprints in the shape of small hands that seem to have been pressed into the rocks as if they were soft clay. They are said to be real handprints.

'Impossible!' exclaim rationalists. 'A flesh-and-blood hand can't be pressed into stone.'

At Zazliai, Lithuania, a granite rock is venerated because it bears footprints to which a wonderous origin is attributed.

'Nothing but a legend!' say rationalists.

In the museum of Cochabamba, Bolivia, there are granite blocks with very distinct handprints in them. It is obvious that hands sank into the stone as easily as a foot sinks into mud. 'They're "touched stones",' say the learned curator, Dr Ibarra Grasso. 'It's impossible to explain how the miracle took place, but the fact is that hands kneaded the granite and left their imprints in it. The phenomenon eludes reason, of course, but it's rational to accept an obvious fact.'

Gregori B, who knows many secrets but does not reveal them to everyone, explained the miracle of kneaded stones to me.[59]

'Ancient builders,' he said, 'knew an herb by means of which they could make hard sandstone, granite and diorite completely malleable. They cut their building blocks out of softened stone and the blocks then hardened in the sun like clay.'

In Peru there are many stones bearing footprints and handprints.

The Stone of Asmodeus

Asmodeus is known in literature as the demon of carnal love. Poor Asmodeus! He was undoubtedly given that bad reputation because he was an Ase, an Aryan god, like Azalel, but that is beside the point here.

His father was Tubalcain, son of Lamech, and according to tradition he was the first to forge iron and brass. Legend also says that he tried to dethrone Solomon but was finally vanquished, which gives a moral ending to the story.

The Hebrews regarded him as the prince of demons and impurity. As an example of his cleverness they reported that when Solomon forced him to work on the temple in Jerusalem he finished building it without using a hammer, an axe or any other metal tool; he used only a certain stone that cut other stones as a diamond cuts glass. Unfortunately the secret of that stone, like the secret of the herb that made granite malleable, has been lost in the mists of legend.

The Baalbek Bottle

A mysterious bottle, endowed with powers as extraordinary as those of the stone of Asmodeus, attracted a great deal of attention, in occult circles at least, at the beginning of this century. It was hermetically closed and seemed to contain a liquid. It had been found in a necropolis at Kerak, near Baalbek, where there are still ruins of a temple dedicated to Baal.

Mr Eddet, the owner of the land, had a silkworm-breeding house whose foundations he wanted to strengthen. At a certain depth the workmen uncovered an enormous stone that served as the door of a room with a vaulted ceiling. They moved the stone aside, went into the tomb and found a solid gold tray with the bottle standing on it. Urns were arranged symmetrically around the tray and the tomb gave the impression of having been made for the sole purpose of sheltering the mysterious bottle.

The urns contained gold coins; the workmen took them, but Mr Eddet was able to keep the bottle and have it examined by Maspero. The eminent Egyptologist declared that it was the only one of its kind and that it dated from before the time of Christ. Eddet took several photographs of it before placing it in the vault of the Beirut bank. Since then, no one knows what became of it, but rumour claims that it contained either the blood of Christ or the Philosopher's Stone.

The Powers of the Invisible

In France and America, experiments have recently been made on the strange ways in which the invisible can act on the subconscious mind.

During a colour television programme in the United States an advertising message for red toilet soap (no brand was specified) was projected at the rate of one image every four seconds. The images were inserted in an ordinary film, a Western, that was projected at twenty-four images per second.

It has been determined that the eye does not see continuous movement when a film is projected at a rate slower than fifteen images per second. To leave a margin of certainty, films are usually projected at twenty-four images per second.

If a filmed Western has a proportion of twenty-three

images relating to the plot plus one image advertising red soap, it will seem normal to the viewer. His eye will see the twenty-three images of that plot but remain insensitive to the twenty-fourth. His subconscious mind, however, will register the isolated, invisible image and he will unconsciously respond to the advertisement. This was proved in the United States because the sale of red soap increased considerably during the period of the experiment.

It is thus possible not only to broadcast invisible advertising on television, but also to exert indiscernible pressure on personal choice, and therefore to direct public opinion. The same thing can perhaps be done with sound; if it is not possible now, it will be some day.

Antigravity Cavorite

Like Jules Verne, H. G. Wells was a great initiate who, by projecting himself into the future, perceived scientific developments, some of which have already been achieved.

During a dinner of the Round Table group,[60] my friend Melchior de Lisle recalled the alloy known as 'cavorite', invented by Wells in one of his stories, which by blocking gravity enabled Professor Cavor to go to the moon.

There is a group in the United States, with an office and a publication, devoted to research intended to produce the miraculous alloy. It was Edison, a remarkable inventor but a poor theorist, who suggested the idea of founding the group to a millionaire inclined towards eccentricity, and research has continued since then.

At the end of the last century the group believed that cavorite has been surpassed by an invention that created a great stir at the time, but now seems to have faded into oblivion: the Keely apparatus.

Keely Conquers Gravity

In 1887 a sensational experiment was performed in a laboratory in Philadelphia before twelve magnates of the mining industry. An unknown inventor named Keely disintegrated blocks of gold-bearing quartz in a few seconds by placing them in contact with a small machine that he held in his hand. Each block crumbled into fine dust in which particles of gold could easily be disintegrated. The experiment was successfully repeated in the Catskill Mountains, with the result that the magnates bought abandoned mines, which had repercussions on the gold market.

Such was the story that reached France in the last century. It aroused little interest among scientists, but theosophical circles, at least, were strongly impressed by it, since *Le Lotus*, the journal of the French Theosophical Society, published a long article on the subject in its issue of September, 1888. I will give the main points of that article below.

Keely was a mysterious, reticent man. His knowledge of the exact sciences was relatively small but he undoubtedly knew much more about the theory and practice of the supernatural. He had made many inventions and his personal powers were extraordinary. He once wrapped a wire around an iron cylinder weighing several tons, then connected the wire to a machine he had invented. When an electric current was passed through it, he lifted the cylinder with one finger and carried it as easily as if it were a cork.

'He transported in this way, with one hand,' says the article in *Le Lotus*, 'a machine supplying the power of five hundred horses, from one end of his workshop to the other, without even making a scratch on the floor. The astounded engineers said that they could not have transported it without a derrick, which would have required removing the roof of the workshop.

'He recently applied his force to optics. By means of three wires placed across the lens of a microscope, he made its magnifying power equal to that of the great telescope in the Lick Observatory, the largest in the world.

'Why have our astronomers and opticians not hurried to examine Keely's microscope?

'Mrs Bloomfield More wrote in the Philadelphia *Inquirer* of January 20, 1888, that he had so little concern with financial gain that if it were not for his obligations to the Keely Motor Company, whose aid he has accepted, the secrets he has so closely guarded would by now have been made public knowledge.'

Other witnesses saw Keely spin a hollow globe at 'terrifying speed' and testified that his microscope made it possible to 'see the functioning of an animalcule's heart'. He also invented a telescope with which one could see 'any object with an area of more than ten square feet on the surface of the moon'.

A Strange Attitude

In March, 1888, Dr Franz Hartmann came to Philadelphia from Italy at Keely's invitation. Keely granted him only two short interviews and explained the principle of his invention in terms whose meaning was known only to himself, so that Hartmann admitted he had understood nothing.

During the second interview, Keely's assistants advised Hartmann not to interrupt him with questions, but only to sit at his feet and listen. The explanation was extremely confused; Keely spoke of such things as the 'etheric force,' the '*prima materia* of alchemists' and the 'accord of the mass, sum and substance of those elementary forces which correspond to the vibratory wave.'[61] Finally, having failed to produce the miracles he had announced, he showed Hartmann his 'disintegrator'. Hartmann later wrote that, from the way the apparatus functioned, he was convinced Keely was able to make a wheel turn by means of sound.

Even if we accept that statement we must admit that the evidence given was far from supporting the wondrous feats certified by certain anonymous 'witnesses'.

Finally, I will give M. Gautier-Walter's opinion on that strange affair:

> 'Keely's invention was authentic,' he told me, 'but, like the revelations of initiates, it was premature, and it was therefore counteracted by decision of the four Masters of

the World who have their headquarters in their palace in the Gobi Desert, at the place where the White Island was once located.'

The Vibratory Disintegrator

Nothing in the whole affair was ever proven to be either true or false, but it is at least interesting to consider the characteristics of the device called a 'vibratory disintegrator', which was small enough to be held in the hand. The article in *Le Lotus* describes it as follows:

> It is a hollow ring suspended from a hook, with eighteen resonators inside it. On its surface are vibrating needles or rods arranged in a circle, in decreasing order of size, on three external resonators connected by wires. Suspended in the middle is a second ring containing two visible circular rows of graduated pipes like those of an organ. At the very centre is a disc spinning at very high speed.
>
> Attached to the lower part of the apparatus is a small hollow globe to which the wire that conducts force is connected. This wire is made of silver, gold and platinum.
>
> The disintegrator is charged by pinching one of the tuning needles a single time with one's fingernails, and the force developed is, practically speaking, infinite.
>
> This apparatus can disintegrate all matter.

The Levitation of the Saints

In our time, some interesting work on antigravity and levitation is being done in Toulouse, France, by Jean Goujon (whom I have no intention of placing in the same category as Keely).

Goujon centres his research on the properties of sources that emit coherent waves (the diaphragm of a loudspeaker, for example) when all points of their surface vibrate in phase. Numerous experiments have enabled him to state that such sources create around themselves an attracting field identical to a gravitational field. It would take too long to explain the theory mathematically, but it results in this formula: a surface with an area of one square metre and a linear vibration of 350 metres per second can lift five tons.

Starting from this quasi-postulate, Goujon attacks the problem that haunted Keely and H. G. Wells's Professor Cavor: levitation.

It is hard to sum up the principles of such research in a few lines without seeming terribly heretical to readers with scientific training, but here is what I have retained from Goujon's presentation of his work:

> If, by means of an appropriate screen, we suppress transmission of the coherent sound wave towards the ground, the resultant is directed downward and tends to make the whole system rise . . .
>
> A simultaneous combination of sound, electromagnetic and 'primary' waves should be able to cause levitation or antigravity.

This theory might explain the mysterious force of the levitations performed by saints and magicians.

According to Jean Goujon, the subject does not act from inside himself, but from outside, by the effect of a 'soul wave', an idea that will violently clash with the views of rationalists.

Marcel Pagès and Antigravity

Marcel Pagès is undoubtedly the antigravity technician who is most renowned in the world of research. According to Umberto Bonfiglioli, secretary general of the European Centre of Gravitation Research, no one else has gone as far as Marcel Pagès in study of the problem.

Pagès was first attracted by the combined forces of gyroscopes and centrifugal force which increase in proportion to the square of velocity, developing enormous tensions in a rotating mass. He worked on the problem with the engineer Emile Drouet, and in 1921 he made a disc fly by antigravity.

He concerned himself for a time with Jean Goujon's theory, but concluded that although results are appreciable in air, effects in a vacuum require the use of enormous powers.

In the near future, though probably not in the next few years, flight by means of propellers, jet engines and rockets will be made obsolete by antigravity.

Yet it seems that antigravitational craft are already flying across our skies: the enigmatic 'unidentified flying objects' (UFOs).

Chapter 15

WE ARE EXTRATERRESTRIALS

Unidentified flying objects are being seen in the sky but we cannot say what they are, and such sightings tend to overheat the imagination, stir up delusions and cast doubt on the reality of the phenomenon.

It is hard to accept the idea that civilisations much more advanced than ours should play hide-and-seek with farmers in their fields and motorists on lonely roads. It seems reasonable to assume that if there were contact between two planets it would have a rational, scientific form and not a foolish one – but it may be that a form appears foolish to us only because it is beyond our understanding.

Suggestion Expeditions

One of the many hypotheses that can be formulated on the subject of unidentified flying objects is that of suggestion expeditions with the mission of preparing our minds for the coming of extraterrestrials.

It may be pointed out that the preparation is extraordinarily long, since it has been going on for centuries, but is that a valid objection? Our earthly notion of time may be completely different from that of beings who inhabit planetary systems far distant from ours. If the insects known as ephemerids had a more highly developed intelligence, they would feel disdain for the slow, deliberate entomologist who studies them under a microscope for a whole day – that is, half their lifetime.

The problem can also be considered from another viewpoint: even at a speed greater than that of light, a journey between two planets thousands of light-years apart may be a difficult, hazardous venture with a very small chance of success. If so, it may be that, for reasons unknown to us, contacts abort at the level of our atmosphere, or perhaps even at the surface of our planet.

Some commentators have advanced the theory that extraterrestrials are already among us, but in a multi-dimensional universe that never coincides with our three-dimensional world. They would thus be invisible, beyond the perception of all our senses, yet omnipresent and capable of helping us, by guiding the research of scientists, for example, and inspiring artists and writers. Even though they had the power to do so, they would have no desire to integrate themselves into our inferior world. They would use us as producers of certain forms of energy necessary to their subsistence, while waiting for us to raise our intellectual level to the point of becoming their equals.

Are we still at the stage of sleep or external suggestion, as certain philosophers maintain?

If the truth about extraterrestrials were of that order, it would be hard to understand the nature and meaning of the phenomenon as it is now observed. Why those flashes, those lights moving across the sky and – perhaps – those landings, if the visitors from space operate in the invisible?

When they came to our planet in the past they did not behave like shy, fearful explorers, ready to flee at the slightest breath of wind; on the contrary, they made a spectacular entrance into earthly social life and brought important elements of civilisation and science.

Twentieth-century people are disconcerted and confused; they cannot make sense of that illogical, incoherent situation in which seemingly sincere testimony is mingled with wildly implausible reports.

The same uncertainty was experienced at many different times in the past.

Twelve thousand and five thousand years ago, astronauts came to our planet; there is no longer any doubt of that, but for the past three thousand years the sky has been mysteriously haunted by flying objects. Some of them have secretly landed while others, the famous 'clouds', have played an important part in human history without landing, but it seems that no extraterrestrial has been willing to manifest his presence publicly.

Since our problem is the same as that of our ancestors, I believe that a study of ancient UFOs may bring a little order into the confusion in which we now find ourselves.

The Tulli Papyrus

Among the papers of the late Professor Alberto Tulli, former director of the Egyptian museum of the Vatican, his brother Monsignor Gustavo found a papyrus in bad condition, dating from the Middle Kingdom. He gave it to Prince Boris de Racheweltz, an eminent Egyptologist, and asked him to translate it. Despite the gaps in the text, it told a strange story:

> . . . in the course of the third month of winter in the year 22, at the sixth hour of the day, the scribes of the House of Life saw a circle of fire in the sky. [Although] it had no head, the breath of its mouth had a foul smell. Its body had the length and width of a staff and it had no voice.
>
> The hearts of the scribes were filled with terror and confusion and they lay face down . . . [gap] . . . they came to tell the pharaoh. His Majesty ordered . . . [gap] . . . was examined . . . [gap] . . . and he meditated on what had happened and was recorded on papyruses in the House of Life. When a few days had passed, these things [circles of fire] became more numerous than ever in the sky. They shone more brightly than the rays of the sun and extended to the limits of the four pillars of the skies . . . [gap]
>
> The position of these circles of fire in the sky was all-powerful. The army looked at them with the pharaoh in the middle.
>
> It was after supper. Then the circles of fire rose higher in the sky towards the south. Fish and birds fell from the sky. It was a wonder unknown since the founding of this

> country [Egypt]. And the pharaoh had incense brought, in order to make peace on the earth . . . [gap] . . . and what had happened the pharaoh ordered that it be written in the annals of the House of Life . . . [gap] . . . so that it would be remembered forever.

I may be accused of holding reports from the past in higher regard than those of our own time. I freely admit it, but it must be granted that it is easier to believe a report sanctioned by a pharaoh's edict than one that simply describes the landing of anonymous extraterrestrials in a field of daisies!

Shining Beams and Flying Men

Pliny the Elder speaks of 'three moons' that appeared during the consulate of Domitius and Faunius, 'nocturnal suns', 'burning shields' and 'stars that dart in all directions not without causing violent atmospheric eddies'.

He also mentions 'shining beams' which appeared at the time of the naval defeat that cost the Lacedaemonians control of Greece. It is not absurd to believe that those flying machines may have helped one side to the detriment of the other – after all, the 'cloud' of the Lord repeatedly brought victory or good fortune to the Hebrews.

Traditions of the Indians of Minnesota and Canada, reported by George Hunt Williams, say that round, silent vehicles came down to their lakes before the arrival of the Europeans. When the conquerors came, the aviators disappeared with their machines, after saying that they would return.

In Europe there are no documents on aviation before the eighteenth century, but such documents are not rare in Asia and they abound in Central America. The Palenque slab, for example, bears an image of a space rocket. And only an incorrigible Doubting Thomas can fail to recognise the flying machines in the Mayan codices and manuscripts.

Those Strange Nephilim

The word *nephilim* in the Bible is usually translated as 'giants'. In Genesis 6:1–2 we read that the 'sons of the gods' – or astronauts – 'saw that the daughters of men were beautiful; so they took for themselves such women as they chose.' Then, in Verse 4: 'In those days, when the sons of the gods had intercourse with the daughters of men and got children by them, the Nephilim were on earth. They were the heroes of old, men of renown.'

The meaning is clear: the Nephilim, by breeding with the women of Armenia, Iran, the Caucasus, the Rocky Mountains and the Andes, engendered children who were stronger and more intelligent than native earthly children.

But the translation of *nephilim* as 'giants' is only approximate. According to Vaschalde, the word means 'giants' or 'marvellous beings'; literally, 'makers of wonders'.

And those Nephilim must have come back to earth five thousand years ago, in the time of the Phoenician Baal, because Moses admonished the Hebrews about them (Deuteronomy 32: 16–17): 'They roused his jealousy with foreign gods and provoked him with abominable practices. They sacrificed to foreign demons that are no gods, gods who were strangers to them; they took up with new gods from their neighbours, gods whom your fathers did not acknowledge.'

It is easy to understand Moses' anger: he had to hide the identity of the ancient gods, the Nephilim who had come from another planet, and make the Hebrews worship a single, abstract, unknowable God – and now Baal and Astarte had come on the scene! And the Hebrews, like the peoples of Asia Minor, struck by the arrival of those extraterrestrial initiators, had begun worshipping them. They sacrificed to those 'new gods' whom their fathers had, of course, never worshipped. The newcomers were also Nephilim, 'makers of wonders,' but they were 'new'. Here we have the essential point: why should anyone change gods when he already has the right one?

An Astronaut Named Azazel

Finally converted to the single God imposed on them by Moses, the Hebrews used all sorts of ruses to combat the 'newcomers' and their worshippers, foremost of whom were Azazel and the Philistines. They discredited them in the Bible, which was a sure way to make them repugnant, and presented them as disciples of the devil.[62]

The true identity of Azazel is given in the Book of Enoch, after the landing of the angel-astronauts:

Chapter VII, Verse 9: 'Here are the names of their leaders: Samyaza . . . Urakabarameel, Akibeel, Tamiel, Ramuel, Daviel, Azkeel . . . Asazel, Arazeal.'

The extraterrestrials cohabited with earthly women and taught them sorcery and enchantment.

Chapter VIII, Verse 1: 'Azazel also taught men to make swords, knives, shields, breastplates, mirrors . . . '

Azazel was thus the great initiator of mankind, but he was also the great seducer who made women coquettish and adulterous and, rightly or wrongly, the Hebrews considered him responsible for the deterioration of morality, and consequently for the Deluge that punished it. To institute their single God, they had to eliminate this troublemaker, which they did, but not without certain misgivings, since Azazel, alone with the Almighty, benefited from the offering of a goat during the ceremony of expiation.

The Hebrews had good reasons for ceasing to regard the angel-astronaut as a god, but they were wrong to efface him from the history of civilisation. That was their mistake. They felt guilty about it for thousands of years and secretly tried to atone for it by rendering a certain homage to him. It is important to note that Azazel is the name of the being of whom the Hebrews asked remission of their sins.

The Philistines and Baal

Other enemies of the Hebrews were the Philistines and Baal and Ishtar, gods of Phoenicia and Assyro-Babylonia.

The *Encyclopédie* says that 'the Philistines are badly

mistreated in the Bible, which is quite naturally explained by the courageous defence they opposed to the enterprises of the Hebrews; nothing is more hateful to conquerors than a nation that resists the servitude they want to impose on it.'

Like the Hebrews, the Philistines were Aryans, but they continued worshipping the gods of their ancestors, the very gods who had to be eliminated for the sake of the single God. As they had done with Azazel, the Hebrews accused the enemy gods – Dagon (the initiator identical to Oannes), Baal, Moloch, etc. – of all sorts of crimes. Hence the hatred, in the Bible, of the 'star', which among the peoples of Asia Minor never represented the sun, but the pre-eminent heavenly body. Always the diabolical Venus!

And, like the Hebrews, the ancient civilisations of Egypt and Greece maintained a conspiracy of silence or slander around Baal and the astronaut Azazel in order to give their own ancestors the usurped title of first initiators.

We Are Extraterrestrials

We know that Venus was the homeland of the astronauts of five thousand years ago, but where did the first expedition come from, the expedition of Azazel?

What was the origin of the pre-Deluge people who founded Atlantis and Mu?

Were they descended from apes, as prehistorians claim? No links connecting man to an animal ancestor have ever been found. If any had been discovered, it would be known and museums would give proof of it. Look for such links in Paris, Saint-Germain-en-Laye, Les Eyzies, Berlin, London, Tokyo – your search will be unsuccessful.

Yet there are many known links that connect most animals to their ancestors: the crocodile to the snake, the snake to the fish, the dog to the wolf, the wild pig to the domesticated pig, and so on.

But for man: nothing! Or at least nothing connecting man to a lower animal. Prehistorians do have a few links, the only ones that are genuine: *relatively recent skulls of people more intelligent than we are*, since their cranial capacity of 1,600 cubic centimetres is larger than ours, which average only 1,550!

A sensible man would conclude logically that we have no known animal ancestor and that our present human type seems to have descended from an ancient, more highly evolved type. Yes, that is what a sensible man would think, but not a prehistorian!

Furthermore, since the world has existed for a length of time that we cannot even conceive, I am led to think that if fossil men do not exist on earth, they must exist somewhere else.

If I had stated that heretical hypothesis a few centuries ago, I would have been burned at the stake!

Hundreds of ancient texts clearly show that extra-terrestrials came to our planet in the past, and I believe that the present problem of unidentified flying objects should be studied in the light of the historical data we have on the subject.

That is being done by André Castou, an ardent investigator who lives in Normandy.

André Castou's Idea

At first sight Castou's idea is rather astonishing, but judge for yourself:

> There are two kinds of flying saucers [he writes], large ones and small ones, occupied respectively by giants and dwarfs.
>
> Flying saucers do not come to observe what is happening on earth; they spy on each other.
>
> An enormous saucer is piloted by Pan in person; the leader of the small flying saucers, the most numerous, is Gwyon (or Korrig the Dwarf).
>
> There is antagonism between the giants and the dwarfs. Pan has on his side Silenus, Saturos, Azazel and the ancient monsters. The saucer carrying Pan gives off bright red flashes, in the middle of which is a ball of copper-coloured fire.

Castou bases his view on the fact that the pilots of flying

saucers seen in our time are described in the same way as the giants and dwarfs of mythology.

Spending his nights watching the sky, he sees many flying objects that would otherwise escape observation. It can be said of him that he is one of the 'Vigilant Ones' that sacred writings urge us all to be.

'There are no orthotenic lines,' he says. 'Flying saucers move in all directions.'

It goes without saying that his ideas are opposed by 'saucer fans' as well as their adversaries.

How could mythological and therefore nonexistent beings come through the centuries to our time and take part in a phenomenon whose scientific nature surpasses, for the moment, our most daring knowledge? We might as well believe that we will soon see centaurs galloping across our meadows, that mermaids will sun themselves on our beaches, that a sphinx will begin asking riddles of passengers in our railroad stations.

Let me add to Castou's case the fact that he often sees ten, twenty or even thirty flying saucers in a single night!

As far as the public is concerned, the case is already closed: Castou is a victim of hallucinations. For my part, however, I am inclined toward a more fantastic but also more logical explanation: Castou is a medium and he speaks in allegories; he does not express his own conscious thoughts, but those of entities that act through him.

Gwyon the Dwarf

What Castou says is most likely false in a literal sense, but in a spiritual sense it has overtones of ineffable truth. Pan, Azazel and Gwyon are only resurgences of the original adventure in which the Masters of the World, probably because of the shape of their interstellar spacecraft, were called dragons and flying serpents. With the dwarfs, elves and Korrigans represented by Gwyon, the theme of clairvoyance was pursued with the same rigour.

In Celtic mythology, Gwyon is the initiated dwarf, a personification of human knowledge, the inventor of 'the means of perpetuating thought through time and space'. He came from the Milky Way, which the ancient Celts called the City of Gwyon, or Ker Gwyon, and his father was said to be Don, who lived in the constellation of Cassiopeia. All these details may be clues.

Gwyon was thus similar to Azazel and Prometheus; like them, he was an astronaut, but he was *much smaller*. That was the only difference. It may be a racial difference, and may be part of the explanation of the war between Atlantis and Mu.

The people of Atlantis were probably large and those of Mu small, since statues of giants are found on Easter Island, and, as is shown by the statues of Corsica and Sardinia, a vanquished people does not make images of itself to oppose to the victorious enemy, but magnified, exaggerated images of the conquerors themselves. The little men of Easter Island thus sculpted giants of the enemy race, and not representatives of their own race.

It is these reasons, linked to the problem of unidentified flying objects, that make me take André Castou's views into consideration. Phenomena identical to those observed in the past are now occurring again, or will do so in the near future. As a clairvoyant or medium, Castou has a presentiment of them and announces them in allegorical form, but without being consciously involved in the operation. That is what I mean when I say that occult forces act through him.

Life Is Possible on Venus

Astrophysicists have recently ceased to be certain that Venus is uninhabited. According to Professor Alexander Lebedinsky of the Soviet Union, the surface temperature of the planet must be about 110 degrees Fahrenheit, even though radioelectric measurements indicate 600 to 700 degrees.

Similar observations can be made on the relatively cool surfaces of the gas tubes used in neon signs: the radioelectric radiation of those tubes is equivalent to several thousand degrees.

Lebedinsky assumes that in the lower layers of the Venusian atmosphere there are latent electric phenomena similar to those of gas tubes, because of the planet's slow rotation (it turns on its axis only once in every 247 earthly days). On Earth, where rotation is more rapid, electric atmospheric phenomena take on a stormy character.

The physicists William Plummer and John Strong believe that Venus may have vast areas with bearable temperatures and that man may be able to live there.

It should also be pointed out that climatic conditions on Venus five thousand years ago, or a few centuries before its stabilisation in the solar system, may have been quite different from what they are now, and more favourable to life.

In any case, it would be arbitrary to ignore all the evidence in favour of the idea that Venus was the base from which ancient astronauts came to Earth. The Phoenicians, Assyro-Babylonians, Mayas and Incas could not have conspired together to propagate a lie.

Extraterrestrial: Brains Without Bodies

In 1960 the United States inaugurated Project OZMA for the purpose of listening scientifically for any radio messages that might be sent by extraterrestrial civilisations.

Professor Huang of China, well known to American astronomers, feels that there are probably thousands of other inhabited planets.

Dr Freeman Dyson, a physicist at Princeton University, has stated the hypothesis that astronauts may have to live in a state of hibernation during long interstellar journeys. The astronomer Ronald Bracewell, more adventurous, believes that extraterrestrial civilisations may have created a race specially adapted to their mission as pioneers of the cosmos, a race of space messengers who might be described as brains without bodies and whose function is to gather as much information as possible on other civilisations.

Flying Saucers at Will

Despite the great amount of expensive research that has been done in their country, many Americans do not believe in flying saucers. Twelve American scientists have studied seven hundred and fifty sightings, and they have artificially reconstructed glows of the kind that were taken for UFOs; or so they claim. The glows are said to be phenomena of refraction, reflection or inversion. In the first two cases, a layer of cool air retransmits rays of light from a star to the earth. In inversion, a layer of warm air is compressed between two layers of cool air and acts like a glass surface.

Physicists of the University of North Carolina at Raleigh have created flying saucers at will, making them move singly or in groups and change direction, speed and shape.

These experiments are of great interest, even if they explain only the majority of luminous sightings, which must be the case.

It is certain that the sky is the scene of many strange but perfectly natural phenomena.

On August 15, 1854, one of them puzzled the little town of Jaroslau, Poland, as reported in this newspaper article:

> As the moon rose, it swung left and right and continued to do so more rapidly as it moved higher above the horizon. Suddenly it dropped with extraordinary speed to the line of the horizon, then rose with the same speed to the height it had previously reached.

It was probably a phenomenon of aberration well known to astronomers, which may also explain the famous 'sun miracle' at Fatima, assuming it was not an hallucination.

It is certain, however, that not all unidentified flying objects are hallucinations or atmospheric phenomena. As André Castou says with regret, few people study the problems effectively. It would be easy to set up a network of astronomical observatories all over the globe, but this has not been done.

'Flying saucer fans' make ineffectual investigations and

accept all sorts of wild tales as gospel truth. We are told that Martians have dark skin and blue eyes and are a thousand times more highly evolved than we are; that ten thousand brochures revealing the secrets of flying saucers have been destroyed by the American government; that in São Paolo, Brazil, a Martian gave a fisherman a calling card made of an unknown metal; that in Mexico whole crowds of people see flying saucers zooming across the sky at all hours of the day.

How can anyone believe such nonsense?

There is one line of inquiry that has never been pursued with regard to the many people who claim to have seen landings by Martians or 'little green men', and in my opinion it would be of great importance: those people should be asked what they ate and drank in the hours before the events they allegedly witnessed.

Many visions can surely be explained by hallucinogenic drugs. Aside from alcohol, a number of mushrooms, decoctions and unsuspected chemical combinations are the effective ingredients in initiatic potions capable of producing hallucinations. There are too many people who see flying saucers, elves, the Holy Virgin, Jesus Christ and even God himself!

Celestial Writing

Since the dawn of known times, people have claimed to read signs in the sky.

In an old book entitled *Lecture des Estoilles et de tout ce qui est en l'air*, the chronicler Jacques Gaffarel presents an amusing idea:

> Can we read anything in clouds and other atmospheric phenomena? Reading presupposes some sort of visible signs, whether it be letters, characters, marks, figures, sticks, torches, spears, javelins, knots, nets, colours, holes, points, animals or some other perceptible thing. All those signs or figures can be represented by clouds, and they can read in three ways: by known letters and characters, by hieroglyphs and by marks or signs.

Gaffarel assigned Hebrew letters to the stars, and he then had only to assemble them into words and sentences!

This method does not seem very promising in our time but it at least has the merit of suggesting an experiment that would consist in photographing the movements of luminous unidentified flying objects. These movements might be instructive if they proved to form signs, drawings or even letters. I cannot help thinking of the Zend and Sanskrit languages, which were said to have been derived from an unknown language brought from another planet by the ancestors of the ancient Aryans; or of Hebrew writing, if it was actually inspired by 'angels'.

The Mystery of the Little Green Men

The mysterious Mr N Y, who has sent me some interesting documentation on the extraterrestrials of Proxima Centauri (see *The Legacy of the Gods*), but who refuses to reveal his identity, maintains that the secret services of the major nations are aware of 'the existence of lens-shaped flying craft that are now being tested at several space research centres'.

He also offers an explanation of the strange little green men whom hundreds of people claim to have seen getting out of or into spacecraft:

> The aberration of light from a *vaidorge* (spacecraft used by the inhabitants of Proxima Centauri) as it emerges from contraction to appear in the expanding universe also produces its effect on astronauts when they come out of a spacecraft. The phenomenon can be compared to that which is caused by deformation in a concave mirror . . . That is what happens when one has the privilege of seeing beings come out of a contracting universe. Since light rays are then seventeen times less rapid than the event, the observer's eye registers images that have already passed for the experimenters (effect of distortion).
>
> Those whom you call 'little green Martians' are actually Baals (inhabitants of the planet Baavi in the

system of Proxima Centauri) who are perfectly well constituted, most of them being between six and a half and seven and a half feet in height.

N Y claims to be in contact with these extraterrestrials. His explanation of the 'little green men' is attractive because it reconciles seemingly contradictory reports.

The Little Men of Tibet

We are living in an era that is tragic but richer in fantastic events than any other historical period. The time has come when revelations will astonish men and disrupt their beliefs and faith.

By an odd coincidence – but is it really a coincidence? – the strangest discoveries are being made in the two areas where civilisation flourished before the Deluge: America and eastern Asia.

Space rockets in Tibet? Here is a story from Japan, as reported in the German magazine *Das Vegetarische Universum* and the Belgian magazine *Bufoi*:

Twenty-five years ago, in the caves of Baian Kara Ula, in the mountainous region of the border between Tibet and China, archaeologists discovered tablets of writing consisting of round, flat discs cut out of granite rocks by an unknown method. Near the caves were graves aligned in very precise order. The skeletons in them were identified as belonging to the race of the Dropas and Khams, whose members, about four feet three inches tall, could not be classified in any existing category. That race is totally different from the Chinese, Mongols and Tibetans.

Old Chinese legends tell of short, slender, yellow men who 'came from the clouds' and who because of their extreme ugliness – they had extraordinarily large heads and spindly bodies – were at first shunned, then finally massacred by 'men riding swift horses' (probably Mongols).

Analysis of the skeletons found at Baian Kara Ula indicated an age of about twelve thousand years. The first archaeological reports spoke of 'an extinct breed of apes'. This idea, applied to individuals who had dug graves and left a large number of stone implements, seemed so implausible that one of the men who had stated it, the archaeologist Chi Pu Tei, was severely taken to task by the press. He defended himself by maintaining that the discs with writing on them might have been brought to the caves by civilised people from an earlier time than the Dropas.

The Dropas Landed Twelve Thousand Years Ago

In 1965 Professor Tsum Um Nui resumed study of the problem and made some amazing discoveries.

Seven hundred and sixteen stone discs were found in the caves of Baian Kara Ula. Each of them had a hole in its centre, like our modern phonograph records. Starting from this hole was a double groove that ended at the outer edge of the disc, which makes the resemblance to a phonograph record still stronger.

After patient work, the Peking Academy of Prehistory elucidated the mystery of the discs, but the revelations they gave were so important that Professor Tsum Um Nui was only recently authorised to present a summary of them.

The discs bore a grooved writing which described the odyssey of space travellers at a time when, according to conventional doctrine, it was impossible for spacecraft to exist.

Here is part of the version published by Professor Tsum Um Nui:

> The Dropas came down from the sky in their aerial gliders. Ten times, until sunrise, men, women and children took refuge in caves. Finally they understood from signals that the visitors from the sky had peaceful intentions and the Dropas were able to approach them.

Other texts in grooved writing, attributed to the Khams, contained a kind of ballad that spoke of 'airships destroyed in the course of a landing in hostile mountains' and told how the astronauts were unable to build new ones because they did not have the necessary materials.

Discs that Will Soon Speak

But the revelations of the stone discs do not stop there. Chinese scientists cautiously scraped the precious objects and analysed the particles obtained. They contained a high percentage of cobalt and other metals. When the discs were tested with an oscillograph they set off an amazing rate of vibrations, as if they were charged with a great electrical force. It is thought that transforming them into a type of wave that is still unknown might reveal a message more valuable than that of the grooved writing.

Another discovery supports the idea of interplanetary travel: on the walls of the caves of Baian Kara Ula are engraved drawings representing the rising sun, the moon and the stars, linked to the earth by a myriad of dots showing the route travelled by the astronauts of twelve thousand years ago.

Not everything has yet been said about that fascinating mystery.

The Chinese government, which is still keeping secret the titanic pyramids of Shensi and the documents found in the monasteries of Lhasa, has for political reasons sequestered the speaking discs of the Tibetan astronauts.

Enigmatic objects fly across our sky; monuments whose purpose is unknown to us stand on the surface of our land, and beneath it are buried structures belonging to no known civilisation.

Mystery is all around us and neither our science nor our history can give an answer to it.

In spite of everything, man attempts to formulate explanations that will satisfy his curiosity, and in the face of opposition, silence or disapproval from those who do not want the veil to be lifted, he tries to break open the door that leads to knowledge of things which nature ripens in time and divulges only in small doses.

Documents are speaking, initiates are breaking the seals of tablets hidden in sanctuaries . . . Man will soon know much more about his unknown past.

I have opened books and solicited knowers, and other revelations have been announced. I hope the reader will look with unprejudiced eyes at what is only an honest attempt to lead him away from the sterility of official doctrine and make him realise that if the Masters of the World came to our planet in the past, the time of their return is near, or may already have come.

FOOTNOTES

Chapter 1

[1]Belisama, 'flamelike', is the planet Venus, which the Ancients described as having a 'mane of fire' because they saw it in the form of a comet. The Celtic goddess Belisama is therefore much more recent than Belinus, Esus or Teutates.

[2]The Hindu mathematician and astronomer Aryabhatta, who lived at the beginning of the Christian era, knew the rotation of the earth on its axis, the length of the year and the real causes of eclipses, and said that the light of the moon was borrowed from the sun. But the Vedas had stated these things two thousand years before him, and so had the sacred books of most ancient civilisations. The Druids taught a very precise cosmology and said that the universe had been formed by a primordial vibratory wave (represented by a serpent floating on water). According to Strabo, 'they [the Druids] claim to be able to fathom the mysteries of nature and foretell the upheavals that the universe must still undergo.'

[3]Contrary to legend, Emperor Constantine (280?–337) was a pagan. He did not protect the Christians and he recognised Christianity only for political reasons. He did not become converted until just before his death. It is said that during his struggle against his rival Maxentius he saw a luminous cross in the sky, bearing this inscription: *In hoc signo vinces* ('In this sign you shall conquer'). But this miracle is reported by no one but Eusebius.

Chapter 2

[4]This passage clearly implies that gods are human inventions. And the cosmology of the Hawaiian Island (see Chapter 6) states that men were born before the gods.

[5]This is highly significant. Technites was of an extra-

terrestrial race, since only Autochthon was earthly! The problem of interbreeding with beings from another planet is posed here.

[6]It is obviously Thoth who is being referred to here. Cf. the Norse god Thor.

[7]Hypsistos: the Most High. He is Jupiter Hypsistos Hesychius (Melchizedek, according to Valckanaer).

[8]The Latin version of his name is Saturn and the Orientals called him Bel or Baal. In Phoenician his name is Hil or Hel, notes Séguier de Saint-Brisson, who makes this important remark: 'Hil, Hel or Saturn has no relation to the sun. It seems likely that the city of Heliolopolis was a Greek fabrication of the god Saturn Hilo, or Heliolopolis, just as the Algabal of Emesa was Saturn mountain, mountain god or god Saturn.'

The Algabal of Emesa was a black stone whose relation to Saturn is mysterious but obvious. Why, if not for the purpose of deceiving, was that name falsified by changing it to Heliogabalus (from *helios*, 'sun')? The same procedure was successfully used in Peru and Mexico to change the Venusian cults into solar cults.

The primordial sky, say the documents consulted by Sanchuniathon, had four children: Saturn, Jupiter, Mars and Mercury. The fifth child, Astarte, or Venus, was born later. This is one more indication that the planet Venus did not exist in the solar system five thousand years ago.

[9]The Hebrews were initiated by the Egyptians and the Phoenicians, whose myths they borrowed and disguised. The creators of the world, the Elohim or gods, would seem to be the Phoenician heroes mentioned by Sanchuniathon.

[10]This seems to imply that they could have reigned elsewhere, and it evokes the question of intervention by beings from another planet, as in the Bible. Was it for this reason that Astarte wore the head of a bull? Astarte is Venus, Sanchuniathon points out. Venus the planet and the queen who travelled through the universe in a spacecraft. We must not forget, as Sanchuniathon says quite specifically, that Astarte was not a goddess, but a mortal creature. She therefore needed a spacecraft to explore the sky.

[11]This 'heavenly body' was a meteorite. The Temple of Tyre and most other Phoenician temples have a black or green stone, often conical in shape, representing a heavenly body

(Venus). The Syrian goddess Ashtoreth (Astarte) originally had the form of a conical stone. The Algabal, the sacred stone of Emesa in Phoenicia, was the stone of Venus, fraudulently related to sun worship under the name of Heliogabalus.

[12]Sanchuniathon is quite explicit: two wings are symbols and he explains why. As for the other wings, they are used for flying, since these 'gods' are mortal creatures, as has been said several times. They were deified after their death because they introduced inventions useful to mankind. That is what Sanchuniathon told us at the beginning. Thus Cronus flew and Astarte travelled through the universe.

[13]It is clear from this passage that, for Sanchuniathon and the Phoenicians, serpents, dragons and other reptiles were hateful and noxious creatures. Why is it, then, that the serpent was universally venerated in the ancient world? Sanchuniathon explains this: the venerated serpent was not a venomous snake, such as the viper, but a luminous 'serpent' that moved through the air with the speed of lightning.

[14]Philo did not understand the meaning that Sanchuniathon gave to the 'serpent' and to the powerful 'breath' (the blast of an engine) that propelled it at 'a speed that nothing can surpass'.

[15]In Phoenician mythology, as in all others, the serpent is usually a flying serpent, sometimes with the head of a ram. It is thus represented in a number of steles, bas-reliefs and columns in Phoenicia, Babylon, Phrygia, Egypt, Greece, Peru, Mexico, Guatemala, Colombia and the United States. It is always shown as a major symbol, with a meaning that archaeologists are reluctant to accept.

When it is not flying, the serpent speaks. It is the initiator. Among the Egyptians, by a deterioration of the original meaning, it became a cave of initiation in the shape of an incurvated serpent. It is Eve's adviser in the earthly paradise. It is Satan, the good angel, the friend of man, the initiate who came to earth in a flying serpent with propellers or a jet engine – or both, which is precisely represented by a turbo-propeller airplane!

[16]Agathodaemon (from *agathos*, 'good', and *daimon*, 'spirit') was a benevolent deity among the Greeks. It is also the Greek name of the Egyptian Kneph, god of fertility and beneficence, and symbol of the Nile. Kneph was represented in ancient Egypt in the form of a serpent whose head was

crowned with a kind of diadem and whose tail ended with a lotus blossom or a sheaf of grain.

[17]How could this refer to an actual serpent? Is a serpent brilliant, luminous, capable of illuminating solely by its presence? Or is this a reference, instead, to the 'vessel brighter than the sun' that Garcilaso de La Vega speaks of, the extra-terrestrial spacecraft that brought the Venusian Orejona to Peru?

[18]Ophioneus was a Titan who reigned in the sky with his wife Eurynome, before Saturn and Rhea vanquished him and cast him into Tartarus.

In the religious song that Apollonius of Rhodes puts into the mouth of Orpheus (*Argonautica*, 1, 503), Ophion the serpent-king is hurled into the ocean by Cronos. This tradition was known to Pherecydes of Syros, Pythagoras's teacher. I see the image as a representation of the *comet* Venus hurtling through the celestial ocean.

[19]The Celts also placed the serpent in the middle of a circle, or on concentric circles, which signified the creation of the universe, or a stationary universe, by a vibratory wave.

Is the Agathodaemon a wave? Electricity? The Agathodaemon-serpent would seem to be something analogous to primordial energy-matter. It may be the *nwyvre* (serpent) of the Celts.

Chapter 3

[20]Studies of the sea bottoms and the size of the organisms that form plankton; their size is known to be directly related to the surface temperature of the sea. There have also been studies of the isotopic variations of oxygen in organisms as well as varves (actual layers of sediment), which number twelve thousand since the melting of the European glacier, according to the Swedish geologist De Geer.

Chapter 4

[21]This sign apparently dates from only five thousand years ago; that is, from the period when gods travelling on a flying serpent landed in Phoenicia and Assyria.

[22]During or after a flood, the most serious difficulties are, first, lack of drinking water, and then epidemics such as typhus, plague, cholera and typhoid fever. If three or four billion people were drowned in the year 2000, there would be epidemics that would give little chance of survival to those who escaped the flood. Human life would be nearly impossible in the pestilential conditions that would prevail.

In 1966, cases of cholera were reported after the earthquake in eastern Anatolia, despite preventive vaccination and aid from countries all over the world. It can be assumed that if an earthquake killed two thousand people in a town of ten thousand, and if the eight thousand survivors received no outside help, they would all die of an epidemic.

[23]If we are to believe traditions, hybridisation succeeded with the tapir, the cow and the mare. It is also interesting to recall the Biblical story of Esau, whose skin was foul-smelling and covered with hair, and the Lord's order to the Hebrews not to 'have sexual intercourse with any beast' (Leviticus 18:23).

[24]Danu or Donu in Ireland, Don in Great Britain, Dam in the 'unknown language' from which Sanskrit was derived. The ram-headed serpent was the flying initiator. Cf. the flying ram of the Argonauts, the 'flying serpent' and the flying dragons that guarded treasures (the treasures of initiation).

[25]In mythology, the term 'foreigner' (Oannes, Viracocha, Quetzalcoatl, etc.) implies extraterrestrial origin. It is permissible to relate this phenomenon to that of cellular automatism.

In 1953 James Watson and Francis Crick discovered one of the secrets of life: the structure of deoxyribonucleic acid, or DNA, the essential constituent of the chromosomes that carry 'genetic information'. But it was not known how that 'information' localised in the nucleus of the cell could pass into the cytoplasm of the same cell, in which the synthesis of protein takes place. In 1959 F. Jacob and J. Monod solved the problem by conceiving of a short-lived 'messenger' (ribonucleic acid, or RNA) which disappears as soon as its mission has been accomplished. In 1960 they isolated that theoretical messenger, thus proving its existence.

[26]May we not hypothesise that the creative Word is the written word, which is more important to scientific creation than the spoken word? In any case it is undeniable that 'the stifled word' (silence) cannot engender evolution, knowledge and scientific creation. The initiate is therefore he who speaks, not he who remains silent.

[27]Which proves that the vast majority of the survivors were not farmers and plains-dwellers, but hunters from the high plateaux. Intellectuals gave rise to Egyptian civilisation, but, submerged in the uncultivated masses, they could not teach everything they knew.

[28]In the Popul Vuh of the Mexicans, 'The serpent was on the water like a living light.'

In the Kojiki of the Japanese, a book of ancient things or ancient words dating from the year 700, the serpent is the electric wave of thunder.

[29]Aristotle stated that philosophy was born among the Celts.

Pythagoras said that the Druids were the most learned of men, and there can be no doubt that he had sound reasons for saying so. Furthermore, according to Iamblichus, Pythagoras was initiated by the Druids.

The teaching of the Celts appears in the *Bardas*, a book of Bardic songs.

[30]Buddhist doctrine is based on the 'four sublime truths':

1. Pain is inseparable from existence.
2. Pain is the daughter of desire.
3. Existence and pain can cease through Nirvana.
4. To attain Nirvana, one must destroy desire in oneself.

But what is Nirvana, the reward promised by Buddha to wisdom and virtue? It is eternal rest; the word means 'extinction' in Sanskrit. Buddha was a pantheist.

[31]It was long thought that 'naming' someone meant gaining a certain power, which is true in social relations. To name a dog is to have a certain power over him. Believing that one can name God is an error, but it is nevertheless related to the power of the Word.

[32]Although the initiate or scientist may envisage the idea of God as an axis of philosophical choice, he cannot qualify the concept of God with any adjective but 'unknown'.

[33]After Pythagoras, the Greeks lost the meaning of the

transmitted secrets, which explains the end of initiatic revelations and the incomprehension of the Eleusinian Mysteries and the ancestral rites of the Celts.

Chapter 6

[34]The lords of Germelshausen Castle, in the heart of the Thuringian Forest, worshipped a stone divinity whose name was unknown to them. The last of these lords, who was Christian Rosenkreutz's father, probably gave him a certain initiation.

[35]In summer, Lola Rofocale and a few disciples give exhibitions of paintings and sculpture in the caves. Address: Route D 123, Chemellier, 49 Brissac, France.

[36]For further details, see a treatise on occult music written by two of Swami Matkormano's disciples and published by Editions Souffle et Vie, 8 Avenue Albert-Thomas, 94 Vitry, France.

[37]The initiatic traditions and scientific secrets of the Rosicrucians are taught by the Centre AMORC, 56 Rue Gambetta, 94 Villeneuve-Saint-Georges, France.

Chapter 7

[38]On the Marcahuassi Plateau in Peru, the archaeologist Daniel Ruzzo found a whole population of animals carved out of rocks: bears, lions, goats, dogs, sea lions, etc., and a giant bust called 'the head of the Inca.' Ruzzo believes they are relics of the ancient Masma civilisation.

[39]Address: 103 Avenue Henri-Dunant, Bt 57, 60 Nice, France. It was through my friends Guy Tarade and André Millou that I came to know the Falicon pyramid in 1965.

[40]The pyramid of Cholula, Mexico, was built by Xelhua, one of the pre-Deluge giants, in memory of the mountain of Tlaloc, where he had taken refuge with his brothers at the time of the flood. (Rios. Cod. Mex., Vatican.)

Chapter 9

[41]Neanderthal man had a cranial capacity of 1,600 cubic centimeters, whereas the present average is only 1,500. It would thus seem that prehistoric man had more neurons than we do, and was therefore more intelligent.

[42]Scandinavian mead was considered to have a divine origin. It should be noted that American milkweed was imported several thousand years before the 'discovery' of America by Columbus. My friend the parapsychologist Jacques Rubenstein has pointed out the properties of the corniculate lotus, whose boiled blossoms produce cerebral stimulation and develop the powers of memory.

[43]Koridwen is the White Fairy, mother of Taliesin, who retains all knowledge in the primal night. She is not the mother of mankind, but Eve, who was taught by an initiator from another planet.

[44]The rainbow contains only six colours: the three primary colours, blue, yellow and red, and the three secondary colours that result from their mixture; indigo, a mixture of violet and blue, is a tertiary colour.

[45]An allusion to the flying machine of the god Ahura Mazda, who moved between heaven and earth and could thus observe everything that happened. Yima was a Master of the World.

Chapter 10

[46]The emerald, a natural silicate of alumina and beryllium, can have several colours. When it is pink, yellow, or colourless like a diamond it is called beryl. When it is bluish-green it is called aquamarine.

[47]Pythonesses or prophetesses officiated on a tripod and intoxicated themselves with smoke. The pythoness at Delphi, the most famous of all, officiated in a temple at the entrance of a deep cave from which came exhalations whose nature is not clearly known. Strabo called them 'vapours that produce rapture'. They must have been a kind of hallucinogenic smoke.

[48]Robert Carras, a correspondent and friend, suggests an interesting hypothesis. As the result of a cataclysm that generated mutations, plants formerly known for their medicinal powers must have lose their effectiveness, or perhaps

man mutated and deviated so far from his natural path that he is no longer sensitive to them. It is not impossible that milfoil was once a marvellous healing agent, that agrimony cured liver diseases and snakebite, and so on.

[49]I believe that in a certain period Chinese, Hindu, Japanese and Egyptian art also underwent the influence of hallucinogenic drugs and initiatic potions.

Chapter 11

[50]Those Masters of the World were of extraterrestrial origin; they became the first kings of the great dynasties. Among the Incas and Egyptians, royal marriages were consanguine, sometimes even between mother and son, in order to engender descendants of divine blood, since the ancestors were 'gods'.

[51]The theosophists do not, of course, believe that the four Masters of the World in the Gobi Desert have the materialistic goals conjectured by Guy Tarade. The theosophist view is more moral and reassuring.

Chapter 12

[52]*Firdos* ('paradise') is a word of Zoroastrian origin. The Avestan *pairidaez* means 'citadel', 'fence' or 'fortified enclosure'. *Pairi* designates a way of life in harmony with the cosmos.

Chapter 13

[53]Conspiracies have tried to efface the real character of Minerva. She was the Ana, the Mater of the Celtic peoples, and a typically Aryan goddess. In Gaul her name was Belisama and she was the consort of Apollo.

Alfred Maury says that Minerva was 'a Pelasgian goddess, a personification of the moist spirit' (like Venus). She was the Menerfa and Mnerfa of the Etruscans, and her name is linked to the root *men* (*manas* in Sanskrit).

Minerva Glaucopis had green eyes, the colour of the planet Venus, like Kukulkan and Quetzalcoatl. She was the 'flamelike' Belisama (the *comet* Venus), Ishtar and Isis; that is, the initiator from the sky.

[54]Always the same procedure: in 1926, when the archaeological discovery of Glozel ruined the absurd theories of the conspiracies, Glozel was declared to be a fraud. If it had not been for the patriotism of Emile Fradin and Dr Morlet, the marvellous finds of Glozel would have been taken abroad.

In 1872 Heinrich Schliemann, knowing that the Sultan of Turkey wanted to seize his prodigious collection, *gave* it to France or, more precisely, to the city of Paris! The French ambassador at Athens was instructed to carry out the negotiations. Evidence for the existence of Troy, exhibited in Paris – that would not have been prudent! As a result of prolonged administrative formalities, that collection, unique but highly embarrassing to 'historical truths', was not immediately accepted by France, and the Sultan was able to take possession of it.

Schliemann's heretical work tended to prove that Greece, Phoenicia, Chaldea, etc., had a Hyperborean origin; that is, that 'the world was born in Atlantis', and not in Sumer.

[55]C. T. Kopheeb, director of the Leningrad Museum, has said in reply to an inquiry from me that the papyrus from the reign of Sent and the papyrus written by Manetho are not in his museum, but that they may be in the Hermitage Museum, which is much larger. I am still continuing my research in the matter.

[56]Mayan writing has never been translated. Linguists have assigned meanings to a number of its signs, but their interpretations are not certain. We do not even know in which direction the manuscripts should be read: Bollaert says they should be read from bottom to top and from right to left; Diego de Landa says from left to right; Hyacinthe de Charencey says there are no invariable directions (and he must be right). Brasseur de Bourbourg translated part of the Troano Manuscript by reading backward – which did not change much, since he was dealing with ideograms.

[57]The message says, 'Tiahuanaca, in Central America,' which is an excusable geographical error for Heinrich Schliemann, but not for his grandson. A hoaxer would not have thought of making that subtle mistake. The correct version, of course, is 'Tiahuanaco, in Bolivia, South America'.

[58]France, which was a beacon of civilisation a few centuries

ago, has now sunk to the level of a second-class nation, far behind Germany, America, Great Britain and the Soviet Union.

French cultural policy is anarchic and incoherent and seems to be torpedoed by conspiracies in power.

In 1962 I denounced a scandal resulting from notorious negligence: the prehistoric chipped flint tools of France, strewn over the world's largest archaeological sites, were being broken by pieces by agricultural machines. There was, it seems, a governmental order to preserve that world heritage but nothing has been done. The flint cores of Le Grand-Pressigny, for example, are now disappearing.

The same danger threatens France's most valuable treasure: her cathedrals, châteaux and old houses, which ought to give her, along with Greece, Italy and Mexico, a prestige constantly increased by time. But that ancestral heritage will be largely destroyed within ten years by the sonic booms of jet aircraft.

The French government would like to generalise the use of the French language in international conferences, and French-speaking African nations support that effort. But the cultivated classes of Africa (as well as France and French Canada) have to learn English or German in order to read the most important documents of human knowledge! The Vedas, for example, have not been translated into French (there are only extracts and condensations), and most of the best Mayan, Moslem and Scandinavian manuscripts have been translated only into German, English and Russian. And, of course, Celtic mythology has not been translated into French.

Why should African peoples persist in studying French when the French National Library in Paris cannot supply them with the most essential texts of ancient civilisations?

Chapter 14

[59]I regard Gregori B., alias Beltran Garcia, as a great initiate. He has often given me proof of his high knowledge.

[60]A group of investigators and pioneers in unusual phenomena who meet for dinner once a month in a restaurant on the Rue Rodier in Paris. These dinners are secret and the conversation at them is entirely about unusual phenomena.

[81]This is a distinctive trait of the charlatan: speaking a half-spiritualistic, half-scientific jargon that means nothing but serves to conceal his ignorance from guillible listeners.

Chapter 15

[82]The gods of an old religion are always called 'devils' by a new one. A typical case is that of the Hindu and Iranian gods. The good god Indra of the Vedas became the demoniac Andra of the Avesta; the devas (good spirits) of the religion of Brahma were transformed into the daevas (demons) of the religion of Zoroaster. Similarly with the Hebrews and the Christians: the good Azazel and Satan were called demons.